KT-573-404

SECOND EDITION

Ant
The Definitive Guide

PARK LEARNING CENTRE
UNIVERSITY OF GLOUCESTERSHIRE
P.O. Box 220, The Park
Cheltenham GL50 2RH
Tel: 01242 532721

Steve Holzner

O'REILLY®

Beijing · Cambridge · Farnham · Köln · Paris · Sebastopol · Taipei · Tokyo

Ant: The Definitive Guide, Second Edition
by Steve Holzner

Copyright © 2005, 2002 O'Reilly Media, Inc. All rights reserved.
Printed in the United States of America.

Published by O'Reilly Media, Inc., 1005 Gravenstein Highway North, Sebastopol, CA 95472.

O'Reilly books may be purchased for educational, business, or sales promotional use. Online editions are also available for most titles (*safari.oreilly.com*). For more information, contact our corporate/institutional sales department: (800) 998-9938 or *corporate@oreilly.com*.

Editor:	Brett McLaughlin
Production Editor:	Matt Hutchinson
Production Services:	GEX, Inc.
Cover Designer:	Hanna Dyer
Interior Designer:	David Futato

Printing History:

May 2002:	First Edition.
April 2005:	Second Edition.

Nutshell Handbook, the Nutshell Handbook logo, and the O'Reilly logo are registered trademarks of O'Reilly Media, Inc. *Ant: The Definitive Guide*, the image of a horned lizard, and related trade dress are trademarks of O'Reilly Media, Inc.

Java and all Java-based trademarks and logos are trademarks or registered trademarks of Sun Microsystems, Inc., in the United States and other countries. O'Reilly Media, Inc. is independent of Sun Microsystems.

Many of the designations used by manufacturers and sellers to distinguish their products are claimed as trademarks. Where those designations appear in this book, and O'Reilly Media, Inc. was aware of a trademark claim, the designations have been printed in caps or initial caps.

While every precaution has been taken in the preparation of this book, the publisher and author assume no responsibility for errors or omissions, or for damages resulting from the use of the information contained herein.

This book uses RepKover™, a durable and flexible lay-flat binding.

ISBN: 0-596-00609-8

[M]

Ant
The Definitive Guide

Other Java™ resources from O'Reilly

Related titles

Java™ in a Nutshell
Jakarta Struts Cookbook
Programming Jakarta Struts
JUnit Pocket Guide
Learning XSLT

XML in a Nutshell
Java Servlet and JSP Cookbook
Enterprise JavaBeans
JavaServer Faces
Tomcat: The Definitive Guide

Java Books Resource Center

java.oreilly.com is a complete catalog of O'Reilly's books on Java and related technologies, including sample chapters and code examples.

OnJava.com is a one-stop resource for enterprise Java developers, featuring news, code recipes, interviews, weblogs, and more.

Conferences

O'Reilly brings diverse innovators together to nurture the ideas that spark revolutionary industries. We specialize in documenting the latest tools and systems, translating the innovator's knowledge into useful skills for those in the trenches. Visit *conferences.oreilly.com* for our upcoming events.

Safari Bookshelf (*safari.oreilly.com*) is the premier online reference library for programmers and IT professionals. Conduct searches across more than 1,000 books. Subscribers can zero in on answers to time-critical questions in a matter of seconds. Read the books on your Bookshelf from cover to cover or simply flip to the page you need. Try it today with a free trial.

Table of Contents

Preface ix

1. Getting Started **1**
Ant's Origins   2
Getting Ant   2
Ant at Work   4
Anatomy of a Build File   6
Running Ant   23

2. Using Properties and Types **32**
Using Properties to Control Tasks   32
Using Property Files   39
Handling Data Using Types   44

3. Building Java Code **60**
Compiling Code   60
Getting Input from the User   66
Calling Other Ant Tasks   68
Importing Other Build Files   72
Documenting Code   74
Creating JAR Files   81
Setting Build Numbers   84
Setting Timestamps   85

4. Deploying Builds **88**
Packaging Applications for Deployment   88
Preparing to Deploy   99
Deploying Applications   102
Scheduling Automatic Builds   118

5. Testing Builds with JUnit **125**

Using JUnit 127
Running Test Cases 137
Testing in Batches 142
Running the Build File 144
Extending JUnit 148

6. Getting Source Code from CVS Repositories **150**

Source Control and Ant 150
Logging In 153
Working with the Server 154
Getting Version Data 161
Creating Change Logs 161
Finding Changes Between Versions 164
Creating Patches 165

7. Executing External Programs **167**

Executing Java Code 167
Executing External Programs 172
Performing Batch Execution 179
Multithreading Tasks 181
Setting Execution Order 182

8. Developing for the Web **184**

Creating WAR Archives 184
Creating CAB Files 187
Creating Simple Web Deployment 188
Deploying with SCP 189
Deploying to Tomcat 192
Compiling JSPs 196
Deploying to EJB Containers 200

9. XML and XDoclet **206**

Validating XML Documents 206
Loading Properties from XML Files 211
Creating Ant Task DTDs 213
Transforming XML Using XSLT 214
Using XDoclet 218
Developing Enterprise JavaBeans 230

10. Optional Tasks **234**
    Using Sound   234
    Creating Splash Screens   235
    Substituting Text Using Regular Expressions   236
    Handling Dependencies   238

11. Integrating Ant with Eclipse **241**
    Introducing Eclipse   241
    Running Ant Build Files   247
    Using a Different Version of Ant   253
    Using the Ant View   255

12. Extending Ant **257**
    Creating a Simple Custom Ant Task   257
    Extending the Task Class   260
    Creating Custom Listeners   278
    Creating Custom Loggers   280
    Creating Custom Filters   282
    Creating Custom Selectors   284
    Creating New Types   286

Index **291**

Preface

Welcome to Ant, today's premiere build tool. Ant is an extraordinary tool, and it fills a long-standing need among developers. No longer do you have to try to remember the 50 steps to build your project and make sure you do them in the right order or try to get finicky makefiles just right. Now you've got a true build tool that's genuinely easy to work with and outstandingly powerful. If you've never used Ant, you're in for a treat.

We're going to push the envelope in this book, working from the basics through the advanced, doing nearly everything that Ant can do. This book was designed to open up Ant and make it more accessible than any other book on the subject. It's a programmer-to-programmer book, written to make you an Ant pro without wasting time.

If you're a programmer, this book is written to give you exactly what you want to see, which is the good stuff and only the good stuff. There's as much Ant crammed into this book as you need to master the topic, and mastering Ant is the goal.

What's Inside

From cover to cover, this book is pure Ant, covering hundreds of topics and techniques. We start from the most basic Java™ development up to extending Ant yourself; it's all here. Here are a few of the topics covered in this book:

- Getting and installing Ant
- Creating build files
- Running a build
- Handling build failures
- Specifying build targets
- Using property files
- Handling data types and properties

- Handling filesets
- Using selectors, filtersets, and filter chains
- Working with mappers
- Creating conditional targets
- Packaging applications
- Moving, copying, and deleting files
- Building documentation
- Creating JAR files
- Deploying applications
- Using FTP
- Handling remote deployment
- Getting and installing JUnit
- Using JUnit assertions
- Creating a test case
- Running a test case
- Using CVS and Ant
- Accessing CVS
- Initializing CVS
- Running external programs and continuous integration
- Running code in a new JVM
- Calling other programs
- Setting environment variables
- Scheduling Ant builds automatically
- Scheduling builds in Unix and Windows
- Using scripting
- Using AntHill
- Creating email notifications
- Working with XDoclet and XML
- Creating XML build logs
- Handling web development
- Compiling JSP pages
- Using Ant's Enterprise JavaBeans™ (EJB) tasks
- Using XDoclet for EJB development
- Connecting Ant to Eclipse
- Configuring Ant in Eclipse

- Writing Ant tasks
- Handling errors
- Writing custom filters and selectors
- Writing custom Ant loggers and listeners

Here's an overview, chapter by chapter:

Chapter 1, *Getting Started*
> This chapter is all about the basics, including all the details on how to create Ant build files and how to run them.

Chapter 2, *Using Properties and Types*
> This chapter is about two central Ant topics: properties and types. Properties let you configure Ant tasks, and types hold data used by tasks.

Chapter 3, *Building Java Code*
> This chapter focuses on the Java build process, from compiling Java code with the javac task through compressing and packaging the results with tasks such as jar.

Chapter 4, *Deploying Builds*
> This chapter covers tasks to package applications for deployments such as tar, gzip, and zip; tasks to prepare directories for deployment such as delete and mkdir; and tasks to deploy applications such as copy and move for local and network deployment, as well as ftp, telent, sshexec, and mail for remote deployment.

Chapter 5, *Testing Builds with JUnit*
> It doesn't make much sense to deploy code that has been broken by a new build. This chapter using the JUnit framework with Ant, during which you can run tests on your code and deploy it if it satisfies those tests.

Chapter 6, *Getting Source Code from CVS Repositories*
> There's a lot of support built in for Concurrent Version System (CVS) in Ant, and this chapter is all about making code sharing in teams with CVS happen.

Chapter 7, *Executing External Programs*
> Part of the build process involves testing what you've built, and an obvious way of doing that is to run the results of a build. Doing so from Ant involves using the major tasks in this chapter: java, exec, and apply.

Chapter 8, *Developing for the Web*
> This chapter covers the tasks specifically designed for packaging web applications, such as war, cab, ear, and jspc, and for deploying them, such as get, serverdeploy, and scp. I'll also cover the custom Ant tasks targeted to specific servers such as deploy, reload, and undeploy.

Chapter 9, *XML and XDoclet*

You can validate XML documents using XML DTDs and schema using the xmlvalidate task. You can read properties from an XML document using xmlproperty. You can use the xslt/style task to transform XML documents using XSLT. In this chapter, I discuss XDoclet, an open source code generation engine designed to run in Ant. XDoclet can generate code, deployment descriptors such as *web.xml*, and other artifacts for web and EJB applications.

Chapter 10, *Optional Tasks*

Ant comes with a number of optional tasks, and this chapter covers the highlights, including tasks that create sounds to indicate where you are in a build, tasks that display splash screens, tasks that work with regular expressions to match text, and more.

Chapter 11, *Integrating Ant with Eclipse*

Eclipse is the premiere integrated development environment (IDE) for Java programmers. Eclipse is great at visual development, whereas Ant is great for builds. Eclipse comes with Ant built in, and there's an extensive Ant interface in Eclipse. The Ant/Eclipse connection is extremely useful to Java developers, and it's covered in this chapter.

Chapter 12, *Extending Ant*

This chapter covers how to create new Ant tasks, handle task attributes, access property values, work with nested text and elements, make builds fail, work with filesets, use custom tasks as wrappers for external programs, and more.

Conventions Used in This Book

There are some conventions I'll use that you should know about. When there's a new piece of code under discussion, it will appear highlighted; when there's more code to come, you'll see three dots. Here's what that looks like:

```java
import org.apache.tools.ant.Task;
import org.apache.tools.ant.BuildException;

public class Project extends Task
{
    private String language;

    public void execute( ) throws BuildException
    {
        System.out.println("The language is " + language);
    }

    public void setLanguage(String language)
    {
        this.language = language;
```

```
          .
          .
          .
      }
   }
```

Note that I'll use the standard convention for selecting menu items in this book when menu items come into play (as when we use Ant in the Eclipse IDE). For instance, to create a new project in Eclipse, you use the File → New → Project menu item.

The following typographical conventions are used in this book:

Plain text
> Indicates menu titles, menu options, menu buttons, and keyboard accelerators

Italic
> Indicates new terms, URLs, email addresses, filenames, file extensions, path-names, directories, and Unix utilities

`Constant width`
> Indicates commands, options, switches, variables, types, classes, namespaces, methods, modules, properties, parameters, values, objects, events, event handlers, or XML tags

`Constant width italic`
> Shows text that should be replaced with user-supplied values

`Constant width bold`
> Used to highlight blocks of code and commands or other text that should be typed literally by the user

> This icon signifies a tip, suggestion, or general note.

> This icon signifies a caution or warning.

What You'll Need

All the software you'll need in this book can be downloaded from the Internet for free. You'll need Ant—this book was written using Ant 1.6.1—and I'll discuss where to get Ant in Chapter 1. Other software packages are used at various points in the book, such as the AntHill build server or the Eclipse IDE (Chapter 11 is on using Ant in Eclipse), and I'll show where to download all the requisite software as it's needed. It's all free.

Using Code Examples

This book is here to help you get your job done. In general, you may use the code in this book in your programs and documentation. You do not need to contact O'Reilly for permission unless you're reproducing a significant portion of the code. For example, writing a program that uses several chunks of code from this book does not require permission. Selling or distributing a CD-ROM of examples from O'Reilly books *does* require permission. Answering a question by citing this book and quoting example code does not require permission. Incorporating a significant amount of example code from this book into your product's documentation *does* require permission.

We appreciate, but do not require, attribution. An attribution usually includes the title, author, publisher, and ISBN. For example: "*Ant: The Definitive Guide,* Second Edition by Steve Holzner. Copyright 2005 O'Reilly Media, Inc., 0-596-00609-8."

If you feel your use of code examples falls outside fair use or the permission given above, feel free to contact us at *permissions@oreilly.com*.

Safari Enabled

 When you see a Safari® Enabled icon on the cover of your favorite technology book, it means the book is available online through the O'Reilly Network Safari Bookshelf.

Safari offers a solution that's better than e-books. It's a virtual library that lets you easily search thousands of top technology books, cut and paste code samples, download chapters, and find quick answers when you need the most accurate, current information. Try it free at *http://safari.oreilly.com*.

We'd Like to Hear from You

Please address comments and questions concerning this book to the publisher:

> O'Reilly Media, Inc.
> 1005 Gravenstein Highway North
> Sebastopol, CA 95472
> (800) 998-9938 (in the United States or Canada)
> (707) 829-0515 (international or local)
> (707) 829-0104 (fax)

O'Reilly maintains a web page for this book, which lists errata, examples, and any additional information. You can access this page at:

> *http://www.oreilly.com/catalog/anttdg2*

To comment or ask technical questions about this book, send email to:

bookquestions@oreilly.com

For more information about our books, conferences, Resource Centers, and the O'Reilly Network, see the following web site:

http://www.oreilly.com

CHAPTER 1

Getting Started

Build tools are one of the most boring items developers must have available in their development cycle. They aren't sexy, they aren't going to impress your friends, and you'll hardly notice a build tool at all until it's time to redeploy that 1,000-class Java application you've been working on. Then, all the interesting code, killer IDEs, and amazing design patterns aren't worth nearly as much as typing ant and calmly watching your boring build tool handle complicated dependencies, deployment onto multiple servers via FTP and SSH, and log errors. It is here that build tools like Ant truly shine.

At its most basic, all a good build tool does is take source code, compile it, and create a working application. When you're writing a single-class application, this isn't a big deal; in fact, it can be annoying to manage a build system instead of typing javac. But it's a different story when you start working with multiple source files, with multiple dependencies, need to check code out of a central repository automatically, test the code, and deploy it to some remote destination. You can end up with dozens of tasks to complete each time you want to build your application, which is the last thing you want to spend time on when you're already brain-dead from an all-night debugging session. When new members join your team, you'll have to walk through this whole process again, showing them the ropes and hoping they don't break anything in the process. It's for all of these reasons that developers—and especially Java programmers—turn to Ant.

Though there are still powerful alternatives to Ant like make, Jam, Cons, gnumake, and nmake, nothing is as integrated into the Java programming language. Ant is pure Java; you'll find line after line of Java code and *.java* files if you obtain a source release of the tool. Further, some of the most popular projects in the Java universe are built using Ant; everything from Tomcat to JBoss to Turbine can go from source to binary by typing ant.

Ant's Origins

Ant was originally the brainchild of James Duncan Davidson, and the word Ant stands for "Another Neat Tool," a fact that relatively few developers realize. Ant 1.0 first appeared in March 2000. James' original inspiration was to create a build tool that used a simple XML-based format for build files, as opposed to the shell commands and involved formatting that Makefiles used. Ant caught on rapidly, and newer versions followed—Ant 1.1 (July 2000), 1.2 (October 2000), 1.3 (March 2001), 1.4 (September 2001), and 1.5 (July 2003). The version this book uses—version 1.6.1—appeared in February of 2004. Although James Davidson has moved on to work with other build tools, Ant continues to evolve on an almost daily basis.

Ant is an open source, Apache community project, and its home page is at *http://ant.apache.org*. Because it's an open source project, it's always developing. There are multiple authors, called *committers*, which can write to Ant's source code repositories. However, officially sanctioned Ant versions don't appear too rapidly, and when they do, they're usually backward compatible enough to make sure your build files aren't broken.

 One notable exception to this practice is Ant 2.0, which may be out sometime in the next year or so. When it does come out, the Apache Ant team plans on releasing an automated migration tool that will translate 1.x build files to Ant 2.0.

Getting Ant

Ant comes in two editions: binary and source. The binary release is ready to use: just download, uncompress, and go. The source release allows you to see what makes Ant run and to make modifications of your own if you choose. To download either, go to *http://ant.apache.org/* and click a link under the Download title (either Binary Distributions or Source Distributions).

Downloading a binary edition is easiest: Just click the Binary Distributions link and download the *.tar.gz* or *.zip* compressed file.

 If you want bleeding-edge Ant, you can get the nightly builds from *http://cvs.apache.org/builds/ant/nightly/*.

Installing Ant

To install the binary distribution of Ant, expand it. Here's the resulting directory layout (only the *bin* and *lib* directories are needed to run Ant):

```
ant
|__ bin  Ant launch scripts
```

```
|
|___ lib  Ant jars
|
|___ docs Ant documentation
|
|___ etc  XSL for formatting Ant XML output
```

You need to perform the following steps to complete the setup process:

1. Add the Ant *bin* directory to your path.

2. Set the `ANT_HOME` environment variable to the directory where you installed Ant.

 On some operating systems, the Ant scripts can guess `ANT_HOME`—specifically in Unix and Windows NT/2000—but it's better not to rely on them doing so accurately.

3. Set the `JAVA_HOME` environment variable to the directory where your JDK is installed.

If you've expanded Ant in *c:\ant* on Windows, you'll end up with a new directory, *c:\ant\apache-ant-1.6.1*. If you've installed the JDK in *c:\jdk1.4* (and the Java *bin* directory is *C:\jdk1.4\bin*), set the environment variables like this:

```
set ANT_HOME=C:\ant\apache-ant-1.6.1
set JAVA_HOME=C:\jdk1.4
set PATH=%PATH%;%ANT_HOME%\bin
```

In Unix (bash), assume Ant is installed in */usr/local/ant*. Here's how you'd set up the environment:

```
export ANT_HOME=/usr/local/ant
export JAVA_HOME=/usr/local/jdk1.4
export PATH=${PATH}:${ANT_HOME}/bin
```

In Unix (csh), you'd do something like this:

```
setenv ANT_HOME /usr/local/ant
setenv JAVA_HOME /usr/local/jdk1.4
set path=( $path $ANT_HOME/bin )
```

 There are great instructions on how to set environment variables on many different systems in the installation documentation for the Java JDK.

To compile Java code, you'll need a working JDK on your machine. If you only have a Java Runtime Environment (JRE), Ant won't be able to do many things you need it to do. Also note that the Microsoft JVM/JDK is not supported.

In Windows 95, Windows 98, and Windows ME, the batch file used to launch Ant will not work if ANT_HOME holds a long filename (a filename which is not in the 8.3 format). It's best to install Ant in a short 8.3 path, such as *c:\Ant*. If you're using one of these operating systems, you'll need to configure more environment space. Update the following line in your *config.sys* file:

```
shell=c:\command.com c:\ /p /e:32768
```

Testing Ant

With Ant in your path, you should be able to run it at the command line. To test this, type ant -version, which should display the current Ant version:

```
%ant -version
Apache Ant version 1.6.1 compiled on February 12 2004
```

If Ant's not working, you'll see something along these lines:

```
-bash-2.05b$ ant
-bash: ant: command not found
```

Here's the Windows version of the same error:

```
C:\>ant
'ant' is not recognized as an internal or external command,
operable program or batch file.
```

In that case, go back over the installation instructions, and look at the Ant documentation for troubleshooting issues.

Ant at Work

Rather than go on and on about what Ant can do for you, an example can illustrate how easy Ant makes the build process. Assume that you have a Java file called *Project.java*, as shown in Example 1-1.

Example 1-1. A simple Java class

```
public class Project
{
    public static void main(String args[])
    {
        System.out.println("No worries.");
    }
}
```

Assume you want to compile this code and store the results, *Project.class*, in a JAR file, *Project.jar*. With Ant and a build file, this is a piece of cake. By default, Ant looks for a build file named *build.xml*. That file is a valid XML document; Example 1-2 shows the build file for this example.

Example 1-2. A simple Ant build file

```xml
<?xml version="1.0" ?>
<project default="main">

    <target name="main" depends="compile, compress">
        <echo>
            Building the .jar file.
        </echo>
    </target>

    <target name="compile">
        <javac srcdir="."/>
    </target>

  <target name="compress">
        <jar jarfile="Project.jar" basedir="." includes="*.class" />
  </target>

</project>
```

To run this Ant build file, make sure it's in the same directory as *Project.java*, and enter ant at the command-line prompt. Ant has been tested on many platforms, including Linux; Unix versions from Solaris to HP-UX; Windows 9x, NT, 2000, and XP; OS/2 Warp, Novell Netware 6, and MacOS X.

When you run Ant on this first build file, here's what you'd see in Unix (using the bash shell):

```
-bash-2.05b$ ant
Buildfile: build.xml

compile:
    [javac] Compiling 1 source file

compress:
      [jar] Building jar: /home/httpd/vhosts/builder/Project.jar

main:
     [echo]
     [echo]                 Building the .jar file.
     [echo]

BUILD SUCCESSFUL
Total time: 2 seconds
```

You'll get the same results in any supported operating system. For example, here's what you'd see in Windows. Everything except the build time is identical:

```
C:\ant\ch01>ant
Buildfile: build.xml

compile:
    [javac] Compiling 1 source file
```

```
compress:
    [jar] Building jar: C:\ant\ch01\Project.jar

main:
    [echo]
    [echo]              Building the .jar file.
    [echo]

BUILD SUCCESSFUL
Total time: 4 seconds
```

For the most part, Ant builds are independent of operating system, and for that reason, % is used as a generic command prompt in this book. If anything is operating-system-dependent, it will be listed explicitly.

When Ant finishes executing the build file, you'll have *build.xml*, *Project.java*, the compiled *Project.class*, and *Project.jar*, all in the same directory. *Project.jar* will contain a manifest file and *Project.class*. Fortunately, Ant handles 10, 20, or 100 source files in this same way, making your life easy at build time.

Anatomy of a Build File

Ant projects all revolve around one or more build files. By default, Ant looks for a build file named *build.xml*. Because Ant files are XML documents, they start with an XML declaration, as all valid XML documents must:

```
<?xml version="1.0" ?>
        .
        .
        .
```

 For the complete XML 1.0 syntax, look at *http://www.w3.org/TR/ REC-xml/*. XML 1.1 is out now as well, but Ant build files are based on XML 1.0, and the difference between these versions is small anyway, centering mostly on the manner in which certain Unicode characters are supported.

Projects

Every Ant build file contains exactly one *project*. You set up an Ant project in a build file with the project element, which is the *document element*—i.e., the element that contains all other elements:

```
<?xml version="1.0" ?>
<project>
        .
        .
        .
</project>
```

As Ant build files are just XML, you'll need to know which attributes are allowed on the top-level project element.

 You'll also want to know about the elements that can be nested within project. Those are dealt with throughout the rest of this chapter and in Chapter 2.

The three allowed attributes for the project element are shown in Table 1-1.

Table 1-1. The project element's supported attributes

Attribute	Description	Required
name	Defines the project name	No
default	The target to invoke if no target is explicitly specified	Yes
basedir	The base directory from which all relative paths are resolved	No

Note that the default attribute is required. This attribute points to the Ant target that you want run by default; in other words, this controls what happens when you type ant at the command prompt, without any other special instructions. In the following case, the default target is main:

```
<?xml version="1.0" ?>
<project default="main">
    .
    .
    .
</project>
```

Targets

An Ant *target* is a group of tasks that you want Ant to perform. These tasks are grouped together into one easily remembered unit, which is the target. For example, you might have a target deploy which opens an FTP connection to a remote server, uploads various files, and closes the connection. Though multiple tasks may be involved (opening the connection, performing an upload, closing the connection, and perhaps checking for error messages), it's easiest to think of this as one unit of work. Considering this as a single target makes it reusable and easily accessed from various portions of your build file.

Another example might be a target named init that initializes a build by deleting output directories and recreating them so they'll be empty, as well as copying over license files that should be a part of every build. You might use a target named compile to compile dozens of source files across various directories and store the results in various output directories. In all these cases, the target handles piecing together various individual tasks.

Ant build files are made up of targets like these. For example, to create the main target, you use the target element, along with the name attribute:

```
<?xml version="1.0" ?>
<project default="main">

    <target name="main">
        .
        .
        .
    </target>

</project>
```

You can see the possible attributes for the target element in Table 1-2.

Table 1-2. The target element's attributes

Attribute	Description	Required
name	Defines the target name	Yes
depends	Comma-separated list of targets to execute before this target	No
if	Name of a property needed to run this task	No
unless	Name of a property that can *not* be set before running this task	No
description	Description of this target's purpose	No

Tasks

You populate an Ant target with *tasks*; a task is an XML element that Ant can execute to make something happen. For example, the echo task echoes text messages to the console:

```
<?xml version="1.0" ?>
<project default="main">

    <target name="main">
        <echo>
            Building the .jar file.
        </echo>
    </target>

</project>
```

To create an Ant target, you place Ant tasks like echo inside a target element; in this case, the main target only has one task, but you can include hundreds.

Built-in tasks

As you'd expect, Ant comes with a large number of built-in tasks, and you can see them all in Table 1-3 (many of these tasks may contain subelements).

In cases where a task is listed and followed by another task name in brackets (as in apply [execon]), the first task is the current name you should use; the second task is an older name that performs similar functionality but is now deprecated. Always use the task *not* in brackets to ensure your code is current.

Table 1-3. Core Ant tasks

Task name	Description
ant	Executes Ant
antcall	Executes a target from the current build file
antstructure	From a given build file, creates a DTD reflecting all of the tasks Ant currently knows about
apply [execon]	Invokes a native executable
available	Sets a Boolean value in a property according to the availability of desired resource
basename	Sets a property to the last element of a specified path in an effort to determine a file's name without directory structure
buildnumber	Manages build numbers
bunzip2	Expands GZip or BZip2 archives
bzip2	Packs GZip or BZip2 archives
checksum	Creates checksums for one or more files
chmod	Modifies file permissions on Unix
concat	Concatenates multiple files
condition	Checks the result of a condition and sets the result to in a property
copy [copydir, copyfile]	Copies files
cvs	Interacts with a CVS repository
cvschangelog	Converts a series of CVS change logs into an XML report
cvspass	Adds entries to a *.cvspass* file
cvstagdiff	Creates an XML report highlighting the differences between tags
cvsversion	Finds the CVS software version
defaultexcludes	Modifies the list of default exclude patterns, affecting which files are automatically excluded from processing by file-related tasks
delete [deltree]	Delete files and folders
dependset	Deletes target files that are older than new source files
dirname	Assigns a file's directory path to a property
ear	Extends the jar task to support handling files for an Enterprise Application Archive (EAR)
echo	Echoes text to System.out or to a file
exec	Invokes a native executable
fail	Halts and exits a build by throwing a BuildException
filter	Sets a token filter that can be used by filter-related tasks such as copy

Table 1-3. Core Ant tasks (continued)

Task name	Description
fixcrlf	Adds or remove tabs, carriage returns, linefeeds, and EOF characters from a set of files
genkey	Adds a new key to a given *keystore*
get	Retrieves files using FTP, HTTP, and more from a URL
gunzip	Unpacks a GZip file
gzip	Packs a GZip file
import	Allows the use of other Ant files
input	Displays a message and reads a line of input from the console, allowing for user input during the build process
jar	Creates a JAR archive similar to Java's jar command
java	Executes the Java interpreter to run a class or application
javac	Compiles the specified source file(s)
javadoc [javadoc2]	Invokes the javadoc tool to create documentation
loadfile	Sets a property file to the entire contents of a text file
loadproperties	Loans an entire property file into Ant properties
macrodef	Defines a new task as a macro built-up upon other tasks
mail	Sends SMTP mail messages
manifest	Creates an archive's manifest file
mkdir	Makes a new directory
move [rename]	Moves a file to another directory
parallel	Contains other Ant tasks that can be run simultaneously by multiple Java threads
patch	Uses the patch command (assuming it is on the path) to apply *diff* files to a source file (or files)
pathconvert	Converts paths between platforms
presetdef	Defines a new task based on an existing task with certain options preset as defaults
property	Sets one or more properties to new values
record	Runs a listener that records the logging output of the build process to a file
replace	Replaces a string with another in all files in a directory
rmic	Invokes the rmic compiler
sequential	A container task that can contain other Ant tasks and run them in sequence
signjar	Uses the JarSigner to securely sign ZIP and JAR archives
sleep	Suspends execution for a specified period of time
sql	Runs SQL statements against a database
subant	Runs Ant within all subdirectories of the project directory
sync	Synchronizes two directory trees
tar	Makes a new TAR archive
taskdef	Creates a new task definition and adds it to the current project
tempfile	Sets a temporary filename to an Ant property

Table 1-3. Core Ant tasks (continued)

Task name	Description
tstamp	Sets time-based properties to the current time
typedef	Creates a new task or data type for use in the current project
unjar	Unpacks a JAR file
untar	Unpacks a TAR file
unwar	Unpacks a WAR file
unzip	Unpacks a ZIP file
uptodate	Sets a property value to true if a given target file is newer than a set of source files
waitfor	Halts a build and continues when specified conditions are met
war	Creates WAR archive files (an extension of the jar task)
whichresource	Locates a class or resource, either on the current class path or the system class path
xmlproperty	Loads Ant properties from an XML property file
xslt [style]	Transforms a set of documents via XSLT
zip	Creates and packs a new ZIP archive

Optional tasks

Besides these built-in tasks, called the *core tasks*, Ant supports many optional tasks, which you can see in Table 1-4. These tasks may require the support of additional JAR files, which you load into the Ant *lib* directory. For example, ftp uploads files to remote servers; you need to place the JAR files *jakarta-oro.jar* and *commons-net.jar* in your Ant *lib* directory to use the task. Another optional task is csc, which compiles Microsoft C# code:

```
<csc optimize="true" debug="false"
    warnLevel="4"
    unsafe="false" targetType="exe" incremental="false"
    mainClass = "Main" destFile="app.exe" >
    <src dir=".src" includes="*.cs" />
    <reference file="${testCSC.dll}" />
    <define name="RELEASE" />
</csc>
```

 To determine which additional JAR files an optional task needs, see *http://ant.apache.org/docs/manual/index.html#librarydependencies*, which lists the needed libraries for each optional task and where to get them.

Table 1-4. Optional Ant tasks

Task name	Description
antlr	Runs the ANTLR Translator Generator Language Tool.
attrib	Changes the permissions and/or attributes of a file.
cab	Creates CAB files (Microsoft archives).

Table 1-4. Optional Ant tasks (continued)

Task name	Description
chgrp	Changes file groups on Unix.
chown	Changes file ownership.
depend	Determines which class files are out-of-date compared to their source.
echoproperties	Lists the project's properties.
ftp	Supports a basic FTP client.
icontract	Generates a property file for iContract, an application for controlling assertions.
image	Performs bulk image manipulation.
jarlib-available	Checks for the presence of an extension.
jarlib-display	Displays the "Optional Package" and "Package Specification" information for JAR files.
jarlib-manifest	Generates a manifest with required dependencies.
jarlib-resolve	Searches for the location of a JAR file, setting the location to an ANT property.
javacc	Invokes the JavaCC compiler.
javah	Generates C header and source files for the Java Native Interface (JNI).
JPCoverage	Runs the JProbe coverage analyzer.
JcovMerge	Merges JProbe coverage snapshots.
JcovReport	Takes a JProbe coverage snapshot and creates a report.
jdepend	Uses the JDepend parser to generate code quality metrics.
jjdoc	Invokes the JJDoc documentation generator (used with JavaCC).
jjtree	Inserts parse tree building actions into source code using the JJTree preprocessor for the JavaCC compiler.
jlink	Deprecated. Merges archive contents. Use the zip and jar tasks with the zipfileset and zipgroupfileset attributes instead.
jprobe	Runs various tools from the JProbe suite.
jspc	Deprecated. Compiles JSP pages to Java source code. Use Tomcat's jspc task instead.
junit	Runs unit tests using JUnit.
junitreport	Merges separate XML files generated by the JUnit task into a single XML file.
maudit	Highlights stylistic and potential execution problems using the Metamata Metrics/WebGain Quality Analyzer.
mimemail	Deprecated. You can still send mail using the mail task.
mmetrics	Generates metrics using the WebGain's Metameta Metrics Quality Analyzer.
mparse	Takes a grammar file, and compiles it with MetaMata's MParse compiler.
native2ascii	Takes a native encoded file and converts it to ASCII.
netrexxc	Compiles all NetRexx source files.
propertyfile	Creates or modifies property files.
pvcs	Gets latest source code from a PVCS repository.
renameextensions	Deprecated. You can achieve the same results by using the move task and using a glob mapper.

Table 1-4. Optional Ant tasks (continued)

Task name	Description
replaceregexp	Replaces matched text with new text.
rexec	Controls a rexec session from Ant.
rpm	Builds Linux RPM installation files.
scp	Moves files to and from a remote SSH server.
script	Executes an Apache BSF script.
Scripdef	Defines Ant tasks from scripts.
serverdeploy	Runs a hot-deployment tool for a J2EE server.
setproxy	Configures web proxy properties.
sound	After a build, plays a sound file letting you know whether the build succeeded or failed.
splash	Displays a splash screen.
sshexec	Executes a command on a remote server using SSH.
stylebook	Uses Apache Stylebook to generate book documentation.
symlink	Makes, deletes, or edits Unix symbolic links.
telnet	Controls a Telnet session from ANT.
test	Executes a JUnit test.
translate	Translates keywords in files using values in resource bundles.
vajload	Loads files for Visual Age for Java source control.
vajexport	Exports packages for Visual Age for Java source control.
vajimport	Imports files for Visual age for Java source control.
wljspc	Compiles JSP pages using WebLogic's JSP compiler.
xmlvalidate	Validates XML files and reports any errors.

In addition to these tasks, specific Ant tasks for .NET are shown in Table 1-5.

Table 1-5. .NET Ant tasks

Task name	Description
Csc	Invokes the C# compiler.
vbc	Invokes the VB.NET compiler.
jsharpc	Invokes the J# compiler.
ildasm	Disassembles from .NET intermediate language back to source code.
ilasm	Assembles code into .NET intermediate language.
WsdlToDotNet	Given a WSDL file, this task will generate C# or VB code.
ImportTypelib	COM library importer.

Specific tasks for the Clearcase version control system are listed in Table 1-6.

Table 1-6. Clearcase Ant tasks

Task name	Description
CCCheckin	Checks in files
CCCheckout	Checks out files
CCUnCheckout	Unchecks out files
CCUpdate	Executes cleartool update
CCMklbType	Executes cleartool mklbtyle
CCMklabel	Executes cleartool mklabel
CCRmtype	Executes cleartool rmtype
CCLock	Executes cleartool lock
CCUnluck	Executes cleartool unlock
CCMkbl	Executes cleartool mkbl
CCMkattr	Executes cleartool mkattr
CCMkdir	Executes cleartool mkdir
CCMkelem	Executes cleartool mkelem

Many specific Enterprise JavaBeans (EJB) tasks are shown in Table 1-7.

Table 1-7. EJB-related Ant tasks

Task name	Description
blgenclient	Generates a client JAR for Borland application servers
ddcreator	Creates EJB deployment descriptors, given a group of WebLogic deployment descriptors
ejbc	Invokes WebLogic's ejbc tool
Iplanet-ejbc	Invokes iPlanet's ejbc tool
ejbjar	Invokes the ejbjar tool (used for many application servers)
wlrun	Starts a WebLogic server
Wlstop	Stops a WebLogic server

The Perforce source control tasks are shown in Table 1-8.

Table 1-8. Perforce Ant tasks

Task name	Description
P4Sync	Synchronizes files with the Perforce server.
P4Change	Gets a list of current changes from the Perforce server.
P4Edit	Checks out files for editing.
P4Submit	Checks in files.
P4Have	Lists all client-viewable files.
P4Label	Makes a label based on the files in the current workspace.
P4Labelsync	Syncs with a label.

Table 1-8. Perforce Ant tasks (continued)

Task name	Description
P4Counter	Gets or sets a counter value. (Counters can be used to keep track of build events, such as the number of builds that have been executed.)
P4Reopen	Reopens a checked-out file.
P4Revert	Reverts file(s) that have been changed to their original content.
P4Add	Adds file(s) to the list to be submitted to the server.
P4Delete	Deletes file(s).
P4Integrate	Integrates file(s). You must specify the source file(s) and the target file(s).
P4resolve	Resolves file(s) in case others have made changes to the file(s) when you were working on it.
P4Fstat	Views differences with the server.

Many tasks for Microsoft Visual Source Safe are detailed in Table 1-9.

Table 1-9. Visual Source Safe tasks

Task name	Description
vssget	Gets a copy of a particular VSS file
Vsslabel	Makes a new label for the current version of a file
Vsshistory	Displays a file's history in the project
Vsscheckin	Checks in files to VSS
Vsscheckout	Checks out files from VSS
Vssadd	Adds a new file to VSS
Vsscp	Changes the project considered the current project by VSS
Vsscreate	Makes a new project

Continuing with source control repository tasks, Table 1-10 shows tasks for working with Starteam source control.

Table 1-10. Starteam Ant tasks

Task name	Description
STCheckout	Checks out files from StarTeam projects
STCheckin	Checks in files to StarTeam projects
STLabel	Creates a new label for this project
STList	Displays a list of files in the project

Table 1-11 shows tasks for the Continuous source control server.

Table 1-11. Continuous/Synergy Ant tasks

Task name	Description
CCMCheckin	Checks in files to the source manager
CCMCheckout	Checks out files from the source manager
CCMCheckinTask	Checks in all files in the current task
CCMReconfigure	Reconfigures an existing command
CCMCreateTask	Creates a task

Finally, Table 1-12 lists optional tasks for supporting SourceGear's SourceOffSite Visual Source Safe plug-in.

Table 1-12. SourceOffSite Ant tasks

Task name	Description
Sosget	Gets a read-only copy of a file
Soslabel	Creates a label for the current project
Soscheckin	Checks in files to the source manager
Soscheckout	Checks out files from the source manager

In addition to the built-in and the optional tasks, Ant supports third-party and custom tasks (yes, that's a large number of tasks you can use!). As you'd expect, third-party tasks add functionality to Ant; as an example, take a look at the third-party tasks available for free at *http://ant-contrib.sf.net/*, which includes a set of tasks for use with Ant and C++. Creating Ant tasks is easier than you might think, and you're going to create your own in Chapter 11.

Dependent Tasks

Typically, you create an Ant build file with a default target named something like main; this target then acts as a master target, handling program flow for the entire build process. It tells Ant to run other targets and specifies their ordering. This is accomplished through the target element's depends attribute.

For example, you might want to add a target named compile to compile your code and add another target called compress to put the compiled code into a JAR file:

```
<?xml version="1.0" ?>
<project default="main">

    <target name="main">
        <echo>
            Building the .jar file.
        </echo>
    </target>
```

```
    <target name="compile">
        <javac srcdir="."/>
    </target>

    <target name="compress">
        <jar jarfile="Project.jar" basedir="." includes="*.class" />
    </target>

</project>
```

Ensure that the compile and compress targets run (in that order) by assigning the string "compile, compress" to the default target's depends attribute:

```
<?xml version="1.0" ?>
<project default="main">

    <target name="main" depends="compile, compress">
        <echo>
            Building the .jar file.
        </echo>
    </target>

    <target name="compile">
        <javac srcdir="."/>
    </target>

    <target name="compress">
        <jar jarfile="Project.jar" basedir="." includes="*.class" />
    </target>

</project>
```

When you run Ant, it'll look for *build.xml* and execute the default target, which the project element indicates is main. The main target's depends attribute tells Ant to run the compile target and then run the compress target *before* running the body of the main target.

 Though you use this attribute to indicate the order targets should run in, targets can still fail, which means you're not guaranteed that they will all behave as expected. Generally, a failed target will stop the Ant build process, but that's not always the case.

Bear in mind that dependencies can be nested inadvertently. For example, take a look at this build file fragment:

```
<target name="find"/>
<target name="inspect" depends="find"/>
<target name="test" depends="inspect"/>
<target name="purchase" depends="test, inspect, find"/>
```

If target purchase was the default target, you might think that targets test, inspect, find, and purchase were executed in that order. However, target test depends on target inspect, which depends on find, and so on. An Ant target gets executed *once* even when multiple targets depend on it. Because the dependencies of a task are executed before the task, the actual order of execution here is find, inspect, test, and then purchase.

Properties

In addition to targets and tasks, the third pillar of an Ant build file is its *properties*. Properties are name-value pairs that act much like constants in Java code. You set the value of a property with the property element and can refer to that property by name throughout your build file. You can insert the value of a property in task attributes by dereferencing the property name with ${*property-name*}.

For example, if you had a property named bin corresponding to the output directory of your build and wanted to refer to that directory, you could refer to it as ${bin} when you assign it to task attributes in your build file. If you wanted to refer to the *archives* subdirectory in that output directory, you could refer to it as ${bin}/archives. The advantages to this approach should be obvious to anyone who's had to change a directory name in 300 different places throughout an application.

 A forward slash will work as a directory delimiter even on Windows systems; Ant is smart enough to know what you mean.

Property attributes

Properties are used the same way as constants are in Java: they let you collect definitions in one centralized place rather than having them dispersed throughout a build file. When you want to change property values, you can make changes in one location and know that they will propagate throughout the build file. You can see the attributes of the property element in Table 1-13.

Table 1-13. The property element's attributes

Attribute	Description	Required
classpath	The classpath to use when looking for a resource.	No
classpathref	The classpath to use when looking for a resource, which can then be given as a *reference* to a path element later in the build file.	No
environment	The prefix to use when retrieving environment variables. For example, if you specify environment="env", you will be able to access operating-system-specific environment variables as property names like ${env.PATH}.	A resource, file, url, or environment attribute is required when not using the name attribute.
file	The name of a property file to load values from.	A resource, file, url, or environment attribute is required when not using the name attribute.

Table 1-13. The property element's attributes (continued)

Attribute	Description	Required
location	Sets the property to the absolute filename of the given file. If an absolute path is supplied, it's left unchanged (with / and \ characters converted for the current platforms). Otherwise, the supplied filename is taken as a path relative to the project's base directory and then expanded.	A value, location, or refid element is required when using the name attribute.
name	The name of the property to set.	No
prefix	The prefix to add to properties loaded from a file or a resource. A . is appended to the prefix if none is specified.	No
refid	A *reference* to a (previously) defined object.	A value, location, or refid element is required when using the name attribute.
resource	The resource name of the property file, used for searching the classpath.	A resource, file, url, or environment attribute is required when not using the name attribute.
url	The URL from which to read properties.	A resource, file, url, or environment attribute is required when not using the name attribute.
value	The value of this property.	A value, location, or refid element is required when using the name attribute.

As an example, you can store a message that displays "Building the .jar file." in a property named message:

```
<?xml version="1.0" ?>
<project default="main">

    <property name="message" value="Building the .jar file." />
    .
    .
    .
</project>
```

 You declare properties *outside* your targets. As of Ant 1.6, *all* tasks can be declared outside of targets (earlier versions only allowed property, typedef and taskdef to be used outside of a target element). When you define tasks external to a specific target, those tasks are evaluated *before* any targets are executed.

You can echo the message to the console like this:

```
<?xml version="1.0" ?>
<project default="main">
```

```
<property name="message" value="Building the .jar file." />
    .
    .
    .
<target name="main" depends="compile, compress">
    <echo>
        ${message}
    </echo>
</target>

</project>
```

Properties are frequently used to hold pathnames, and the property element's location attribute is useful in this context. Suppose you're storing your source code in a subdirectory of the current directory named *source* and want to deploy the *.jar* file created by this build file to a directory named *bin*. You can create properties corresponding to these directories:

```
<?xml version="1.0" ?>
<project default="main">

    <property name="message" value="Building the .jar file." />
    <property name="src" location="source" />
    <property name="output" location="bin" />

    <target name="main" depends="init, compile, compress">
        <echo>
            ${message}
        </echo>
    </target>
        .
        .
        .
</project>
```

The default target in this build file, main, depends on an init target where the mkdir task (detailed in Chapter 3) is used to create the output directory:

```
<?xml version="1.0" ?>
<project default="main">

    <property name="message" value="Building the .jar file." />
    <property name="src" location="source" />
    <property name="output" location="bin" />

    <target name="main" depends="init, compile, compress">
        <echo>
            ${message}
        </echo>
    </target>

    <target name="init">
        <mkdir dir="${output}" />
    </target>
```

```
        .
        .
        .
</project>
```

Now you can compile the Java source code from the ${src} directory, placing the created *.class* file in the ${output} directory, and create the *Project.jar* file in the ${output} directory, all using properties:

```
<?xml version="1.0" ?>
<project default="main">

    <property name="message" value="Building the .jar file." />
    <property name="src" location="source" />
    <property name="output" location="bin" />

    <target name="main" depends="init, compile, compress">
        <echo>
            ${message}
        </echo>
    </target>

    <target name="init">
        <mkdir dir="${output}" />
    </target>

    <target name="compile">
        <javac srcdir="${src}" destdir="${output}" />
    </target>

    <target name="compress">
        <jar destfile="${output}/Project.jar" basedir="${output}"
            includes="*.class" />
    </target>
</project>
```

The relative paths used will be expanded in a platform-specific way, something like this in Unix:

```
-bash-2.05b$ ant -f properties.xml
Buildfile: properties.xml

init:
    [mkdir] Created dir: /home/steve/bin

compile:
    [javac] Compiling 1 source file to /home/steve/bin

compress:
      [jar] Building jar: /home/steve/bin/Project.jar

main:
     [echo]
     [echo]                   Building the .jar file.
     [echo]
```

```
BUILD SUCCESSFUL
Total time: 2 seconds
```

Here's the Windows version:

```
C:\ant\ch01>ant -f properties.xml
Buildfile: properties.xml

init:
    [mkdir] Created dir: C:\ant\ch01\bin

compile:
    [javac] Compiling 1 source file to C:\ant\ch01\bin

compress:
      [jar] Building jar: C:\ant\ch01\bin\Project.jar

main:
     [echo]
     [echo]                 Building the .jar file.
     [echo]

BUILD SUCCESSFUL
Total time: 4 seconds
```

Built-in properties

Ant gives you access to the same system properties you'd have access to in Java code, as if they were Ant properties. For example, if you want to determine the name of the operating system, you can refer to ${os.name} in your build file.

 For a list of system properties, see the Java documentation of the System.getProperties( ) method.

Ant has some additional Ant-specific properties:

ant.file
   Contains the absolute path of the build file

ant.java.version
   Contains the JVM version Ant is using (can hold only 1.1, 1.2, 1.3, 1.4 and [as of Ant 1.6] 1.5)

ant.project.name
   Holds the name of the project that is executing (set with the name attribute of project)

`ant.version`
> Contains the version of Ant running

`basedir`
> Holds the absolute path of the project's base directory (set with the `basedir` attribute of project)

Running Ant

Running Ant from the command-line is simple:

```
%ant [options] [target [target2 [target3] ...]]
```

Command-Line Options

options are one or more of the command-line options that begin with a hyphen, listed in Table 1-14; *target*, *target2*, etc., are the specific targets you want to run in the event you don't want to defer to the project element's default target.

 Entering **ant -help** on the command line generates a list of command-line options.

Table 1-14. Ant command-line options

Name	Description
`-buildfile` *file*, `-f` *file*, or `-file` *file*	Runs the build file specified by *file*.
`-D`*property=value*	Sets a property called *property* with a value of *value*, and passes it to Ant.
`-debug`, `-d`	Prints debugging information.
`-diagnostics`	Prints diagnostics about Ant.
`-emacs`, `-e`	Creates plain, emacs-friendly logging information.
`-find` *file*, `-s` *file*	Searches for the build file (named *file*) along the directory structure towards the root.
`-help`, `-h`	Prints help information.
`-inputhandler` *class*	Specifies the class that will handle user text input.
`-keep-going`, `-k`	Continues to execute targets even if prior targets fail. Only targets that do not depend on failed targets are attempted.
`-l` *file*	Logs output to *file*.
`-lib` *path*	Specifies the classpath on which to search for JARs and library classes.
`-listener` *classname*	Adds an instance of *classname* as a listener, which is alerted when build events occur (e.g., starting and stopping of the build process).
`-logger` *classname*	Specifies the class to handle logging of Ant's output.

Table 1-14. Ant command-line options (continued)

Name	Description
-noinput	Turns off interactive input.
-projecthelp, -p	Prints the project's help information (if there is any).
-propertyfile *file*	Loads properties from the specified file.
-quiet, -q	Reduces Ant messages to the minimum possible.
-verbose, -v	Specifies verbose output.
-version	Prints the version of Ant being used.

Ant Is Just Java

Ultimately, Ant is just Java code, and can be run with java like any other Java class:

```
java -Dant.home=/home/steven/ant org.apache.tools.ant.Main
    [options] [target [target2 [target3] ...]]
```

You can use the Ant Launcher, which first appeared in Ant 1.6:

```
java -Dant.home=/home/steven/ant org.apache.tools.ant.launch.Launcher
    [options] [target [target2 [target3] ...]]
```

Executing Ant

If you want to use a build file named *build.xml* and want to run the default target, enter ant in the directory containing the build file:

```
%ant
```

For example, if you ran the build file from Example 1-2, that command gives this result:

```
-bash-2.05b$ ant
Buildfile: build.xml

compile:
    [javac] Compiling 1 source file

compress:
      [jar] Building jar: /home/httpd/vhosts/builder/Project.jar

main:
     [echo]
     [echo]              Building the .jar file.
     [echo]

BUILD SUCCESSFUL
Total time: 2 seconds
```

Each build file requires a default target, but you can specify the target(s) you want Ant to run via the command line. For example, add a target named clean to the build file (using Example 1-2 as a starting point):

```
<project default="main">
    <target name="main" depends="compile, compress">
        <echo>
            Building the .jar file.
        </echo>
    </target>

    <target name="compile">
        <javac srcdir="."/>
    </target>

<target name="compress">
        <jar jarfile="Project.jar" basedir="." includes="*.class" />
    </target>

    <target name="clean">
        <delete file="*.class"/>
        <delete file="*.jar"/>
    </target>
</project>
```

You can then specify the clean target from the command line:

```
%ant clean
```

If you want to run multiple targets, you can list them (in the order they should be run):

```
%ant clean compile compress
```

> If you don't want to allow a target to be run from the command line, you can start the target name with a hyphen (e.g., -clean). This will make Ant think the target is a command-line option, and since -clean isn't a valid command-line option, Ant will refuse to run that target directly.

By default, the build file that Ant looks for is *build.xml*, but you can name the file as you want.

> The downloadable example code for Ant has multiple build filenames to make the separation of examples clearer.

For example, if you have a build file named *project.xml* that you want to use, you can specify that Ant should use that build file with -f (or -file or -buildfile):

```
%ant -f project.xml
```

If you use the -find *file* option, Ant will search for a build file first in the current directory, then in the parent directory, and so on, until a build file with the supplied name is found or the root of the filesystem is reached.

Customizable Environment Variables

Ant scripts, which start Ant, use some customizable environment variables:

JAVACMD
> Holds the full path of the Java executable. Use this to launch a different JVM than JAVA_HOME/*bin/java(.exe)*.

ANT_OPTS
> Command-line arguments that should be passed to the JVM unchanged.

ANT_ARGS
> Ant command-line arguments. These may be used, for example, to point to a different logger, a new listener, or to include the -find flag in all invocations of Ant.

 The Ant wrapper script for Unix will read the file *~/.antrc* before it starts running. On Windows, the Ant wrapper batchfile *ant.bat* invokes %HOME%*antrc_pre.bat* at the start of the Ant process and %HOME%*antrc_post.bat* at the end of that process. You can use these files to set or unset environment variables that should only be used during the execution of Ant.

Failed Builds

Every Ant developer has builds that fail for one reason or another. Ant does its best to pinpoint the problem. For example, say you misspelled the name of the javac task:

```
<?xml version="1.0" ?>
<project default="main">
    <target name="main" depends="compile, compress">
        <echo>
            Building the .jar file.
        </echo>
    </target>

    <target name="compile">
        <jjavac srcdir="."/>
    </target>
    .
    .
    .
```

Ant will diagnose this problem when it runs and give you some feedback:

```
%ant
build.xml:10: Could not create task or type of type: jjavac.

Ant could not find the task or a class this task relies upon.

This is common and has a number of causes; the usual
solutions are to read the manual pages then download and
install needed JAR files, or fix the build file:
 - You have misspelt 'jjavac'.
   Fix: check your spelling.
 - The task needs an external JAR file to execute
   and this is not found at the right place in the classpath.
   Fix: check the documentation for dependencies.
   Fix: declare the task.
 - The task is an Ant optional task and optional.jar is absent
   Fix: look for optional.jar in ANT_HOME/lib, download if needed
 - The task was not built into optional.jar as dependent
   libraries were not found at build time.
   Fix: look in the JAR to verify, then rebuild with the needed
   libraries, or download a release version from apache.org
 - The build file was written for a later version of Ant
   Fix: upgrade to at least the latest release version of Ant
 - The task is not an Ant core or optional task
   and needs to be declared using <taskdef>.

Remember that for JAR files to be visible to Ant tasks implemented
in ANT_HOME/lib, the files must be in the same directory or on the
classpath

Please neither file bug reports on this problem, nor email the
Ant mailing lists, until all of these causes have been explored,
as this is not an Ant bug.

Total time: 0 seconds
```

Sometimes errors won't stop a build, and you may want to change that behavior so the build will terminate when there's been any kind of problem. Most tasks have a failonerror attribute, which is set to false by default. Setting this attribute's value to true makes the build fail if the task encounters an error, allowing you to stop a build if a specific task generates errors.

Keep in mind that this won't affect your build in the case where you've previously executed the build and your output files are up to date. By default, Ant tasks check to see if the output files they're supposed to create are current (i.e., the output file is more recent than the files used to create it); if they are, Ant tasks won't recreate them because Ant considers the target executed. For example, here's what you'd see when you run the example build file a second time; Ant displays the names of the various targets but, because they're up to date, it doesn't execute them:

```
%ant
Buildfile: build.xml

compile:

compress:

main:
     [echo]
     [echo]                Building the .jar file.
     [echo]

BUILD SUCCESSFUL
Total time: 3 seconds
```

 Ant doesn't come with a built-in debugger, which can make it tough to troubleshoot build files. However, one of the items under development in the Java Eclipse IDE is an Ant build file debugger. Chapter 11 has more on integrating Ant into Eclipse.

Verbose Output

You can control the amount of output Ant gives you when it runs with the -verbose, -quiet, and -debug command-line options. If you ask Ant to be quiet, it won't display anything except for build failure or success, total build time, and any text you specifically output via the echo task. Here's an example of a quiet build:

```
%ant -quiet
     [echo]
     [echo]                Building the .jar file.
     [echo]

BUILD SUCCESSFUL
Total time: 2 seconds
```

On the other side of the coin, the -verbose option gives you a lot more information than normal, including whether Ant is skipping up-to-date output files, what OS or JDK you're using, and a lot more. Here's what you might see from a verbose build on Unix:

```
-bash-2.05b$ ant -verbose
Apache Ant version 1.6.1 compiled on February 12 2004
Buildfile: build.xml
Detected Java version: 1.4 in: /opt/j2sdk1.4.2_02/jre
Detected OS: Linux
parsing buildfile /home/build.xml
Project base dir set to: /home
Build sequence for target `main' is [compile, compress, main]
Complete build sequence is [compile, compress, main, clean, ]
```

```
compile:
    [javac] Project.class skipped - don't know how to handle it
    [javac] Project.jar skipped - don't know how to handle it
    [javac] Project.java omitted as Project.class is up to date.
    [javac] build.xml skipped - don't know how to handle it

compress:
      [jar] Project.class omitted as Project.class is up to date.

main:
     [echo]
     [echo]                 Building the .jar file.
     [echo]

BUILD SUCCESSFUL
Total time: 1 second
```

This output shows that Ant is skipping up-to-date output targets. Here's similar output in Windows:

```
%ant -verbose
Apache Ant version 1.6.1 compiled on February 12 2004
Buildfile: build.xml
Detected Java version: 1.4 in: C:\jdk1.4
Detected OS: Windows 2000
parsing buildfile C:\ant\ch01\build.xml with URI = file:///C:/ant/ch01/build.xml

Project base dir set to: C:\ant\ch01
Build sequence for target `main' is [compile, compress, main]
Complete build sequence is [compile, compress, main, clean, ]

compile:
    [javac] Project.class skipped - don't know how to handle it
    [javac] Project.jar skipped - don't know how to handle it
    [javac] Project.java omitted as Project.class is up to date.
    [javac] build.xml skipped - don't know how to handle it

compress:
      [jar] Project.class omitted as Project.class is up to date.

main:
     [echo]
     [echo]                 Building the .jar file.
     [echo]

BUILD SUCCESSFUL
Total time: 2 seconds
```

The -debug options prints out even more information—often pages of it—which isn't reproduced here. Included in a debugging build is information about classes as they're loaded, classes that Ant looked for but couldn't find, the locations where Ant is picking up library files, and almost everything else you could think of.

Another useful command-line option for displaying information is the -projecthelp option, which prints out a list of the build file's targets. Targets that include a description attribute are listed as Main targets; those without a description are listed as "Subtargets," and then the "Default" target is listed.

Here's the example build file, with the addition of a description attribute for each target element:

```xml
<?xml version="1.0" ?>
<project default="main">
    <target name="main" depends="compile, compress" description="Main target">
        <echo>
            Building the .jar file.
        </echo>
    </target>

    <target name="compile" description="Compilation target">
        <javac srcdir="."/>
    </target>

    <target name="compress" description="Compression target">
        <jar jarfile="Project.jar" basedir="." includes="*.class" />
    </target>
</project>
```

Here's what you'd see when running Ant with the -projecthelp option:

```
%ant -projecthelp
Buildfile: build.xml

Main targets:

 compile   Compilation target
 compress  Compression target
 main      Main target
Default target: main
```

Logging and Libraries

You can log the output of running Ant using the -logfile option. For example, here's how you'd sent output to a file named *file.log*:

```
%ant -logfile file.log
```

You can log part of a build file's results with the record task; for example, if you were using the javac task to compile code and wanted to log the output of this task to a file named *log.txt*, you could start and stop that logging this way:

```xml
<record name="log.txt" action="start"/>
    <javac ... />
<record name="log.txt" action="stop"/>
```

Another handy option is the -lib option, which adds additional directories to be searched for *.jar* or *.class* files. Here's an example, which adds */home/ant/morejars* to the library search path:

```
%ant -lib /home/ant/morejars
```

The -lib option is useful when you're working on a system where you don't have access to the Ant *lib* directory as is often the case when dealing with Internet Service Providers (ISPs). Using this option, you can make sure Ant has access to JAR files needed for Ant's optional tasks without having to load them into directories you don't have permission to access.

 Before Ant 1.6, all JARS in *ANT_HOME/lib* would be added to the CLASSPATH used to run Ant. Since Ant 1.6, two directories are scanned—*ANT_HOME/lib* and *.ant/lib*—in the Java user home directory. You can place additional library files in this directory if you don't have access to *ANT_HOME/lib*. The location of the Java user home directory depends on your JVM settings. In Unix, it's usually your home directory (so you'd store additional Ant libraries in, for example, */home/<username>/.ant/lib*). In Windows, it's usually *C:\Documents and Settings\<username>* (so you'd store additional Ant libraries in *C:\Documents and Settings\<username>\.ant\lib*). To determine where your Java user home is, use this element in a build file:

```
<echo>${user.home}</echo>
```

CHAPTER 2

Using Properties and Types

In Chapter 1, you learned about properties and tasks in Ant. However, long tables with short descriptions do not an Ant expert make. In this chapter, you begin to get the details on using Ant's extensive feature set, which relies on two conerstones: properties and types. You received an introduction to them in the previous chapter, but here's where to get a real working knowledge.

In the examples from last chapter, building was a linear process: you compiled some files, you JARed them up, and then you were done. In the real world, things are almost never so straightforward. You need to be able to check for specific files and perform different tasks depending on the existence of those files. You need to respond to error conditions, and let the user know what has happened when errors do occur. You often need to deal with groups of files, copy them over en masse, and more. These kinds of tasks involve using properties and types.

Using Properties to Control Tasks

Ant provides extensive support for controlling the build process; though Ant is not a programming language, it has a number of control structures, and those control structures rely on properties. As if and try/catch allow you to handle several logic paths in Java, Ant's control tasks allow you the same flexibility within the context of a build process.

Setting Conditions

The foundation to any type of control processing is some form of the if statement. This typically involves two steps:

1. Check or determine if a certain condition is true.
2. If the condition is true, perform one action; if it is false, perform another.

In Java, this all happens in a single line of code; in Ant, the condition must be set in one step, and the evaluation of that condition occurs in another step. First, you need to set a condition based on some criteria; not surprisingly, condition is the name of the task Ant provides. condition allows you to specify one or more true/false tests (sometimes called *criteria*). If all the criteria evaluate to true, a property, supplied to the condition task, is set to true; if one or more of the criteria evaluate to false, the property is assigned a false value. You can check that property's value later in the build file.

In this example, the build file checks to see if two files exist using the available task (covered later in the chapter) and sets the property all.set (to true) if the files are found:

```
<condition property="all.set">
  <and>
    <available file="file1.java"/>
    <available file="file2.java"/>
  </and>
</condition>
```

Here's another example where the build file checks to see if it's running on Mac OS but not Mac OS X, which Ant treats as part of the Unix family:

```
<condition property="MacOs.Not.MacOsX">
  <and>
    <os family="mac"/>
    <not>
      <os family="unix"/>
    </not>
  </and>
</condition>
```

Here's how you can set a property; in this case, called do.abort—if the do.delete property value equals "yes":

```
<condition property="do.abort">
  <equals arg1="yes" arg2="${do.delete}"/>
</condition>
```

You can see the attributes of the condition task in Table 2-1.

Table 2-1. The condition task's attributes

Attribute	Description	Required	Default
property	The property you want to set.	Yes	
value	The value you want to set the property to.	No	true

This task depends on nested elements for evaluation; you can see the possibilities in Table 2-2.

Table 2-2. Elements that can be nested within the condition task

Nested element	Functionality
and	True if all of its contained conditions are true.
available	Identical to the `available` task, which checks for the availabilty of files.
checksum	Identical to the Ant `checksum` task, which generates a checksum for files. If you compare two files that you think are the same, but their checksums are different, the files are different as well.
contains	Checks if one string (`string`) contains another (`substring`). Optionally, you can make the test case sensitive with the `casesensitive` attribute. The default is to make comparisons case insensitive.
equals	Checks whether two strings are identical. The strings are given using the (required) attributes `arg1` and `arg2`. The optional attributes are `casesensitive` and `trim`.
filesmatch	Checks to see whether two files have identical contents. The required attributes are `file1` and `file2`.
http	Checks for a valid response from a web server at the specified URL. The required attribute is `url`, and the optional attribute is `errorsBeginAt` (the lowest HTTP response code that is an error).
isfalse	Behaves the same as `istrue` but returns the logically opposite value.
isreference	Checks if a particular reference has been defined. The required attribute is `refid`; the optional attribute is `type`, which holds the name of the data type or task you expect this reference to be.
isset	Checks if a given property has been set. The required attribute is `property`.
istrue	Checks if a string equals any of the strings Ant considers true, that is, `true`, `yes`, or `on`. There is one required attribute: `value` (holds the value to test).
not	Logically negates the results of a condition.
or	True if at least one of the contained conditions is true.
os	True if the operating system matches the attributes you specify. The attributes (all optional) of this element are `family` (windows, dos, unix, mac, win9x, sunOS, etc.), `name`, `arch` (meaning architecture), and `version`.
socket	Checks for the existence of a TCP/IP listener. The required attributes are `server` (an IP address or DNS name) and `port`.
uptodate	Identical to the `uptodate` task. True if the target file is at least as up-to-date as its source code. The required attributes are `property` (the property to set), `srcfile` (source file to check), and `targetfile` (the file you want to check for up-to-dateness).

Here's an example that sets the property omit.debug.info to true if the property build.type contains *either* of the words "release" or "gold" *and* if the property explicitly.include.debug.info is false:

```
<condition property="omit.debug.info">
    <and>
        <or>
            <contains string="${build.type}" substring="release"/>
            <contains string="${build.type}" substring="gold"/>
        </or>
        <isfalse value="${explicitly.include.debug.info}"/>
    </and>
</condition>
```

Here's another example, which sets the property use.property.file true if the files build.properties *and* version.properties are available, *or* if the file *core.jar* is not current:

```
<condition property="use.property.file">
    <or>
        <and>
            <available file="build.properties"/>
            <available file="version.properties"/>
        </and>
        <not>
            <uptodate srcfile="core.java" targetfile="core.jar"/>
        </not>
    </or>
</condition>
```

Performing Conditional Actions

Actions can be conditionally executed based on two factors: if a certain condition has been met (using the if attribute) and if a certain condition has not been met (using the unless attribute). You can determine if a task runs using if and unless to check the values of properties. Three elements support if and unless attributes: target, patternset (which can group file-matching patterns such as "*.java," "*.class," and so on; see the section "Working with Patterns"); fail target is the simplest, as shown here:

```
<target name="buildModule" if="code.complied.OK"/>
    .
    .
    .
</target>
```

The buildModule target is executed only if the code.complied.OK property is true.

Example 2-1 demonstrates the unless attribute. In this case, the build file won't compile the source files if the file *enduser.agreement* exists, which sets a property named final.version.

Example 2-1. Using the unless attribute (ch02/if/build.xml)

```
<?xml version="1.0" ?>
<project default="main">

    <property name="message" value="Building the .jar file." />
    <property name="src" location="source" />
    <property name="output" location="bin" />
    <available file="${output}/enduser.agreement" property="final.version"/>

    <target name="main" depends="init, compile, compress">
        <echo>
            ${message}
```

Example 2-1. Using the unless attribute (ch02/if/build.xml) (continued)

```
        </echo>
    </target>

    <target name="init">
        <mkdir dir="${output}" />
    </target>

    <target name="compile" unless="final.version">
        <javac srcdir="${src}" destdir="${output}" />
    </target>

  <target name="compress">
        <jar destfile="${output}/Project.jar" basedir="${output}"
            includes="*.class" />
  </target>
</project>
```

Stopping Builds

You can make a build fail at runtime using property values and the fail task.

 The fail task has been made more useful since Ant 1.5 with the addition of support for the if and unless attributes.

For example, this build will fail with a message unless the specified classes are found in the classpath:

```
    <target name=
        <condition property="classes.available">
            <and>
                <available classname="org.steven.SAXparser" />
                <available classname="org.steven.DOMparser" />
            </and>
        </condition>
        <fail message="Could not find all classes." unless="classes.available" />
            .
            .
            .
    </target>
```

You can see the available attributes of fail in Table 2-3.

Table 2-3. The fail task's attributes

Attribute	Description	Required
message	A message indicating why the build exited	No
if	Fails if the property of the given name is true in the current project	No
unless	Fails if a property of the given name is false in the current project	No

Property-Setting Tasks

A few tasks allow you to indirectly set properties; that is, you specify a task (like available) and assign the result of that task's processing to a property. These function are like the condition task, though the syntax is different.

Availability of resources

The available task sets a property to true if a resource is available at runtime. The resource can be a file, a directory, a class in the classpath, or a JVM system resource. If the resource is available, the property value is set to true; otherwise, the property is not set.

For example, the following build fragment will set the property Math.present to true if org.steve.Math is in Ant's classpath:

```
<available classname="org.steve.Math" property="Math.present"/>
```

Here's another example, which sets file.present to true if the file build.properties exists in the current directory:

```
<available file="build.properties" property="file.present"/>
```

You can see the attributes of this task in Table 2-4. You can set the property value to something other than the default by using the value attribute.

This task is handy for setting properties that avoid or allow target execution depending on system parameters or the presence of various files. For example, you may want to load in properties from a property file (see the section "Using Property Files" in this chapter) rather than use default values if that property file exists.

Table 2-4. The available task's attributes

Attribute	Description	Required	Default
classname	Class to search for.	One of classname, file, or resource	
classpath	Classpath to use when searching for classname or resource.	No	
classpathref	A reference to the classpath to use for searches.	No	
file	The file to search for.	One of classname, file, or resource	
filepath	The path to use when searching for a file.	No	
ignoresystemclasses	Set to true to ignore Ant's runtime classes in searches, using only the specified classpath instead. Affects the classname attribute.	No	false
property	The name of the property to set with the results of the search.	Yes	

Table 2-4. The available task's attributes (continued)

Attribute	Description	Required	Default
resource	The resource to look for.	One of `classname`, `file`, or `resource`	
type	The type of file to look for. Set this to a directory (`type="dir"`) or a file (`type="file"`).	No	
value	Specifies the value you want to set the property to for a successful match.	No	true

Checking file modification dates

The uptodate task sets a property to true under certain conditions. In this case, the property is set to true if a target file, or set of target files, is more current than a source file or set of source files. You can specify the file you want to check with the targetfile attribute and the source file that is used to create it with the srcfile attribute. If you want to check a set of source files, use nested srcfiles elements. If the target (or targets) is current, based on the source file or files, the property whose name you specify will be set to true.

In this example, the property Do.Not.Build will be set to true if the target file, *classes.jar,* is current when compared to its source *.java* files:

```
<uptodate property="Do.Not.Build" targetfile="classes.jar" >
    <srcfiles dir= "${src}" includes="*.java"/>
</uptodate>
```

You can use the ** wildcard to stand for the current directory and any subdirectory of that directory, which makes it easy to work with a directory hierarchy in depth. For example, if you want to check the ${src} directory for *.java* files, as in the previous example, and any subdirectory of ${src}, you could set includes to **/*.java. Doing so would match the *.java* files in the ${src} directory and in any subdirectories of ${src}. Here's how that might look:

```
<uptodate property="Do.Not.Build" targetfile="classes.jar" >
    <srcfiles dir= "${src}" includes="**/*.java"/>
</uptodate>
```

Here's an example checking against a single source file, using the srcfile attribute:

```
<uptodate property="Do.Not.Build" targetfile="classes.jar" >
    <srcfile includes="/usr/local/bin/classes.java"/>
</uptodate>
```

You can see attributes for the uptodate task in Table 2-5.

Table 2-5. The uptodate task's attributes

Attribute	Description	Required	Default
property	The name of the property to set with the results of this task	Yes.	
value	The value you want to set the property to if the target is current	No.	true
srcfile	The file you want to check against the target file(s)	Yes, unless a nested srcfiles element is present	
targetfile	The file you want to check for current status	Yes, unless a nested mapper element is present	

Using Property Files

In larger build files, you might be working with dozens of properties, and storing them in property files is common. Setting tens, or hundreds, of properties all within a build file is a bad habit to get into and almost impossible to maintain.

Using property files means that you can quickly tailor a build file to different sets of circumstances by swapping property files. And you can store property values; though we've been using mostly true/false properties to make conditional processing easier, they can hold all kinds of textual data, such as copyright notices and legal information, in a central repository everyone can share.

 You can specify a property file to use on the command line with the -propertyfile option.

Take a look at Example 2-2, which uses a property file to hold a property named message. This example points to the property file with the property task's file attribute, which can hold the fully qualified name of the file. You can use the property task's url attribute to point to a property file.

Example 2-2. Using a property file (ch02/properties/build.xml)

```xml
<?xml version="1.0" ?>
<project default="main">

    <property file="build.properties" />
    <property name="src" location="source" />
    <property name="output" location="bin" />

    <target name="main" depends="init, compile, compress">
        <echo>
            ${message}
        </echo>
    </target>
```

Example 2-2. Using a property file (ch02/properties/build.xml) (continued)

```
    <target name="init">
        <mkdir dir="${output}" />
    </target>

    <target name="compile">
        <javac srcdir="${src}" destdir="${output}" />
    </target>

  <target name="compress">
          <jar destfile="${output}/Project.jar" basedir="${output}" includes="*.class" />
  </target>
</project>
```

Here are the entire contents of another sample file, *build.properties*, which uses a *name=value* format for each property:

```
message=Building the .jar file.
```

Using the build file from Example 2-2, here's the output from running Ant; note the value of the message property was picked up correctly from *build.properties*:

```
%ant
Buildfile: build.xml

init:
    [mkdir] Created dir: /home/steve/ch02/properties/bin

compile:
    [javac] Compiling 1 source file to /home/steve/ch02/properties/bin

compress:
     [jar] Building jar: /home/steve/ch02/properties/bin/Project.jar

 main:
     [echo]
     [echo]                 Building the .jar file.
     [echo]

BUILD SUCCESSFUL
Total time: 3 seconds
```

Properties in external files are stored as text strings, suitable for properties of the kind you'd set with the property task's value attribute.

Ant has an optional task, propertyfile, that lets you edit property files. This can be useful when you need to make unattended modifications to configuration files when deploying to servers.

Loading Text

You use the `loadfile` task to load a text file into a single property. Here's an example that loads the property `message` with the text in the file *message.txt*:

```
<loadfile property="message"
    srcFile="message.txt"/>
```

You can see the attributes of this task in Table 2-6.

Table 2-6. The loadfile task's attributes

Attribute	Description	Required	Default
srcFile	Indicates the source file	Yes	
property	Indicates the property you want to store the text in	Yes	
encoding	Indicates the encoding you want to use when reading text from the file	No	
failonerror	Set to `true` if you want to halt the build if this task failed	No	true

Overriding Properties

Take a look at Example 2-3, defining a property named `message` twice: first with the value `"Building the .jar file."` and then with the value `"Compiling and compressing."`.

Example 2-3. Overriding a property (ch02/overriding/build.xml)

```
<?xml version="1.0" ?>
<project default="main">

    <property name="message" value="Building the .jar file." />
    <property name="src" location="source" />
    <property name="output" location="bin" />
    <property name="message" value="Compiling and compressing." />

    <target name="main" depends="init, compile, compress">
        <echo>
            ${message}
        </echo>
    </target>

    <target name="init">
        <mkdir dir="${output}" />
    </target>

    <target name="compile">
        <javac srcdir="${src}" destdir="${output}" />
    </target>

  <target name="compress">
        <jar destfile="${output}/Project.jar" basedir="${output}" includes="*.class" />
  </target>
</project>
```

This attempts to override the property with a new definition. Once you define a property in a build file, it behaves much like a constant—ie., you can't redefine it inside the build file. So, when you run Ant using this build file, you'll see the first version of the property:

```
init:
    [mkdir] Created dir: /home/steve/ch02/properties/bin

compile:
    [javac] Compiling 1 source file to /home/steve/ch02/properties/bin

compress:
      [jar] Building jar: /home/steve/ch02/properties/bin/Project.jar

main:
    [echo]
    [echo]              Building the .jar file.
    [echo]

BUILD SUCCESSFUL
Total time: 3 seconds
```

When Ant sees a property defined, whether in a build or a property file, it considers that property defined. You can't change it.

Except in one way. (Of course! Who wants a language without exceptions?)

If you want to override a property in a build file, you can set properties on the command line. That can be done with the -Dproperty=value option, where property is the name of the property and value is the value for that property. If you specify a property set in the build file, the value specified on the command line will override the value specified in the build file.

Here's how to do that:

```
%ant -Dmessage="Compiling and compressing"
Buildfile: build.xml

init:
    [mkdir] Created dir: /home/steve/ch02/properties/bin

compile:
    [javac] Compiling 1 source file to /home/steve/ch02/properties/bin

compress:
      [jar] Building jar: /home/steve/ch02/properties/bin/Project.jar

main:
    [echo]
    [echo]              Compiling and compressing
    [echo]
```

```
BUILD SUCCESSFUL
Total time: 3 seconds
```

The value on the command line overrides both of the values within the build file.

Setting Properties Using Environment Variables

You can access environment variables with the property element's environment attribute, which sets the prefix to use for environment variables ("env" is customary in Ant files); after you set that prefix, you can reference environment variables by name using that prefix. Here's an example build file that displays the value of ANT_HOME:

```
<project default="main">

    <property file="build.properties" />
    <property name="src" location="source" />
    <property name="output" location="bin" />
    <property environment="env" />

    <target name="main" depends="init, compile, compress">
        <echo>
            ${env.ANT_HOME}
        </echo>
    </target>
        .
        .
        .
```

Here's the result of running Ant using this build file:

```
%ant
Buildfile: build.xml

init:

compile:

compress:

main:
     [echo]
     [echo]                 C:\ant\apache-ant-1.6.1
     [echo]

BUILD SUCCESSFUL
Total time: 2 seconds
```

It's easy to pass environment variables from the command line as well; use -DVAR=%ENV_VAR% (Windows) or -DVAR=$ENV_VAR (Unix). You can then access these variables inside your build file as ${VAR}.

You've got a good handle on properties at this point, and they're a major building block of Ant build files. The next step up is to work with the built-in Ant *types*.

Handling Data Using Types

Ant supports a number of types, and the rest of this chapter is devoted to understanding them and how to work with them. These types work much like data types in programming languages, and as you're going to see, types and properties are intertwined. The data structures you create using types can be assigned to properties, and the data you use to set up those data structures is often stored in properties. Now that you've got properties under your belt, it's time to move on to types.

Much of what a build tool like Ant does is work with files in directory structures, so you might expect that many of the Ant types have to do with handling files and directories. You can see the available Ant core (that is, built-in) types in Table 2-7.

Table 2-7. Core Ant types

Type	Description
Assertions	Enables, or disables, Java 1.4 assertions
Description	Holds a description of the project that can be viewed if you use the Ant -projecthelp command
DirSet	Contains a group of directories
FileList	Contains a named list of files
FileSet	Contains a groups of files
File mappers	Maps original filenames to a new set of names
FilterChains	Contains a group of ordered FilterReaders
FilterSet	Contains a group of filters
PatternSet	Contains a group of filename-matching patterns
Path-like structures	Includes a wide variety of support for specifying file paths
Permissions	Contains the security permissions given to the code as executed in the JVM where Ant is currently running
PropertySet	Groups a set of properties together
Selectors	Groups files in a fileset selected using criteria other than filename, as provided by the include and exclude tags
XMLCatalog	Contains a catalog of public XML resources, such as DTDs or entities
ZipFileSet	Contains a special form of a fileset, using ZIP files

Many Ant tasks in the upcoming chapters depend on the types you see in Table 2-7, so it's worth going through them in detail, especially the ones that handle files. Understanding Ant types is central to using Ant; if you don't understand paths and FileSets, for example, you'll be severely hampered by what you can do with Ant.

Path-Like Structures

In Ant, paths are often handled by the path type, called a *path-like structure*. As you can imagine, you have to work with paths frequently. For example, a task like javac supports the path attributes srcdir, classpath, sourcepath, bootclasspath, and extdirs, all of which are handled as path-like structures. That means you can set them as attributes:

```
<javac destdir="${build}"
       classpath="classes.jar"
       srcdir="${src}"/>
       debug="on">
</javac>
```

You can set paths as nested elements, not just as attributes, and you do that with the src, classpath, sourcepath, bootclasspath and extdirs elements. For the javac task, the srcdir attribute becomes the src element. Nested elements are a good idea when you have multiple paths you want to work with that would otherwise be assigned to the same attribute. Here's an example:

```
<javac destdir="${build}"
       classpath="classes.jar"
       debug="on">
  <src path="${src}"/>
  <src path="${src2}"/>
</javac>
```

In addition, when you want to specify path-like values, a nested element can be used with internal pathelement elements, which specify paths, like this:

```
<javac destdir="${build}"
       classpath="classes.jar"
       debug="on">
  <src path="${src}"/>
  <src>
    <pathelement path="${src2}"/>
    <pathelement path="${src3}"/>
  </src>
</javac>
```

In pathelement, the location attribute specifies a single file or directory relative to the project's base directory (or an absolute filename), while the path attribute holds colon-separated or semicolon-separated lists of locations (such as "classes.jar;classes2.jar").

 You can separate directories with a / or a \ on any platform.

If you want to build your own paths and reference them later, you can use the path element with enclosed pathelement elements. For example, to create a new path and give it the ID build.classpath, you can use this path element and then refer to the new path with the refid attribute that path-like structure elements support:

```
<path id="build.classpath">
    <pathelement path="${classes}"/>
    <pathelement path="${classes2}"/>
</path>

<target name="compile">
    <javac destdir="${build}"
        classpath="classes.jar"
        debug="on">
    <src path="${src}"/>
    <classpath refid="build.classpath"/>
    </javac>
</target>
```

If a task supports path-like structures, you can specify paths using the attributes of the task, nested elements with names that correspond to those attributes, or with a reference to a path you've explicitly created with path.

Working with Groups of Files

FileSets are types that represent groups of files, and they're common in Ant because handling a group of files is a common thing to do. The fileset element can contain nested include, includesfile, exclude and excludesfile elements; here's an example using fileset, as well as include and exclude:

```
<fileset dir="${source}">
    <include name="**/*.java"/>
    <exclude name="**/*test*"/>
</fileset>
```

Here's an example that lets you include certain files using the filename selector (more on selectors later in this chapter):

```
<fileset dir="${source}">
    <filename name="**/*.java"/>
    <filename name="test.cpp"/>
</fileset>
```

Many Ant tasks support file sets, such as the copy task (see Chapter 4); here's an example, which copies all but *.java* files from the src directory to the dest directory:

```
<copy todir="../dest">
    <fileset dir="src">
        <exclude name="**/*.java"/>
    </fileset>
</copy>
```

You can see the attributes of the fileset type in Table 2-8.

FileSets can appear inside tasks that support file sets or at the same level as target (as when you want to assign a file set to a property).

Table 2-8. The fileset type's attributes

Attribute	Description	Required	Default
casesensitive	Specifies whether the include and exclude patterns be treated in a case-sensitive way.	No	true
defaultexcludes	Specifies whether default excludes will be used or not (yes or no). Default excludes *are* used when omitted.	No	true
dir	Specifies the root of the directory tree used to create this FileSet..	dir or file must be specified.	
excludes	Specifies a list (comma- or space-separated) of patterns of files that you want to exclude.	No	
excludesfile	Specifies a file; each line of this file is used as an exclude pattern.	No	
file	A shortcut for creating a single file fileset.		
followsymlinks	Specifies whether you want symbolic links to be followed. Defaults to true.	No	
includes	Specifies a list of patterns for files that you want included. Comma- or space-separated.	No	
includesfile	Specifies the name of a file; each line in the file will be used as an include pattern.	No	

As mentioned, the fileset element can contain include, includesfile, exclude and excludesfile elements, and you can see the allowed attributes of these elements in Table 2-9. The fileset element can contain patternset and selector elements, which you'll see later in this chapter.

Table 2-9. The include, includesfile, exclude and excludesfile type's attributes

Attribute	Description	Required
If	If the corresponding property is true, use this pattern.	No
Name	Pattern to include/exclude (for include and exclude types) or the name of the file holding the patterns to include/exclude (for includesfile and excludesfile types).	Yes
unless	If the corresponding property is *not* set, use this pattern.	No

Some tasks form *implicit* file sets, such as the javac task. This means that a task supports all attributes of fileset (see Table 2-8). You don't have to use a nested fileset element at all if you don't want to because the built-in attributes of the task give you all the support you need. Each time we come across such a task, I'll be sure to mention this.

 The FileSet dir attribute becomes srcdir in the javac task because a dir attribute would be ambiguous in the javac task: Is it the source or destination directory?

Default excludes

Some files are excluded by default from file sets since they correspond to system or temporary files of various kinds. Here are the patterns excluded by default (recall that ** means the current directory, or any subdirectory of the current directory):

- **/*~
- **/#*#
- **/.#*
- **/%*%
- **/._*
- **/CVS
- **/CVS/**
- **/.cvsignore
- **/SCCS
- **/SCCS/**
- **/vssver.scc
- **/.svn
- **/.svn/**
- **/.DS_Store

 If you do not want these default excludes applied, you can disable them with defaultexcludes="no" in types such as FileSets. You can modify the list of default excludes by using the defaultexcludes task.

Working with Groups of Directories

Directory sets (DirSets) are types corresponding to groups of directories. This type is great for grouping directories together and handling them at one time with various tasks. DirSets can appear inside various tasks or at the same level as target; like file sets, directory sets can contain nested include, includesfile, exclude, excludesfile, and patternset elements. Here's an example:

```
<dirset dir="${build.dir}">
    <include name="apps/**/classes"/>
    <exclude name="apps/**/*Test*"/>
</dirset>
```

You can find the attributes of this type in Table 2-10.

Table 2-10. The dirset type's attributes

Attribute	Description	Required	Default
casesensitive	Specifies whether you want to use case sensitivity.	No	true
dir	Contains the root of the directory tree you want to use.	Yes	
excludes	A list of the patterns matching directories you want exluded. Comma- or space-separated list.	No	
excludesfile	Specifies a name of a file; each line of the file is interpreted as an exclude pattern.	No	
followsymlinks	Set to true if you want symbolic links to be followed.	No	true
includes	A list of the patterns matching directories you want included. Comma- or space-separated list.	No	
includesfile	Specifies a name of a file; each line of the file is interpreted as an include pattern.	No	

Creating Lists of Files

FileLists are types corresponding to explicitly named lists of files. While FileSets act as filters, returning only those files that exist in the filesystem and match specified patterns, FileLists are useful for specifying files individually. Here's an example:

```
<filelist
    id="docfiles"
    dir="${doc}"
    files="type.html,using.html"/>
```

You can see the filelist attributes in Table 2-11.

 FileLists are not supported by as many tasks as FileSets are. You might try using a FileSet with nested filename elements to add individual files to the FileSet.

Table 2-11. The filelist type's attributes

Attribute	Description	Required
dir	The base directory you want to use for this file list	Yes
files	A comma-separated list of filenames to include in the file list	Yes

Working with Patterns

A powerful way of working with multiple files is to use patterns, such as the pattern "*.java," which will match all files with the extension *.java*, "*.class," which matches files with the extension *.class*, and so on. If you want to work with multiple patterns simultaneously in Ant, patterns can be grouped into sets and later referenced by their id attribute. These sets are defined with the `patternset` type, which can appear nested into a FileSet or an implicit FileSet.

Here's an example, where I'm creating a file set, using a pattern set, that will match all of a project's documentation files, excluding beta documentation:

```
<fileset dir="${src}" casesensitive="yes">
    <patternset>
        <include name="docs/**/*.html"/>
        <include name="prof/**/*.html" if="professional"/>
        <exclude name="**/*beta*"/>
    </patternset>
</fileset>
```

You can see the attributes of this type in Table 2-12.

Table 2-12. The patternset type's attributes

Attribute	Description
excludes	A list of the patterns matching files you want exluded. Comma- or space-separated list.
excludesfile	Specifies a name of a file; each line of the file is interpreted as an `exclude` pattern.
includes	A list of the patterns matching files you want included. Comma- or space-separated list.
includesfile	Specifies a name of a file; each line of the file is interpreted as an `include` pattern.

PatternSets can include nested `include`, `includesfile`, `exclude`, and `excludesfile` elements, and you can nest PatternSets within one another.

Selectors

Besides all the types we've seen, selectors are powerful types and go far beyond selecting files based on filenames. They let you select files that make up a file set based on many criteria, such as what text a file contains, the date a file was modified, the size of a file, and more. Selectors have become one of the coolest things in Ant, and you can see Ant's core selectors, which come built into Ant, in Table 2-13.

Table 2-13. The core selectors

Selector	Means
contains	Selects files that contain particular text
containsregexp	Selects files whose contents contain text that matches a given regular expression
date	Selects files that were modified before a particular date and time, or that date and time
depend	Selects files that were modified more recently than files you compare them to
depth	Selects files based on how far down they appear in a directory tree
different	Selects files that are different from a set of target files you specify
filename	Selects files using a pattern to match filenames
modified	Selects files if an algorithm gives a different result from that stored

Table 2-13. The core selectors (continued)

Selector	Means
present	Selects files based on their presence, or absence, at some other location
size	Selects files larger or smaller than a particular size
type	Selects files based on their type: regular files or directories

You can nest selectors inside file sets to select the files you want. For example, here's how to create a file set of HTML documentation files that contain the text "selector" using the contains selector:

```
<fileset dir="${docs}" includes="**/*.html">
    <contains text="selector" casesensitive="no"/>
</fileset>
```

The date selector lets you choose file sets based on date, as here, where I'm selecting all documentation files before 1/1/2005:

```
<fileset dir="${docs}" includes="**/*.html">
    <date datetime="01/01/2005 12:00 AM" when="before"/>
</fileset>
```

You can use the filename selector much like the include and exclude tags inside a fileset. Here's an example:

```
<fileset dir="${source}" includes="**/*">
    <filename name="**/*.cpp"/>
</fileset>
```

The containsregexp selector limits the files in a fileset to only those whose contents contain a match to the regular expression specified by the expression attribute:

```
<fileset dir="${source}" includes="*.java">
    <containsregexp expression="$println(.);"/>
</fileset>
```

The type tag selects files of a certain type: directory or regular. Here's an example:

```
<fileset dir="${src}">
    <type type="dir"/>
</fileset>
```

FileSets are no longer about filenames. Now you've got access to more data, including what's inside files.

 Selectors can be defined outside of any target by using the selector tag and using them as references.

File Filters

Filters let you filter the data in files, modifying that data if you want to. FilterSets are groups of filters, and you can use filters to replace tokens in files with new content.

For example, say that your files contain a token, like @DATE@; you can use filters and a filter set to copy those files with the copy task, while replacing that token with the current date. You can find the attributes of the filter set type in Table 2-14; to use FilterSets, you can use the filter task, which is coming up next (with examples).

 When a filter set is used in an operation, the files are processed in text mode and the filters applied line by line. This means that the copy operations will typically corrupt binary files.

Table 2-14. The filter set type's attributes

Attribute	Description	Required	Default
begintoken	The string, usually a character, that specifies the beginning of a token (e.g., @ in @AUTHOR#)	No	@
endtoken	The string, usually a character, that specifies the end of a token (e.g., # in @AUTHOR#)	No	@
id	The ID you want to use for this filter set	No	
refid	The ID of a filter set you want to use while creating this filter set	No	

You specify the filters inside a filter set with the filter task, coming up next.

Using the filter task

The filter task supports the actual filters in a filter set. Here's a filter set example where the build file instructs Ant to copy *build.java* from the ${archives} directory to the ${source} directory, and replace the token @DATE@ in the files with today's date:

```
<copy file="${archives}/build.java" toFile="${source}/build.java">
    <filter set>
        <filter token="DATE" value="${TODAY}"/>
    </filter set>
</copy>
```

Here's the same example where the token to replace is %DATE;:

```
<copy file="${archives}/build.java" toFile="${source}/build.java">
    <filter set begintoken="%" endtoken=";">
        <filter token="DATE" value="${TODAY}"/>
    </filter set>
</copy>
```

You can define a FilterSet and reference it later:

```
<filter set id="today.filter" begintoken="%" endtoken=";">
    <filter token="DATE" value="${TODAY}"/>
</filter set>
```

```
<copy file="${archives}/build.java" toFile="${source}/build.java">
    <filter set refid="today.filter"/>
</copy>
```

 If you just want to replace text in a file, you can use the Ant replace task. Here's an example:

```
<replace file="${src}/index.html"
         token="author" value="Ted"/>
```

You can use the concat task, designed to concatenate files together, to concatenate text to the end of a file, like this:

```
<concat
    destfile="readme.txt">Copyright (C) 2005</concat>
```

You can see the attributes of this task in Table 2-15.

Table 2-15. The filter task's attributes

Attribute	Description	Required
filtersfile	The file from which you want filters to be read (you format this file like a property file).	Token and value attributes must be provided, or only the filtersfile attribute.
token	The token string to match (omit the beginning and end tokens).	Token and value attributes must be provided, or only the filtersfile attribute.
value	The string to replace the token with.	Token and value attributes must be provided, or only the filtersfile attribute.

Filtering and Modifying Text with FilterChains and FilterReaders

A FilterReader filters text and can modify that text. A FilterChain is a group of FilterReaders, applied in order, and functions much like piping one command to another in Unix. Using FilterReaders and FilterChains, you can process text data in advanced ways. A number of Ant tasks support filterchain elements:

- concat
- copy
- loadfile
- loadproperties
- move

You can create filter chains with your own Java classes or with one of the elements you see in Table 2-16.

Table 2-16. FilterChain nested elements

Element	Does this
classconstants	Filters and outputs constants as defined in a Java class.
concatfilter	Appends a file to the filtered file, or prepends a file to the filtered file. Two optional attributes: prepend (name of the file to prepend) and append (name of the file to append).
deletecharacters	Deletes characters that you specify in the filtered content. The required attribute, chars, holds the characters to delete.
escapeunicode	Changes non US-ASCII characters into the matching Unicode escape sequence (\ plus four digits).
expandproperties	Replaces Ant properties (of the form ${ . . . }) with the property's actual value.
filterreader	Defines a generic filter. Has one parameter, the required classname attribute. Supports classpath and param nested elements.
headfilter	Reads the header, that is, the first few lines, from the filtered data. Supports two optional attributes: lines (number of lines to read) and skip (number of lines from the beginning to skip).
linecontains	Filters out those lines that don't include lines that contain specified strings. One required attribute: contains (the substring to search for).
linecontainsregexp	Filters out lines that don't contain text-matching specified regular expressions. One required attribute: regexp (Pattern of the substring to be searched for).
prefixlines	Adds a prefix to every line. Required attribute: prefix (the prefix to use).
replacetokens	Filters text and replaces text between begintoken and endtoken with the text you specify.
stripjavacomments	Strips Java comments.
striplinebreaks	Strips line breaks from the filtered data. Set the optional linebreaks attribute to the line break text.
striplinecomments	Filters out lines that start with comments, as you specify. Set the comment attribute to the string that starts the line.
tabstospaces	Filters out tabs and replaces them with spaces (default is 8).
tailfilter	Reads the tail of the text, that is, the last few lines from the filtered text. Supports two optional attributes: lines (number of lines to read) and skip (number of lines from the end to skip).
tokenfilter	Tokenizes the filtered text into strings. One optional attribute: delimOutput (overrides the tokendelimiter returned by the tokenizer).

Each of these filters correspond to a Java class; for example, the head filter corresponds to org.apache.tools.ant.filters.HeadFilter. Here are a few examples: Suppose you want to read the first three lines of the file given by ${sourcefile} into the property sourcefile.header. You could use filterreader and the Ant filter reader class org.apache.tools.ant.filters.HeadFilter:

```
<loadfile srcfile="${sourcefile}" property="sourcefile.header">
    <filterchain>
        <filterreader classname="org.apache.tools.ant.filters.HeadFilter">
            <param name="lines" value="3"/>
```

```
        </filterreader>
      </filterchain>
    </loadfile>
```

Ant gives you a shortcut with filter readers like this one, where you can use a task named headfilter to do the same thing:

```
<loadfile srcfile="${sourcefile}" property="sourcefile.header">
  <filterchain>
    <headfilter lines="3"/>
  </filterchain>
</loadfile>
```

The linecontains filter reader includes only those lines that contain all the strings you specify with contains elements. Here's an example, where I'm filtering only lines containing "apples" and "oranges":

```
<linecontains>
  <contains value="apples">
  <contains value="oranges">
</linecontains>
```

The linecontainsregexp filter reader includes only those lines that match the regular expression you've specified. For example, here's how to match only lines that contain lowercase letters:

```
<linecontainsregexp>
    <regexp pattern="^[a-z]$">
</linecontainsregexp>
```

The stripjavacomments filter reader strips away comments from the data, using Java syntax guidelines. Here's an example:

```
<loadfile srcfile="${src.file}" property="java.text">
    <filterchain>
        <stripjavacomments/>
    </filterchain>
</loadfile>
```

The striplinecomments filter reader removes all those lines that begin with strings that represent comments as specified by the user. For example, here's how to remove all lines that begin with #, REM, rem, and //:

```
<striplinecomments>
    <comment value="#"/>
    <comment value="REM "/>
    <comment value="rem "/>
    <comment value="//"/>
</striplinecomments>
```

The tabstospaces filter reader replaces tabs with spaces; here's an example:

```
<loadfile srcfile="${src.file}" property="src.file.detabbed">
    <filterchain>
        <tabstospaces/>
    </filterchain>
</loadfile>
```

The classconstants filter readers recovers constants defined in Java *.class* files. For example, say that you have a constant named MAXFILES:

```
public interface Files
{
    public static final String MAXFILES ="4";
}
```

To load the MAXFILES constant and make it accessible by name, you can use the loadproperties task and the classconstants filter reader:

```
<loadproperties srcfile="Files.class">
  <filterchain>
    <classconstants/>
       .
       .
       .
  </filterchain>
</loadproperties>
```

As you can gather from the name, you can use multiple filter readers in a filter chain, and we'll add the prefixlines filter reader to prefix constants we recover with the text "Files.":

```
<loadproperties srcfile="Files.class">
  <filterchain>
    <classconstants/>
    <prefixlines prefix="Files."/>
  </filterchain>
</loadproperties>
```

Now you've recovered the constant Files.MAXFILES from a compiled *.class* file, and can display it with echo:

```
<echo>${Files.MAXFILES}</echo>
```

Transforming One Set of Files to Another with Mappers

Mappers are another Ant type, and they're used to map one set of files to another. For example, one of the mappers available in Ant is the regexp mapper that lets you grab a set of files and rename them. You can use mappers in copy, move, apply, uptodate, and a number of additional tasks.

Here's an example, where I'm copying a file set from a directory named *development* to a directory named *backup*, renaming *.java* files to *.backup* files. This works because whatever matches to the expression inside the parentheses in the regular expression in the from attribute can be referenced in the to attribute as \1; a match to a second pair of parentheses may be referenced as \2, and so on:

```
<copy todir="backup">
    <fileset dir="development" includes="**/*.java"/>
    <mapper type="regexp" from="([a-z]*).java" to="\1.backup" />
</copy>
```

Another mapper is the `flatten` mapper, which lets you copy files while stripping off any directory information from the filenames. That's how mappers typically work; you specify a file set and then add a mapper to refine or manipulate the set of files you want to work with.

To use a mapper, you use the Ant `mapper` element, which has the attributes you see in Table 2-17.

 The mapper `classpath` attribute holds a path, which means you can use a nested `classpath` element if you prefer.

Table 2-17. Mapper attributes

Attribute	Description	Required
classname	Specifies the mapper using a class name	Either type or classname
classpath	Specifies the classpath you want used when searching for classname	No
classpathref	Specifies the classpath to use	No
from	Sets the value of the from attribute	Depends on implementation
to	Sets the value of the to attribute	Depends on implementation
type	Specifies a built-in mapper	Either type or classname

Experience shows that Ant will *not* automatically convert / or \ characters in the to and from attributes to the correct directory separator for your current platform. If you need to specify a directory separator here, use ${file.separator}.

What mappers can you use with the mapper element? You can see the available Ant mappers in Table 2-18.

Table 2-18. Ant mappers

Mapper	Does this
flatten	Flattens the target filename to the source filename but with all directory information stripped off from the front. To and from attributes are ignored.
glob	Lets you support wildcards (*) in the to and from attributes.
identity	Copies over the filename by making the target filename the same as the source filename. To and from attributes are ignored.
merge	Takes the target filename from the to attribute (from will be ignored).
package	Helps with Java package names by replacing directory separators with dots.
regexp	Lets you use regular expressions on the to and from values.
unpackage	Replaces any dots in the name of a package with legal directory separators (available since Ant 1.6).

When you use the identity mapper, the target filename is the same as the source filename, in other words, this one's transparent to Ant. Here's the way you'd use this mapper in a file set:

```
<mapper type="identity"/>
```

The flatten mapper is more interesting; this one strips all leading directory information off, allowing you to copy all files in a directory tree to a single directory. Here's an example:

```
<copy todir="backup">
    <fileset dir="development" includes="**/*.java"/>
    <mapper type="flatten" />
</copy>
```

The merge mapper copies multiple files to the same target file. Here's an example:

```
<mapper type="merge" to="backup.tar"/>
```

In the glob mapper, you can use filename patterns in the to and from attributes, and those patterns may contain at most one asterisk (*):

```
<copy todir="backup">
    <fileset dir="development" includes="**/*.java"/>
    <mapper type="glob" from="*.java" to="*.old"/>
</copy>
```

The regexp mapper lets you use regular expressions in the to and from attributes. You can create regular expression matches using parentheses in the to attribute value and refer to the matched values as \1 through \9 in the from attribute value. We've seen an example of this mapper at work:

```
<copy todir="backup">
    <fileset dir="development" includes="**/*.java"/>
    <mapper type="regexp" from="([a-z]*).java" to="\1.backup" />
</copy>
```

For more on regular expressions, see *Mastering Regular Expressions* by Jeffrey Friedl (O'Reilly).

The package mapper is an interesting one as it replaces directory separators found in the matched source pattern with dots in the target pattern placeholder, reproducing Java package syntax. This inspiration here is that this mapper was designed to be useful to flatten directory structures where files have the fully qualified classname as part of their name (this mapper was designed for use with the uptodate and junit tasks). Here's an example:

```
<mapper type="package"
    from="*Beta.java" to="Beta*Beta.xml"/>
```

For example, if you used this mapper element on *org/steve/tools/ant/util/AntTask-Beta.java*, it will create *Beta.org.steve.tools.ant.util.AntTaskBeta.xml*, flattening the directory structure but still letting you see where files come from.

The unpackage mapper, new since Ant 1.6, is the reverse of the package mapper; that is, it replaces dots in a package name with directory separators. Here's an example:

```
<mapper type="package"
    from="Beta*Beta.xml" to="*Beta.java"/>
```

This is a useful one if you want to restore the original directory structure after flattening it with the package mapper. This example will take files such as *Beta.org.steve.tools.ant.util.AntTaskBeta.xml* back to *org/steve/tools/ant/util/AntTaskBeta.java*.

CHAPTER 3

Building Java Code

Ant is the premiere build tool for Java developers, and this chapter focuses on the Java build process, from compiling Java code with the javac task through compressing and packaging the results with tasks such as jar and tar. Along the way, I'll discuss several central build issues, such as keeping track of the build number, storing that number in a JAR file's manifest file, getting input from the user and acting on that input, calling one Ant target from another, creating Javadoc with the javadoc task, and more.

Compiling Code

The javac task compiles Java source code. You've seen javac at work many times in this book but haven't exhausted what this task has to offer by any means. You can get an idea how extensive a task it is by its huge number of attributes, shown in Table 3-1.

Table 3-1. The javac task's attributes

Attribute	Description	Required	Default
bootclasspath	Specifies where to find any bootstrap class files.	No	
bootclasspathref	Specifies where to find any bootstrap class files, given as a reference.	No	
classpath	Specifies the classpath you want to use.	No	
classpathref	Specifies the classpath you want to use, given as a reference to a path.	No	
compiler	Specifies the compiler you want to use. If you don't set this attribute, this task will use the compiler pointed to by the build.compiler property, if set. If that property is not set, the default compiler for the current JVM is used.	No	

Table 3-1. The javac task's attributes (continued)

Attribute	Description	Required	Default
debug	Specifies whether or not your code should be compiled to include debug data. Corresponds to the compiler's -g option.	No	no
debuglevel	Specifies keywords that will be added to the command line with the -g switch. Possible values are none or a comma-separated list of these keywords: lines, vars, and source. This attribute requires debug to be set to true; if it's not, this attribute is ignored.	No	
depend	Specifies that you want to use dependency tracking if your compiler supports it.	No	
deprecation	Specifies that you want the compiler to display deprecation information.	No	no
destdir	Specifies the destination directory for the generated class files.	No	
encoding	Specifies the encoding of your Java files.	No	
excludes	Specifies a list of files that you want to exclude. A comma- or space-separated list of files.	No	
excludesfile	Specifies a file containing a list of files you want to exclude.	No	
executable	Specifies the path to the javac executable that will be used when fork is used. Defaults to the compiler currently used by Ant.	No	
extdirs	Specifies the location of installed extensions, if any.	No	
failonerror	Specifies if you want the build to fail if there are compilation errors.	No	true
fork	Specifies if to execute javac in a forked process.	No	no
includeAntRuntime	Specifies whether you want to make the Ant run-time libraries accessible to the compiler.	No	yes
includeJavaRuntime	Specifies whether you want to make the default runtime Java libraries accessible to the executing JVM.	No	no
includes	Specifies a list of files that you want to include. A comma- or space-separated list of files.	No	

Table 3-1. The javac task's attributes (continued)

Attribute	Description	Required	Default
includesfile	Specifies a file containing a list of files you want to include.	No	
listfiles	Specifies whether you want to list the source files to be compiled.	No	no
memoryInitialSize	Specifies the starting size of the memory for the JVM. Applies only if javac is run externally.	No	
memoryMaximumSize	Specifies the maximum size of memory you want to use for the JVM, if you're forking it.	No	
nowarn	Specifies whether you want to pass the -nowarn switch to the compiler.	No	off
optimize	Specifies whether you want to compile using optimization, using the -O switch.	No	off
source	Specifies whether you want to use the -source switch. Legal values are 1.3, 1.4, and 1.5.	No	no -source argument will be used
sourcepath	Specifies the source path to use.	No	The value of the srcdir attribute (or nested src elements)
sourcepathref	Specifies the source path you want to use, given in reference form.	No	
srcdir	Specifies where to find the Java source files you want to compile.	Yes, unless nested src elements are present	
target	Specifies that you want to generate class files for particular Java version (e.g., 1.1 or 1.2).	No	
tempdir	Specifies the directory where temporary files should go. Used only if the task is forked and the length of the command line arguments is over 4 KB. Available since Ant 1.6.	No; default is the current working directory	
verbose	Specifies that you want the compiler to generate verbose output.	No	no

This is where the meat is for most Java authors. This task—which should be one of your staples—makes sure the source directory will be recursively scanned for Java source files to compile and compiles them. Only Java files that have no correspond-ing *.class* file or where the class file is older than the *.java* file will be compiled.

The javac task forms an implicit FileSet and supports all attributes of fileset (note that dir becomes srcdir) as well as the nested include, exclude and patternset ele-ments. And because the javac task's srcdir, classpath, sourcepath, bootclasspath, and extdirs attributes are path-like structures, they can be set via nested src, classpath, sourcepath, bootclasspath and extdirs elements.

Compiling Source Files

Here are a few javac examples, starting with a standard example that compiles all *.java* files in and under the ${src} directory and stores the *.class* files in the ${bin} directory. In this case, the classpath includes *common.jar*, and we're compiling with debug information turned on:

```
<javac srcdir="${src}"
    debug="on"
    destdir="${bin}"
    classpath="common.jar"
/>
```

This next example compiles *.java* files in and under the ${src} and ${src2} directories, storing *.class* files in ${bin}, including *common.jar* in the classpath, and turns debug information on. In this case, only files in *packages/archive/*** and *packages/backup/*** will be included and those in *packages/archive/betapackage/*** will be excluded:

```
<javac srcdir="${src}:${src2}"
    destdir="${build}"
    includes="packages/archive/**,packages/backup/**"
    excludes="packages/archive/betapackage/**"
    classpath="common.jar"
    debug="on"
/>
```

Ant only uses the names of the source and class files to find the classes that need a rebuild. It doesn't read the source codes, and so has no knowledge about nested classes. If you want to specify dependencies that Ant is having trouble with, use the Ant depend task (covered in Chapter 6) for advanced dependency checking.

One of the new aspects of Ant 1.6 is support for Java 1.5. Specify "1.5" to the javac attribute of javac (expect new version to accept "5.0" in addition to the slightly older "1.5" version.

Selecting which files to compile

You can make javac compile only files that you explicitly specify, as opposed to all files under the specified source directory. You do that by disabling the javac task's default searching mechanism by unsetting the sourcepath attribute and specifying the files you want to include and exclude explicitly, as here, where I'm including only *.java* files in the ${src} directory:

```
<javac sourcepath="" srcdir="${src}"
    destdir="${bin}" >
    <include name="*.java" />
</javac>
```

Forking the compiler

Forking the Java compiler makes it run in a new process, something that's often useful if you want to use another compiler or want to configure the compiler's runtime environment. When the compiler is used in unforked mode in Windows, it may lock the files in the classpath of the javac task. That means you won't be able to delete or move those files later in the build. If you need to change that, fork the compiler, using the fork attribute.

Here's an example that compiles all *.java* files under the ${src} directory, stores the *.class* files in the ${bin} directory, and forks the javac compiler into its own thread process:

```
<javac srcdir="${src}"
    fork="yes"
    destdir="${bin}"
/>
```

Here's an example showing how you can tell Ant which Java compiler you want to run after forking:

```
<javac srcdir="${src}"
    destdir="${bin}"
    fork="yes"
    executable="/opt/java/jdk1.3/bin/javac"
    compiler="javac1.3"
/>
```

 In the early days, if you were using Ant on Windows, a new DOS window would pop up for every use of an external compiler. If you use a JDK after 1.2, this won't be a problem.

Setting Command-Line Options

You can explicitly specify command-line arguments for the compiler with nested compilerarg elements:

```
<javac srcdir="${src}"
    destdir="${build}"
    classpath="xyz.jar"
    debug="on">
    <compilerarg value="-1 -a"/>
</javac>
```

The attributes of the compilerarg element appear in Table 3-2.

Table 3-2. The compilerarg attributes

Attribute	Description	Required
compiler	Specifies the required version of the compiler you want to use; if the compiler is not of this version, the argument won't be passed to it. For possible values, see the section "Using a Different Java Compiler."	No
file	Specifies the name of a file as a command-line argument.	Exactly one of value, line, file, or path
line	Specifies a list of command-line arguments, delimited by spaces.	Exactly one of value, line, file, or path
path	Specifies a path-like string as a command-line argument. You can use ; or : as path separators if you wish. (Ant will convert them to local path separators.)	Exactly one of value, line, file, or path
value	Specifies a command-line argument.	Exactly one of value, line, file, or path

Here's an example that stores the output of the compilation in a directory named *output1.4* if the compiler version is 1.3, 1.4, 1.5, all of which correspond to the "modern" option (see the section "Using a Different Java Compiler" for details on specifying the compiler version):

```
<javac srcdir="${src}"
    destdir="${build}">
    <compilerarg compiler="modern" value="-d output1.4"/>
</javac>
```

Here's an example where the compiler switches to use are in a file named *options*:

```
<javac srcdir="${src}"
    destdir="${build}">
    <compilerarg file="options"/>
</javac>
```

Using a Different Java Compiler

Using javac, you can specify the compiler you want to use with the global build. compiler property (which affects all javac tasks throughout the build) or with the compiler attribute (specific to the current javac task). Here's an example:

```
<javac srcdir="${src}"
    compiler="javac1.3"
    destdir="${out}"
    classpath="servlet-api.jar"
/>
```

Here are the possible values for the `build.compiler` property or the `compiler` attribute:

`classic`
> Specifies that you want to use the standard JDK 1.1/1.2 compiler; you can use `javac1.1` and `javac1.2` as aliases.

`extJavac`
> Specifies that you want to use modern or classic in a JVM of its own.

`gcj`
> Specifies that you want to use the `gcj` compiler from gcc.

`jikes`
> Specifies that you want to use the Jikes compiler.

`jvc`
> Specifies that you want to use the Command-Line compiler from Microsoft's Java/Visual J++. You can use `microsoft` as an alias.

`kjc`
> Specifies that you want to use the kopi compiler.

`modern`
> Specifies that you want to use the JDK 1.3/1.4/1.5 compiler. Here, you can use `javac1.3`, `javac1.4`, and `javac1.5` as aliases.

`sj`
> Specifies that you want to use the Symantec Java compiler. You can use `symantec` as an alias.

Getting Input from the User

At some point in a build, you may need input from the user. For example, you might want to ask before deleting a directory with the `delete` task.

 The delete task is covered in detail in Chapter 4.

To get input from the user, use the `input` task, which creates a new property based on user input.

Example 3-1 puts input to work. This build file asks whether it's OK to delete the *bin* directory, and if it's not, the build fails. It queries the user using the `input` task, and creates a new property, `do.delete`, based on the user's input.

Example 3-1. Using the input task (ch03/input/build.xml)

```xml
<?xml version="1.0" ?>
<project default="main">

    <property name="message" value="Building the .jar file." />
    <property name="src" location="source" />
    <property name="output" location="bin" />

    <target name="main" depends="init, compile, compress">
        <echo>
            ${message}
        </echo>
    </target>

    <target name="init">
        <input
            message="Deleting bin directory OK?"
            validargs="y,n"
            addproperty="do.delete"
        />
        <condition property="do.abort">
            <equals arg1="n" arg2="${do.delete}"/>
        </condition>
        <fail if="do.abort">Build aborted.</fail>
        <delete dir="${output}" />
        <mkdir dir="${output}" />
    </target>

    <target name="compile">
        <javac srcdir="${src}" destdir="${output}" />
    </target>

  <target name="compress">
        <jar destfile="${output}/Project.jar" basedir="${output}" includes="*.class" />
  </target>
</project>
```

Here's what you see when you run Ant using this build file:

```
%ant
Buildfile: build.xml

init:
    [input] Deleting bin directory OK?(y,n)
y
    [delete] Deleting directory /home/steven/input/bin
    [mkdir] Created dir: /home/steven/input/bin

compile:
    [javac] Compiling 1 source file to /home/steven/input/bin

compress:
    [jar] Building jar: /home/steven/input/bin/Project.jar
```

```
main:
    [echo]
    [echo]               Building the .jar file.
    [echo]

BUILD SUCCESSFUL
Total time: 5 seconds
```

The attributes of this task appear in Table 3-3.

Table 3-3. The input task's attributes

Attribute	Description	Required
addproperty	Specifies the name of the property to create, using the input from the user.	No
defaultvalue	Specifies the default value to use for the created property; this default will be used if no input is read.	No
message	Specifies the prompt you want to display to prompt the user to enter text.	No
validargs	Specifies the input values you consider valid, separated by commas. If you use this attribute, the task will not allow input that doesn't match one of these values.	No

Calling Other Ant Tasks

You've seen that you can branch using true/false properties. Ant provides other powerful mechanisms for branching, the antcall task, which you can use to call one Ant task from another, and the ant task, which calls Ant tasks in other build files.

Calling Ant Tasks in the Same Build File

A better way to think of antcall is that you're starting a new instance of Ant and executing targets in it. When you call an Ant target with antcall, its dependent targets are executed in order, something that can be confusing if you think you're calling a single target. Generally, it's best to do things the standard way and let Ant sort out the dependencies as it's supposed to. However, Ant can make life easier, as when you have a build file that creates a distribution for many different servers, and when varying sets of tasks need to be executed for each. (Even in cases like that, however, you can still set things up easily enough with if and unless and true/false properties.)

When you use antcall, you can think of that call as creating a new project; all the properties of the current project are available in that new project by default. The attributes of the antcall task appear in Table 3-4.

Table 3-4. The antcall attributes

Attribute	Description	Required	Default
inheritAll	If true, means the task should pass all current properties to the new Ant project. Properties passed to the new project will override the properties that are set in the new project.	No	true
inheritRefs	If true, means the task should pass all current references to the new Ant project.	No	false
target	Specifies the target you actually want to run.	Yes	

You can set properties in the new project with nested param elements, which supports the same attributes as the property task. Such properties will be passed to the new project, no matter how inheritAll is set.

Properties defined on the command line cannot be overridden by nested param elements.

You can use nested reference elements to copy references from the calling project to the new project. See the attributes of this element in Table 3-5.

References from nested elements will override existing references that have been defined outside of targets in the new project but not those defined inside of targets.

Table 3-5. The reference element's attributes

Attribute	Description	Required	Default
refid	Specifies the id of the reference you want to use in the original project	Yes	
torefid	Specifies the id of the reference you want to use in the new project	No	The value of refid

As of Ant 1.6, you can specify sets of properties to be copied into the new project with nested propertyset elements. This element works much like other Ant sets; you can create a set of properties and refer to them all at once by ID. This element can contain propertyref, mapper, and other propertyset elements.

Example 3-2 is an antcall example. In this case, the example calls a new target, displayMessage, to display some text. The example passes the text to display as a parameter named msg.

Example 3-2. Using antcall (ch03/antcall/build.xml)

```xml
<?xml version="1.0" ?>
<project default="main">

    <property name="message" value="Building the .jar file." />
    <property name="src" location="source" />
    <property name="output" location="bin" />

    <target name="main" depends="init, compile, compress">
        <antcall target="displayMessage">
            <param name="msg" value="${message}"/>
        </antcall>
    </target>

    <target name="displayMessage">
        <echo message="msg=${msg}"/>
    </target>

    <target name="init">
        <mkdir dir="${output}" />
    </target>

    <target name="compile">
        <javac srcdir="${src}" destdir="${output}" />
    </target>

    <target name="compress">
        <jar destfile="${output}/Project.jar" basedir="${output}"
            includes="*.class" />
    </target>
</project>
```

Here's what you see when you run Ant using this build file; the msg parameter was passed to the called target:

```
C:\ant\ch03\antcall>ant
Buildfile: build.xml

init:
    [mkdir] Created dir: C:\ant\ch03\antcall\bin

compile:
    [javac] Compiling 1 source file to C:\ant\ch03\antcall\bin

compress:
      [jar] Building jar: C:\ant\ch03\antcall\bin\Project.jar

main:

displayMessage:
    [echo] msg=Building the .jar file.

BUILD SUCCESSFUL
Total time: 6 seconds
```

This is something like a subroutine call, and when using it, there's a tendency to start turning build files into programs. That's almost always a mistake, however; if you find yourself using antcall frequently, you're probably not using Ant the way it was intended. There's a tendency to start writing build files as if you were writing programming code with subroutines, but the best way to write build files is to let Ant doing its thing and check the dependencies. If this seems like this is the second time you've heard this, it is because it's that important.

Calling Ant Tasks in Other Build Files

The ant task is nearly identical to the antcall task, except that it lets you call targets in other build files. Using this task, you can create subproject build files, which let you divide your builds into a core build file with ant tasks to call the other build files as needed. This kind of technique can be useful when your build files are enormous and things are getting too complex to handle in single files; this is one of the ways that Ant scales to meet project needs.

Here's an example using ant, where I'm setting the value of a property named parameter and loading properties from a file:

```
<ant antfile="subproject/subbuild.xml">
    <property name="parameter" value="4096"/>
    <property file="config/subproject/build.properties"/>
</ant>
```

You can see the attributes of this task in Table 3-6.

Table 3-6. The ant task's attributes

Attribute	Description	Required	Default
antfile	Specifies the build file where the target to call is	No	build.xml
dir	Directory where the build file is	No	The current project's basedir, unless inheritall has been set to false, in which case there is no default value
inheritAll	If true, makes the task pass all current properties to the new Ant project	No	true
inheritRefs	If true, makes the task pass all current references to the new Ant project	No	false
output	Specifies the filename where the task should write output	No	
target	Specifies the target in the Ant project that you want to call	No	The new project's default target

If you don't specify a value for the antfile attribute, the file *build.xml* in the directory given by the dir attribute is used. If no target attribute is supplied, the default target of the new project will be used.

Passing properties to the new project works as it does with the antcall task, except that here you use nested property elements instead of param elements to pass properties. You can use nested reference elements and nested propertyset elements as with antcall.

The basedir attribute of the new project's project element is affected by the attributes dir and inheritAll in ant. Take a look at Table 3-7, which shows how basedir is set based on how you set these two attributes.

Table 3-7. Using dir and inheritAll in ant

dir	inheritAll	basedir in the new project
Value assigned	true	The value of the dir attribute
Value assigned	false	The value of the dir attribute
Omitted	true	The basedir of calling project
Omitted	false	The basedir attribute of the project element of the new project

 If you need to start breaking your build files up, consider the subant task, which executes Ant in various subdirectories.

Importing Other Build Files

With ant, you can execute build files outside the current build file, and you can *include* other build files in the current file. The old way of doing this was to rely on XML and the Ant XML parser to do the work for you. For example, if you wanted to include the entire contents of a document named *shared.xml* at a specific point in a build file, you could start by declaring an XML entity named, say, shared in your build file:

```
<?xml version="1.0"?>

<!DOCTYPE project [
    <!ENTITY shared SYSTEM "file:shared.xml">
]>
        .
        .
        .
```

To insert the contents of the *shared.xml* build file into the current build file, you can use an XML entity reference, &shared;, like this:

```
<?xml version="1.0"?>

<!DOCTYPE project [
    <!ENTITY shared SYSTEM "file:shared.xml">
]>
```

```
<project default="main" basedir=".">

    &shared;

    <target name="init">
        .
        .
        .
    </target>
        .
        .
        .
</project>
```

Since Ant 1.6, however, there is a new import task that can be used to include build files. The referenced files have to be complete Ant build files, which are inserted whole (minus the XML declaration and <project> and </project> tags). Here's how the above example would work using the import task:

```
<?xml version="1.0"?>
<project default="main" basedir=".">

    <import file="shared.xml"/>

    <target name="init">
        .
        .
        .
    </target>
        .
        .
        .
</project>
```

The attributes of the import task appear in Table 3-8.

Table 3-8. The import task's attributes

Attribute	Description	Required	Default
file	Specifies the name of the build file you want to import	Yes	
optional	Specifies whether you want to stop the build if the build file to import does not exist	No	false

> Unlike entity includes, you can deference a property with ${ and } to set the name of the file to import with the import task. In addition, if a target with the same name exists, it takes precedence over the target you're importing.

The import task makes it easier to handle relative paths as defined in the imported build file. It does this by creating a new property corresponding to the absolute path of the imported build file so you can resolve relative file references.

Ant has a property called ant.file that contains the absolute path of the build file (see Chapter 1), so this task creates a new property based on the name of the file you're importing. For example, if you import a build file named *newbuild*, the new location property will be named ant.file.newbuild.

Now that you've built your application with the various tasks seen in this chapter, it's time for some documentation.

Documenting Code

Creating applications in a commercial environment frequently means creating documentation, and Ant is up for that with the javadoc task. This task creates documentation using the Java javadoc tool, a process that involves compilation, which merits including this task in this chapter. This is one of the largest tasks in Ant because of the enormous number of javadoc options.

Here's an example, stored in the *javadoc* folder in the code for this book. Suppose you add a documentation-type comment to the *Project.java* file:

```
/** This application prints out "No worries." */
public class Project
{
    public static void main(String args[])
    {
        System.out.println("No worries.");
    }
}
```

You can create Javadoc for the project using the javadoc task in a new target I'll name doc, which will put the generated Javadoc in a *doc* directory, as you see in Example 3-3.

 Note the XML <![CDATA[...]> sections, which the build file uses to pass data to the javadoc tool.

Example 3-3. Creating javadoc (ch03/javadoc/build.xml)

```
<?xml version="1.0" ?>
<project default="main">

    <property name="message" value="Building the .jar file." />
    <property name="src" location="source" />
    <property name="docs" location="docs" />
    <property name="output" location="bin" />

    <target name="main" depends="init, compile, doc, compress">
        <echo>
            ${message}
        </echo>
    </target>
```

Example 3-3. Creating javadoc (ch03/javadoc/build.xml) (continued)

```
<target name="init">
    <mkdir dir="${output}" />
    <mkdir dir="${docs}" />
</target>

<target name="compile">
    <javac srcdir="${src}" destdir="${output}" />
</target>

<target name="doc">
    <javadoc
        sourcefiles="${src}/Project.java"
        destdir="${docs}"
        author="true"
        version="true"
        use="true"
        windowtitle="Project API">
        <doctitle><![CDATA[<h1>Project API</h1>]]></doctitle>
        <bottom><![CDATA[<i>Copyright &#169; 2005</i>]]></bottom>
    </javadoc>
</target>

<target name="compress">
    <jar destfile="${output}/Project.jar" basedir="${output}" includes="*.class" />
</target>
```

```
</project>
```

You can see the javadoc task at work when the build file runs:

```
%ant
Buildfile: build.xml

init:
    [mkdir] Created dir: /home/steven//ch03/javadoc/bin
    [mkdir] Created dir: /home/steven//ch03/javadoc/docs

compile:
    [javac] Compiling 1 source file to /home/steven//ch03/javadoc/bin

doc:
  [javadoc] Generating Javadoc
  [javadoc] Javadoc execution
  [javadoc] Loading source file /home/steven//ch03/javadoc/source/Project.java...
  [javadoc] Constructing Javadoc information...
  [javadoc] Standard Doclet version 1.4.0

  [javadoc] Building tree for all the packages and classes...
  [javadoc] Building index for all the packages and classes...
  [javadoc] Building index for all classes...

  [javadoc] Generating /home/steven//ch03/javadoc/docs/stylesheet.css...
```

```
compress:
      [jar] Building jar: /home/steven//ch03/javadoc/bin/Project.jar

main:
      [echo]
      [echo]                    Building the .jar file.
      [echo]

BUILD SUCCESSFUL
Total time: 10 seconds
```

And you can see the *index.html* Javadoc result in Figure 3-1. Note the message "This application prints out 'No worries.'"

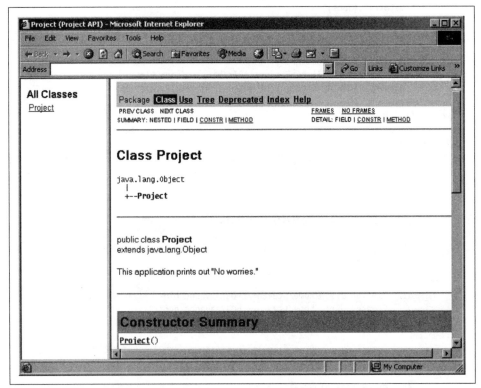

Figure 3-1. New Javadoc for the project

You can see the huge number of attributes of this task in Table 3-9.

 Since the javadoc tool calls the System.exit method, javadoc cannot be run inside the same JVM as Ant. For this reason, javadoc *always* forks the JVM. For more on how to use the javadoc tool, look at the JDK documentation available at *http://java.sun.com/j2se/1.4.2/docs/index.html*.

Table 3-9. The javadoc task's attributes

Attribute	Description	Required	Default
access	Sets the access mode; you can use these values: public, protected, package, or private.	No	protected
additionalparam	Specifies additional parameters for the javadoc command line. Any parameters with spaces should be quoted using ".	No	
author	Specifies you want to include @author paragraphs.	No	
bootclasspath	Specifies you want to override the classpath set by the boot class loader.	No	
bootclasspathref	Specifies you want to override class file references set by the boot class loader.	No	
bottom	Sets the bottom text for each page.	No	
breakiterator	Specifies you want to use the breakiterator algorithm, which is used in debugging. Set to yes or no.	No	no
charset	Specifies the character set to use.	No	
classpath	Specifies the classpath for user class files.	No	
classpathref	Specifies where to find user class files by reference.	No	
defaultexcludes	Specifies whether you want default excludes to be used. Set to yes or no.	No	Default excludes are used.
destdir	Sets the output directory.	Yes	
docencoding	Sets the output file encoding to use.	No	
doclet	Specifies the class file used to start the doclet that will generate the documentation.	No	
docletpath	Specifies the path to the doclet given by the -doclet option.	No	
docletpathref	Specifies the path to the doclet given by the -doclet option by reference.	No	

Table 3-9. The javadoc task's attributes (continued)

Attribute	Description	Required	Default
doctitle	Sets the title for the package index page.	No	
encoding	Specifies the encoding of the source file.	No	
excludepackagenames	Specifies the packages to exclude in the documentation. Give as a comma-separated list.	No	
extdirs	Specifies you want to override the location of installed extensions.	No	
failonerror	Specifies you want to stop the build process if the task exits with a non-zero return code.	No	
footer	Specifies the footer text for each page.	No	
group	Specifies you want to group particular packages in the generated overview page.	No	
header	Specifies the header text you want to use for each page.	No	
helpfile	Specifies the HTML help file you want to use, if any.	No	
link	Specifies you want to create links to the Javadoc output at the given URL.	No	
linkoffline	Specifies you want to link to the documentation at a specific URL using a package list at at another URL.	No	
linksource	Indicates you want to generate hyperlinks to source files; available since Ant 1.6.	No	no
locale	Sets the locale to be used for generating documentation, such as "en_US".	No	
maxmemory	Specifies the maximum amount of memory to allocate to the javadoc task.	No	
nodeprecated	Specifies you do not want to include @deprecated information in the generated documentation.	No	
nodeprecatedlist	Specifies you do not want to generate a deprecated list.	No	

Table 3-9. The javadoc task's attributes (continued)

Attribute	Description	Required	Default
nohelp	Specifies you do not want to generate a link to help documentation.	No	
noindex	Specifies you do not want to generate an index.	No	
nonavbar	Specifies you don't want a navigation bar.	No	
noqualifier	Allows you to use the -noqualifier argument. Set this attribute to "all" or a colon-separated list of packages. Available since Ant 1.6.	No	
notree	Specifies you don't want a class hierarchy to be generated.	No	
old	Specifies you want to generate output using JDK 1.1.	No	
overview	Specifies where to get the overview documentation.	No	
package	Indicates you want to include package/protected/public information.	No	
packagelist	Specifies the name of a file that holds the packages to include in the generated documentation.	No	
packagenames	Specifies a list of packages to include.	No	
private	Specifies you want to show all private classes and members.	No	
protected	Specifies you want to show all protected/public classes and members. This is the default.	No	
public	Specifies you want to show only public classes and members.	No	
serialwarn	Specifies you want to be warned about the @serial tag, if encountered.	No	
source	Sets this attribute to 1.4 to document code that compiles using javac -source 1.4.	No	

Table 3-9. The javadoc task's attributes (continued)

Attribute	Description	Required	Default
sourcefiles	Specifies the source files. Use a comma-separated list.	At least one of sourcepath, sourcefiles, sourcefiles, or a nested sourcepath, fileset, or packageset.	
sourcepath	Specifies where to you want to find source files.	At least one of sourcepath, sourcefiles, sourcefiles, or a nested sourcepath, fileset, or packageset.	
sourcepathref	Specifies where you want to find source files by reference.	At least one of sourcepath, sourcefiles, sourcefiles, or a nested sourcepath, fileset, or packageset.	
splitindex	Specifies you want to split the generated index into one file for each letter.	No	
stylesheetfile	Specifies the CSS stylesheet you want to use.	No	
use	Specifies you want to create class and package usage pages.	No	
useexternalfile	Specifies whether the source filename(s) should be written to a temporary file. Set to yes or no.	No	no
verbose	Specifies you want this task to display messages of what it's doing.	No	
version	Specifies you want to include @version paragraphs.	No	
windowtitle	Sets the title of the browser window for the documentation.	No	

Here's another example. This one passes Java packages starting with gui to javadoc to document them, excludes a few specific packages, sets the header text for each page, groups the packages gui.steve.api.* together on the first page under the title "Group 1 Packages," and includes a link to the Java 1.4.2 docs:

```
<javadoc destdir="api" version="true">

    <packageset dir="code">
        <include name="gui/**" />
        <exclude name="gui/debug/**"/>
    </packageset>
```

```
        <header><![CDATA[Preliminary API Specification]]></header>
        <doctitle><![CDATA[<h1>Test</h1>]]></doctitle>
        <group title="Group 1 Packages" packages="gui.steve.api.*"/>
        <link href="http://java.sun.com/j2se/1.4.2/docs/api/"/>
    </javadoc>
```

Creating JAR Files

The jar task JARs files for you. Example 3-4 is a fairly complex example, which creates a new JAR file with an included manifest, *MANIFEST.MF*, that contains several attributes.

Example 3-4. Using the jar task (ch03/jar/build.xml)

```
<?xml version="1.0" ?>
<project default="main">

    <property name="message" value="Building the .jar file." />
    <property name="src" location="source" />
    <property name="output" location="bin" />

    <target name="main" depends="init, compile, compress">
        <echo>
            ${message}
        </echo>
    </target>

    <target name="init">
        <mkdir dir="${output}" />
    </target>

    <target name="compile">
        <javac srcdir="${src}" destdir="${output}" />
    </target>

    <target name="compress">
        <jar destfile="${output}/Project.jar" basedir="${output}"
            includes="*.class" >
            <manifest>
                <attribute name="Author" value="${user.name}"/>
                <section name="Shared">
                    <attribute name="Title" value="Example"/>
                    <attribute name="Vendor" value="MegaAntCo"/>
                </section>
                <section name="Copyright">
                    <attribute name="Copy" value="(C) MegaAntCo 2005"/>
                </section>
            </manifest>
        </jar>
    </target>
</project>
```

The created JAR file contains *Project.class* and *MANIFEST.MF*; this latter file contains these contents:

```
Manifest-Version: 1.0
Ant-Version: Apache Ant 1.6.1
Created-By: 1.4.2_03-b02 (Sun Microsystems Inc.)
Author: Steven Holzner

Name: Shared
Title: Example
Vendor: MegaAntCo

Name: Copyright
Copy: (C) MegaAntCo 2005
```

Want to sign your JAR file for distribution? Use the jarsign task like this:

```
<signjar jar="jarfile.jar" alias="development"
         keystore="local.keystore"
         storepass="secret"/>
```

The attributes of the jar task are listed in Table 3-10. For more on creating manifests, take a look at the section "Creating Manifest Files."

Table 3-10. The jar task's attributes

Attribute	Description	Required	Default
basedir	Specifies the directory where the task should find files to JAR.	No	
compress	Specifies you want to compress data besides storing it.	No	true
defaultexcludes	Specifies whether you want to use default excludes or not (set to yes or no).	No	yes
destfile	Specifies the new JAR file to create.	Yes	
duplicate	Specifies what you want to do when a duplicate file is found. Possible values are add, preserve, and fail.	No	add
encoding	Specifies the character encoding to use for filenames in the JAR file.	No	UTF-8
excludes	Specifies files to exclude. Give as a comma- or space-separated list.	No	No files (except default excludes) are excluded.
excludesfile	Specifies the name of a file containing exclude patterns, one to a line.	No	
filesetmanifest	Specifies what you want the task to do when a manifest is found in a zipfileset or a zipgroup-fileset file is found. Valid values are skip, merge, and mergewithoutmain.	No	skip
filesonly	Specifies you want to store only files in the JAR file.	No	false

Table 3-10. The jar task's attributes (continued)

Attribute	Description	Required	Default
includes	Specifies files to include. Give as a comma- or space-separated list of patterns.	No	
includesfile	Specifies the name of a file containing include patterns, one to a line.	No	
index	Specifies whether to create an index. This can aid when loading classes.	No	false
keepcompression	Specifies what you want to do with items from existing archives (as with nested JAR files). Available since Ant 1.6.	No	false
manifest	Specifies the manifest file to use. Set to the location of a manifest, or the name of a JAR added through a fileset. If you're using the name of an added JAR file, the task expects the manifest to be in the JAR at *META-INF/MANIFEST.MF*.	No	
manifestencoding	Specifies the encoding used to read the JAR manifest.	No	The platform encoding.
update	Specifies whether if you want to update or overwrite the output file in case it exists.	No	false
whenempty	Specifies what this task should do when when no files match. Possible values are fail, skip, and create.	No	skip

You can refine the set of files to JAR with the includes, includesfile, excludes, excludesfile, and defaultexcludes attributes. The jar task forms an implicit FileSet and supports all attributes of fileset (though dir becomes basedir) as well as the nested include, exclude and patternset elements. You can use nested file sets for more flexibility, and specify multiple ones to merge together different trees of files into one JAR.

The update parameter controls what happens if the *.jar* file exists. When set to yes, the *.jar* file is updated with the files specified. When set to no (the default), the *.jar* file is overwritten.

Besides nested include, exclude and patternset elements, you can nest metainf and manifest elements in the jar task.

Working with the META-INF Directory

The nested metainf element specifies a FileSet. All files included in this fileset will end up in the *META-INF* directory of the JAR file. If this fileset includes a file named *MANIFEST.MF*, the file is ignored (but you'll get a warning telling you what's going on).

Creating Manifest Files

You use this task to write data into a JAR manifest file. The manifest task supports two nested elements: attribute, which you can use to set attributes in a manifest file, and section, which can create a section in a manifest file. The attribute element has two attributes: name (the name of the attribute) and value (the value of the attribute). The section element has one attribute, name (the name of the new section). Here's an example, which creates a manifest with attributes and sections:

```
<target name="compress">
    <jar destfile="${output}/Project.jar" basedir="${output}"
        includes="*.class" >
        <manifest>
            <section name="Credits">
                <attribute name="Author" value="Steve"/>
            </section>
            <section name="Title">
                <attribute name="Title" value="Profits"/>
                <attribute name="Company" value="YourCoInc"/>
            </section>
        </manifest>
    </jar>
</target>
```

For a more substantial example, see Example 3-5 coming up in this chapter. You can see the attributes of this task in Table 3-11.

Table 3-11. The manifest attributes

Attribute	Description	Required	Default
file	Specifies the name of the manifest file to create.	Yes	
mode	Specifies what you want to do with the manifest file. Possible values are update or replace.	No	replace
encoding	Specifies the encoding you want to use when reading a manifest to update.	No	UTF-8 encoding

There's more you can put into JAR manifests as well, such as an automatically incremented build number and a time stamp, both coming up next.

 Need to un-JAR a JAR file? Use Ant's unjar task. Just set the src attribute to the JAR file to un-jar and set the dest attribute to the directory where you want the output.

Setting Build Numbers

Anyone who has released software commercially knows how important it is to keep track of build numbers. The first version of your software might be 1.0.0, an update might be 1.0.1, a major update might be 2.0.0, and so on. The buildnumber task is a basic task that can be used to track these kinds of build numbers.

This task will first attempt to read a build number from a file (by default, *build.number* in the current directory) and set the property build.number to the value that was read in (or to 0 if no value was read). It will increment the number by one and write the new value back to the file.

This task has only one attribute, file, which holds the name in which you want to store the build number. This attribute is not required. I'll take a look at an example using buildnumber after discussing time stamps, the next topic.

Setting Timestamps

The tstamp task sets properties holding the current time so you can time stamp your builds. This task creates the DSTAMP (day stamp), TSTAMP (time stamp) and TODAY properties in the current project. By default, the DSTAMP property is in the format "yyyyMMdd", TSTAMP is in the format "hhmm", and TODAY is in the format "MMMM dd yyyy". If you use this task, it's almost invariably run in an initialization target.

You can see how this works in Example 3-5, which stores the build number and creation date in the project's *.jar* file, using buildnumber and tstamp.

Example 3-5. Using the build number and tstamp tasks (ch03/buildnumber/build.xml)

```
<?xml version="1.0" ?>
<project default="main">

    <property name="message" value="Building the .jar file." />
    <property name="src" location="source" />
    <property name="output" location="bin" />

    <target name="main" depends="init, compile, compress">
        <echo>
            ${message}
        </echo>
    </target>

    <target name="init">
        <buildnumber/>
        <tstamp/>
        <delete dir="${output}"/>
        <mkdir dir="${output}" />
    </target>

    <target name="compile">
        <javac srcdir="${src}" destdir="${output}" />
    </target>
```

```
    <target name="compress">
        <jar destfile="${output}/Project.jar" basedir="${output}"
            includes="*.class" >
            <manifest>
            <attribute name="Author" value="${user.name}"/>
            <section name="Shared">
                <attribute name="Title" value="Example"/>
                <attribute name="Vendor" value="MegaAntCo"/>
                <attribute name="Build" value="${build.number}"/>
                <attribute name="Date" value="${TODAY}"/>
            </section>
            <section name="Copyright">
                <attribute name="Copy" value="(C) MegaAntCo 2005"/>
            </section>
            </manifest>
        </jar>
    </target>
</project>
```

Here's the resulting manifest file from the JAR file, including build number and creation date:

```
Manifest-Version: 1.0
Ant-Version: Apache Ant 1.6.1
Created-By: 1.4.2_03-b02 (Sun Microsystems Inc.)
Author: Steven Holzner

Name: Shared
Title: Example
Vendor: MegaAntCo
Build: 3
Date: June 10 2005

Name: Copyright
Copy: (C) MegaAntCo 2005
```

This task has only one attribute, prefix, which is optional and sets a prefix for the DSTAMP, TSTAMP, and TODAY properties. For example, if prefix="time", these properties will be time.TSTAMP, time.TSTAMP, and time.TODAY, allowing you to name the properties created by this task yourself (at least to the extent of calling giving them names like name.TSTAMP instead of just TSTAMP).

The tstamp task supports a format nested element that lets you set the date and time format. Here's an example that creates a timestamp in the property timestamp:

```
    <tstamp>
        <format property="timestamp" pattern="MM/dd/yyyy hh:mm:ss"/>
    </tstamp>
```

You can see the attributes of the format element in Table 3-12.

The date/time patterns used by format are the same as used by the Java SimpleDateFormat class. For more info on those patterns, see *http://java. sun.com/j2se/1.4.2/docs/api/java/text/SimpleDateFormat.html*.

Table 3-12. The format task's attributes

Attribute	Description	Required
locale	Specifies the locale for the date/time string. Make this of the *language*, *country*, *variant*. The possible values are defined in the Java Locale class.	No
offset	Specifies the offset you want to add to or subtract from the current time, if any.	No
pattern	Specifies the date/time pattern you want to use. The possible values are defined in the Java SimpleDateFormat class.	Yes
property	Specifies the property in which you want to store the date/time string.	Yes
timezone	Specifies the time zone used for generating the time. Possible values are defined in the Java TimeZone class.	No
unit	Specifies the unit of the offset you've specified in offset. Possible values are millisecond, second, minute, hour, day, week, month, or year.	No

CHAPTER 4

Deploying Builds

This chapter starts coverage of one of the things Ant does best: deployment. This chapter covers tasks to package applications for deployment like tar, gzip, and zip; tasks to prepare directories for deployment like delete and mkdir; and tasks to deploy applications like copy and move for local and network deployment, as well as ftp, telent, sshexec, and mail for remote deployment. You'll see other deployment-related tasks, such as touch to set the deployed files' modification dates to a specific value (as is done for commercial software deployments), fixcrlf to fix text file line endings (as in readme, *.sh*, *.bat*, *.html*, or *.ini* files) for different platforms, and more. Finally, you'll learn how to handle build automation, setting up builds to run on their own, at a schedule of your choosing.

There's more on deployment coming up in this book. Ant has a lot of support for deploying web applications, so much so that it'll take more than just this chapter to cover. Chapter 8 covers how to package and deploy web applications, including using get (used to send administrative commands to web servers remotely), serverdeploy, war, and other Ant tasks designed to load web applications to various servers. Chapter 8 and part of Chapter 9 also specifically discuss how to deploy to Enterprise JavaBean™ (EJB) application servers.

Packaging Applications for Deployment

We're going to start with deployment tasks designed to package applications for deployment: tar, gzip, and zip. These are not the only way to package applications; the jar task was covered in Chapter 3 on Java Development, and the war task, a special form of the jar task for web applications that makes allowances for files like the deployment descriptor *web.xml*, will be covered in Chapter 8.

Creating TAR Files

The tar task creates a TAR archive, handy for archiving files for distribution. This task is directory-based and, like other such tasks, forms an implicit FileSet that defines which files—relative to the basedir attribute setting—will be included in the archive.

If you set the compression attribute to gzip or bzip2, you can compress the output .tar file to the specified format. For instance, Example 4-1 compiles code and places the resulting *Project.class* file in a *.tar.gz* file, *Project.tar.gz*, by setting the compression attribute to gzip.

Example 4-1. Tarring a file (ch04/tar/build.xml)

```xml
<?xml version="1.0" ?>
<project default="main">

    <property name="message" value="Building the .tar.gz file." />
    <property name="src" location="source" />
    <property name="output" location="bin" />

    <target name="main" depends="init, compile, compress">
        <echo>
            ${message}
        </echo>
    </target>

    <target name="init">
        <mkdir dir="${output}" />
    </target>

    <target name="compile">
        <javac srcdir="${src}" destdir="${output}" />
    </target>

  <target name="compress">
        <tar
            destfile="${output}/Project.tar.gz"
            basedir="${output}"
            includes="*.class"
            compression="gzip"/>
  </target>
</project>
```

The attributes of this task appear in Table 4-1.

Table 4-1. The tar task's attributes

Attribute	Description	Required	Default
basedir	Specifies the directory from which to get the files to TAR.	No	
compression	Sets the compression method, if any. Legal values are none, gzip and bzip2.	No	none
defaultexcludes	Specifies if you want to use default excludes. Set to yes/no.	No	Default excludes are used.
destfile	Specifies the name of the TAR file you want to create.	Yes	
excludes	Specifies the patterns matching files to exclude, as a comma- or space-separated list.	No	No files (except default excludes) are excluded.
excludesfile	Specifies the name of a file where each line is a pattern matching files to exclude.	No	
includes	Specifies the patterns matching files to include, as a comma- or space-separated list.	No	All files are included.
includesfile	Specifies the name of a file where each line is a pattern matching files to include.	No	
longfile	Specifies how you want to handle long file paths (more than 100 characters). Possible values are truncate, fail, warn, omit and gnu.	No	warn

Here's another example that uses the Ant gzip task after the tar task to create *Project.tar.gz*:

```
<tar tarfile="${dist}/Project.tar" basedir="${output}"/>
<gzip zipfile="${dist}/Project.tar.gz" src="${dist}/project.tar"/>
```

This next example does the same thing, except that it excludes files from the *beta* directory and any *todo.html* files:

```
<tar tarfile="${dist}/Project.tar" basedir="${output}"
    excludes="beta/**, **/todo.html"/>
<gzip zipfile="${dist}/Project.tar.gz" src="${dist}/project.tar"/>
```

The tar task supports nested tarfileset elements. These are specially extended FileSet types that support all the fileset attributes, and the additional attributes you see in Table 4-2.

The tarfileset type gives you control over the access mode, username, and groupname to be applied to the TAR entries. This is handy, for example, when preparing archives for Unix systems where certain files need to have execute permissions.

Table 4-2. The additional tarfileset attributes

Attribute	Description	Required	Default
dirmode	Specifies a three-digit octal string that gives the user and group using normal Unix conventions. Applies to directories only. Available since Ant 1.6.	No	755
fullpath	Using this attribute means the file in the fileset is written with this path in the compressed file.	No	
group	Specifies the group name for the TAR item.	No	
mode	Specifies a 3-digit octal string, which gives the user and group using normal Unix conventions. Applies to plain files only.	No	644
prefix	Specifies a path with which to prefix all files in the compressed file.	No	
preserveLeadingSlashes	Specifies if you want to preserve leading slashes (/) in filenames.	No	false
username	Specifies the username for this TAR item.	No	

This next, longer example uses GNU extensions for long paths and uses `tarfileset` elements to mark some files as executable (specifically, using Unix file mode 755, which means executable and readable by all, and writeable by the owner):

```
<tar longfile="gnu"
    destfile="${dist}" >
    <tarfileset dir="${bin}" mode="755" username="developer" group="ant">
        <include name="${bin}/bootstrap.sh"/>
        <include name="${bin}/build.sh"/>
    </tarfileset>
    <tarfileset dir="${dist}" username="developer" group="ant">
        <include name="${dist}/**"/>
        <exclude name="${dist}/*.sh"/>
    </tarfileset>
</tar>
```

Want to un-TAR a *.tar* archive? Ant has an untar task.

Compressing Using gzip and bzip2

The `gzip` and `bzip2` tasks pack files using the GZip or BZip2 algorithms. Here's an example that GZips a *.tar* file:

```
<gzip src="Project.tar" destfile="Project.tar.gz"/>
```

Here's a similar example that BZips a *.tar* file:

```
<bzip2 src="Project.tar" destfile="Project.tar.bz2"/>
```

Ant supports gunzip and bunzip2 tasks for uncompressing archives.

The supported attributes for these tasks appear in Table 4-3.

Table 4-3. The gzip and bunzip2 tasks' attributes

Attribute	Description	Required
destfile	Specifies the file you want to create.	Exactly one of destfile or zipfile
src	Specifies the file you want to GZip or BZip.	Yes
zipfile	Deprecated. Use destfile.	Exactly one of destfile or zipfile

Creating ZIP Files

The zip task creates ZIP files, useful for packaging files for deployment. The zip task is easy enough to use; here's how to zip all files in the *${dist}/docs* directory into *docs.zip*. If *docs.zip* doesn't exist, it's created; if it does, the files in it are updated:

```
<zip destfile="${dist}/docs.zip"
    basedir="${dist}/docs"
    update="true"
/>
```

This next example zips all files in the *${dist}/docs* directory. Only *.html* files in the directory *api* will be zipped, and files with the name *beta.html* are excluded:

```
<zip destfile="${dist}/docs.zip"
    basedir="${dist}/docs"
    includes="api/**/*.html"
    excludes="**/beta.html"
/>
```

The attributes of this task appear in Table 4-4.

 A JAR archive is a ZIP file with a manifest; if you don't want a manifest in a JAR file, use zip instead of jar.

Table 4-4. The zip task's attributes

Attribute	Description	Required	Default
basedir	Specifies the directory where the files you want to zip are.	No	
compress	Specifies that you don't want to store data but want to compresses it.	No	true
defaultexcludes	Specifies whether you want default excludes to be used or not (yes/no).	No	Default excludes are used

Table 4-4. The zip task's attributes (continued)

Attribute	Description	Required	Default
destfile	Specifies the ZIP file you want to create.	One of destfile or zipfile.	
duplicate	Specifies what you want to do when a duplicate file is found. Valid values are add, preserve, and fail.	No	add
encoding	Specifies the character encoding you want to use inside the ZIP file.	No	The platform's default character encoding.
excludes	Specifies the patterns matching files to exclude, as a comma- or space-separated list.	No	No files (except default excludes) are excluded.
excludesfile	Specifies the name of a file where each line is a pattern matching files to exclude.	No	
filesonly	Stores only file entries.	No	false
includes	Specifies the patterns matching files to include, as a comma- or space-separated list.	No	All files are included.
includesfile	Specifies the name of a file where each line is a pattern matching files to include.	No	
keepcompression	Preserves the compression as it has been in archives you're compressing instead of using the compress attribute. Available since Ant 1.6.	No	false
update	Specifies whether you want to update or overwrite the destination file in case it exists.	No	false
whenempty	Specifies what you want to do when no files match. Possible values are fail, skip, and create.	No	skip
zipfile	Deprecated. Use destfile.	One of destfile or zipfile	

This task supports any number of nested fileset elements to specify the files to be included in the ZIP file. The zip task supports any number of nested zipfileset elements, which support all the attributes of fileset (see Table 2-8) as well as the ones you see in Table 4-5.

Table 4-5. The additional zipfileset attributes

Attribute	Description	Required	Default
dirmode	Specifies a three-digit octal string that gives the user and group using normal Unix conventions. Applies to directories only.	No	755
filemode	Specifies a 3-digit octal string, which gives the user and group using normal Unix conventions. Applies to plain files only.	No	644
fullpath	Using this attribute means that the file in the fileset is written with this path in the compressed file.	No	

Table 4-5. The additional zipfileset attributes (continued)

Attribute	Description	Required	Default
prefix	Specifies a path to with which prefix all files in the compressed file.	No	
src	Specifies a ZIP file instead of a directory as the source of files.	No	

You can nest `zipgroupfileset` elements in a zip task. These elements allow you to add multiple ZIP files in the archive. The attributes for the `zipgroupfileset` type are the same as for the `fileset` type and include the extra attributes for `zipfileset` elements (see Table 4-5).

 Because the zip task forms an implicit FileSet (`dir` becomes `basedir`), you can use nested `include`, `exclude`, and `patternset` elements.

This example zips all files in the *docs* directory into the *docs/guide* directory in the archive, adds the file *readme.txt* in the current directory as *docs/readme.txt*, and includes all the html files in *examples.zip* under *docs/examples*:

```
<zip destfile="${dist}/docs.zip">
    <zipfileset dir="docs" prefix="docs/guide"/>
    <zipfileset dir="${dist}" includes="readme.txt" fullpath="docs/readme.txt"/>
    <zipfileset src="examples.zip" includes="**/*.html" prefix="docs/examples"/>
</zip>
```

 Ant provides an unzip task if you want to decompress ZIP files.

Fixing Carriage Returns

If you've ever deployed documentation files from Unix to Windows or Windows to Unix, you've probably run into problems with line endings. Lines in Unix text files typically end with a newline (/n) while those in DOS and Windows typically end with a carriage return/line feed pair (/r/n). To modify text files before deploying them to other operating systems, use `fixcrlf`. Like other directory-based Ant tasks, this task forms an implicit FileSet and supports all attributes of `fileset` (`dir` becomes `srcdir`) as well as the nested `include`, `exclude` and `patternset` elements.

Say, for example, that you wanted to convert the end of line characters in Unix shell scripts (*.sh*) to be uploaded from Windows to a Unix server to a linefeed, and remove any DOS-style end-of-file (EOF) characters (^Z). You could do that like this:

```
<fixcrlf srcdir="${src}"
    eol="lf"
    eof="remove"
    includes="**/*.sh"
/>
```

Here's how you might go the other way, replacing all end-of-line (EOL) characters with a cr-lf pair in DOS batch (*.bat*) files in preparation to downloading them to Windows:

```
<fixcrlf srcdir="${src}"
    eol="crlf"
    eof="add"
    includes="**/*.bat"
/>
```

This example converts all *.txt* files according to the convention of the host operating system and replaces tabs with spaces:

```
<fixcrlf srcdir="${src}"
    tab="remove"
    includes="**/*.txt"
/>
```

 As demonstrated by the previous example, fixcrlf is good for removing or inserting tabs. That's useful because some software (e.g., Make) is finicky about tabs.

The attributes of this task appear in Table 4-6.

Table 4-6. The fixcrlf task's attributes

Attribute	Description	Required	Default
cr	Deprecated. Use eol.	No	
defaultexcludes	Specifies if you want to use default excludes or not Set to yes/no.	No	Default excludes are used.
destDir	Specifies where you want the modified files.	No	The value of srcDir.
encoding	Specifies the encoding of the files you're working on.	No	The default JVM encoding.

eof	Specifies how you want to handle DOS end-of-file (^Z) characters. Possible values are:
	
	add
	  Makes sure an EOF character is at the end of the file.
	
	asis
	  Leaves EOF characters alone.
	
	remove
	  Removes any EOF character found at the end.
		No	The default is based on platform. In Unix, the default is remove. For Windows/DOS systems, the default is asis.

Table 4-6. The fixcrlf task's attributes (continued)

Attribute	Description	Required	Default

eol	Specifies how you want to handle end-of-line (EOL) characters. Possible values are:
	
	asis
	    Leaves EOL characters alone.
	cr
	    Converts all EOLs to a single CR.
	lf
	    Converts all EOLs to a single LF.
	crlf
	    Converts all EOLs to the pair CRLF.
	mac
	    Converts all EOLs to a single CR.
	unix
	    Converts all EOLs to a single LF.
	dos
	    Converts all EOLs to the pair CRLF.
		No	The default is based on platform. In Unix, the default is lf. For Windows/DOS systems, the default is crlf. For Mac OS, the default is cr.

excludes	Specifies the patterns matching files to exclude, as a comma- or space-separated list.	No	
excludesfile	Specifies the name of a file where each line is a pattern matching files to exclude.	No	
fixlast	Specifies whether you want to add an EOL to the last line of a processed file. Available since Ant 1.6.1.	No	true
includes	Specifies the patterns matching files to include, as a comma- or space-separated list.	No	
includesfile	Specifies the name of a file where each line is a pattern matching files to include.	No	
javafiles	Specifies if the file is a Java code file. Used with the tab attribute. Set to yes/no.	No	no
srcDir	Specifies where to find the files you want to fix.	Yes	

tab	Specifies how you want to handle tab characters. Possible values are:
	
	add
	    Converts sequences of spaces span a tab stop to tabs.
	asis
	    Leaves tab and space characters alone.
	remove
	    Converts tabs to spaces.
		No	asis

tablength	Specifies the tab character interval. Possible values range from 2 to 80.	No	8

The output file is only written if it is a new file, or if it differs from the existing file. The idea is to prevent bogus rebuilds based on unchanged files that have been regenerated by this task.

Checking File Contents Using Checksums

A checksum is a numerical value corresponding to the contents of a file, and it can tell you if the copy of the file you've deployed is a good copy. This task lets you create an MD5 checksum for a file or set of files. Here's an example using this task; in this case, I'm creating an MD5 checksum for *Project.jar*, which will be stored in a file named *Project.jar.MD5*:

```
<checksum file="Project.jar"/>
```

You can generate a similar checksum for the file after it's been deployed to check if it's OK.

Build files can be used to verify checksum values when testing a deployment; for example, you can generate an MD5 checksum for *Project.jar*, compare that value to a value you've hard-coded into a property named checksum, and set the property checksumOK if the two values match:

```
<checksum file="Project.jar" property="${checksum}" verifyProperty="checksumOK"/>
```

You can see the attributes of the checksum task in Table 4-7.

Table 4-7. The checksum task's attributes

Attribute	Description	Required	Default
algorithm	Specifies the algorithm you want to use to compute the checksum.	No	MD5
file	Specifies the file you want to generate the checksum for.	One of file or at least one nested fileset element.	
fileext	Specifies the extension of the file for the generated checksum.	No	Defaults to the algorithm name being used.
forceoverwrite	Specifies whether you want to overwrite existing files.	No	no
property	If verifyproperty is not set, property specifies the name of the property to hold the checksum value. If verifyproperty is set, property specifies the actual checksum value you expect.	No	
provider	Specifies the algorithm provider.	No	
readbuffersize	Specifies the size of the buffer the task should use when reading files, in bytes.	No	8192

Table 4-7. The checksum task's attributes (continued)

Attribute	Description	Required	Default
`todir`	Specifies the directory where you want check-sums to be written. Available since Ant 1.6.	No	Checksum files are written to the same directory as the source files.
`totalproperty`	Specifies the name of the property that you want to hold a checksum of all the generated check-sums and file paths. Available since Ant 1.6.	No	
`verifyproperty`	Specifies the name of the property to be set `true` or `false` depending upon whether the gener-ated checksum matches the existing checksum.	No	

The checksum task can contain nested `fileset` elements. By now, this should be old hat to you.

Setting Creation Time and Date

When you're deploying files, you can set the creation date and time of those files to a single value to make the deployment look more professional (as you'll usually see with commercial software). The touch task will do this for you; besides setting the creation time and date for a single file, you can do the same thing for whole directories of files if you include a fileset.

If you only specify a single file, its modification time and date is set to the current time and date:

```
<touch file="Project.jar"/>
```

Here's an example that sets the modification time and date of all the files in ${src} to January 1, 2005, at 5:00 PM:

```
<touch datetime="01/01/2005 5:00 pm">
    <fileset dir="${src}"/>
</touch>
```

If the file you're touching doesn't exist, touch will create it for you, which is one of the few ways you can use Ant to create empty files (you can create files with text in them with the echo task, using the `file` attribute). Want to give the file a name that's guaranteed to be unique? Use Ant's tempfile task—for example, <tempfile property="temp. file" /> will store the unique name of a file in the `temp.file` prop-erty, and <touch file="${temp.file}" /> will create that file.

You can see the attributes of this task in Table 4-8.

Table 4-8. The touch task's attributes

Attribute	Description	Required
datetime	Specifies the new modification time of the file. Use the formats MM/DD/YYYY HH:MM AM_or_PM or MM/DD/YYYY HH:MM:SS AM_or_PM.	No
file	Specifies the name of the file whose time and/or date information you want to change.	Yes, unless you use a nested fileset element
millis	Specifies the new modification time of the file, given in epoch milliseconds (that is, since midnight, Jan 1, 1970).	No

The touch task can contain nested `fileset` elements to touch multiple files at once.

Preparing to Deploy

Ant supports several tasks for setting up a deployment environment, such as `delete` and `mkdir`. Both these tasks can be used locally or on a network to set up the directory structure you need to deploy applications.

 If you want to create and delete directories remotely, take a look at the `ftp` task, coming up later in this chapter.

Deleting Existing Files

When deploying, `delete` is great to clean up a previous installation or to clean deployment directories before installing. This task deletes a single file, a directory and all its files and subdirectories, or a set of files specified by one or more FileSets.

Using this task, you can delete a single file:

```
<delete file="/lib/Project.jar"/>
```

Or you can delete an entire directory, including all files and subdirectories:

```
<delete dir="${dist}"/>
```

You can use filesets:

```
<delete includeEmptyDirs="true">
    <fileset dir="${dist}"/>
</delete>
```

You've seen `delete` at work in various places throughout the book, as in the build file in the *input* folder for Chapter 3's code (repeated in Example 4-2), where the user is asked for confirmation before deleting anything.

Example 4-2. Using the delete task (ch03/input/build.xml)

```
<?xml version="1.0" ?>
<project default="main">
```

Example 4-2. Using the delete task *3/input/build.xml) (continued)*

```
    <property name="message" va    Building the .jar file." />
    <property name="src" locati    ource" />
    <property name="output" loc    ="bin" />

    <target name="main" depends    t, compile, compress">
        <echo>
            ${message}
        </echo>
    </target>

    <target name="init">
        <input
            message="Deleting b    rectory OK?"
            validargs="y,n"
            addproperty="do.del
        />
        <condition property="do    t">
            <equals arg1="n" ar    {do.delete}"/>
        </condition>
        <fail if="do.abort">Bui    orted.</fail>
        <delete dir="${output}"
        <mkdir dir="${output}"
    </target>

    <target name="compile">
        <javac srcdir="${src}"    ir="${output}" />
    </target>

  <target name="compress">
        <jar destfile="${output    ject.jar" basedir="${output}" includes="*.class" />
  </target>
</project>
```

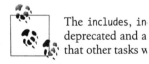 If you use this tas   lelete temporary files created by editors or other
software and it d   t work, try setting the defaultexcludes attribute
to no.

You can see the attributes of t   ask in Table 4-9.

The includes, in   sfile, exclude, and excludesfile attributes are
deprecated and a   ng replaced by fileset. This makes me suspect
that other tasks w   llow this same pattern.

Table 4-9. The delete task's attributes

Attribute	Description	Required	Default
defaultexcludes	Specifies if you want to use default excludes. Set to yes/no.	No	Default excludes are used.
dir	Specifies the name of a directory to delete. All its files and subdirectories will be deleted.	At least one of file or dir (unless a fileset element is specified).	
excludes	Deprecated. Use a fileset element. Specifies the patterns matching files to exclude, as a comma- or space-separated list.	No	No files (except default excludes) are excluded.
excludesfile	Deprecated. Use a fileset element. Specifies the name of a file where each line is a pattern matching files to exclude.	No	
failonerror	Specifies if you want an error to stop the build. Only used if if quiet is false.	No	true
file	Specifies the file you want to delete.	At least one of file or dir (unless a fileset element is specified).	
includeEmptyDirs	Specifies if you want to delete empty directories when using file sets.	No	false
includes	Deprecated. Use a nested fileset element. Specifies the patterns matching files to include, as a comma- or space-separated list.	No	All files are included.
includesfile	Deprecated. Use a nested fileset element. Specifies the name of a file where each line is a pattern matching files to include.	No	
quiet	Suppresses most diagnostic messages.	No	
verbose	Specifies that you want to show the name of each deleted file (true/false).	No	false

The delete task can contain nested fileset elements.

> Here's something you might not have expected: empty directories are
> *not* deleted by default. To remove empty directories, use the
> includeEmptyDirs attribute.

Creating New Directories

Want to create the directory structure for local or network deployment? Use mkdir.
This one's so important that you've seen it in use since Chapter 1. And it's easy to
use with only one attribute, as you can see in Table 4-10.

Table 4-10. The mkdir task's attributes

Attribute	Description	Required
dir	Specifies the directory you want to create	Yes

Want to create a directory? Just do it:

```
<mkdir dir="${dist}"/>
```

 Just realized that you've asked `mkdir` to create a directory whose parent directories don't exist? That's not a problem since `mkdir` creates parent directories as needed.

Deploying Applications

As you'd expect, Ant excels at deploying applications, and there are a number of tasks to choose from. You've saw the `javac` task's `destdir` attribute for deployment back in Chapter 1. In this section, you'll see copy, move, `ftp`, `telnet`, and `sshexec`.

The copy and move tasks are useful for local and network deployments, and tasks like `ftp` are great for remote deployments. Additionally, Chapter 8 will cover deployment to web servers with tasks like get, which you can use to send administrative commands to servers like Tomcat (I'll cover Tomcat's built-in custom Ant tasks), and `serverdeploy`.

 Want to get a file's name without the path attached? Pass the filename to the basename task. Want to get just the path? Use dirname. The pathconvert task converts a nested path or reference to a Path, FileSet, DirSet, or FileList into a path (automatically adjusted for the target platform) and stores the result in a given property.

Deploying by Copying

This task copies a file, or a fileset, to a new file or a new directory. This is Ant's most basic deployment task for local and network deployment. Here are a few examples, starting with copying just one file:

```
<copy file="file.txt" tofile="backup.txt"/>
```

This example copies a file to a new location:

```
<copy file="file.txt" todir="../backup"/>
```

This example copies an entire directory to a new location:

```
<copy todir="../backup">
    <fileset dir="${src}"/>
</copy>
```

This copies a set of files to a new directory:

```
<copy todir="../backup">
    <fileset dir="src">
        <include name="**/*.java"/>
    </fileset>
</copy>
```

Want to copy files and change their names? Use a mapper element like this:

```
<copy todir="../backup">
    <fileset dir="src"/>
    <mapper type="glob" from="*" to="*.old"/>
</copy>
```

Here's how to copy a set of files to a directory, replacing @TODO@ with "DONE" in all copied files:

```
<copy todir="../backup">
    <fileset dir="src"/>
    <filter set>
        <filter token="TODO" value="DONE"/>
    </filter set>
</copy>
```

In Unix, file permissions are not retained when files are copied; files end up with the default UMASK permissions instead. If you need a permission-preserving copy function, use the system copy utilities—see the exec task in Chapter 7 (you'd use <exec executable="cp" ... > here). Or use the chmod task, coming up in this chapter, after the copy.

Example 4-3 uses copy to copy a documentation file to make sure it's included in the final JAR for a project and then deploys the JAR file to a directory named *user*.

Example 4-3. Using the copy task (ch04/copy/build.xml)

```
<?xml version="1.0" ?>
<project default="main">

    <property name="message" value="Deploying the .jar file." />
    <property name="src" location="source" />
    <property name="output" location="bin" />
    <property name="dist" location="user" />

    <target name="main" depends="init, compile, compress, deploy">
        <echo>
            ${message}
        </echo>
    </target>

    <target name="init">
        <mkdir dir="${output}" />
        <mkdir dir="${dist}" />
    </target>
```

Example 4-3. Using the copy task (ch04/copy/build.xml) (continued)

```
<target name="compile">
    <javac srcdir="${src}" destdir="${output}" />
</target>

<target name="compress">
    <copy todir="${output}" file="${src}/readme.txt"/>
    <jar destfile="${output}/Project.jar" basedir="${output}">
        <include name="*.class"/>
        <include name="*.txt"/>
    </jar>
</target>

<target name="deploy">
    <copy todir="${dist}">
        <fileset dir="${output}">
            <exclude name="*.java"/>
            <exclude name="*.class"/>
            <exclude name="*.txt"/>
        </fileset>
    </copy>
</target>
```

```
</project>
```

You can see the attributes of this task in Table 4-11.

Table 4-11. The copy task's attributes

Attribute	Description	Required	Default
enablemultiplemappings	Specifies that you want to use multiple mapper elements. Available since Ant 1.6.	No	false
encoding	Specifies the encoding to use. For use when copying files using filters.	No	Defaults to default JVM encoding
failonerror	Specifies whether you want the task to fail if there is an error.	No	true
file	Specifies the file you want to copy.	Yes, unless a nested fileset element is used.	
filtering	Specifies whether you want to use filtering. Nested filterset elements will always be used; you don't have to set this attribute to true for that.	No	false

Table 4-11. The copy task's attributes (continued)

Attribute	Description	Required	Default
flatten	Specifies you want to ignore the directory structure of source files, copying all files into the directory given by the todir attribute.	No	false
includeEmptyDirs	Specifies you want to copy any empty directories as well.	No	true
outputencoding	Specifies the encoding you want to use when writing files. Available since Ant 1.6.	No	Defaults to the value of the encoding attribute if given, or the default JVM encoding otherwise
overwrite	Specifies whether you want to overwrite existing files.	No	false
preservelastmodified	Specifies you want copied files to have the same modified time as the source files.	No	false
todir	Specifies the directory the files should be copied to.	If you use the file attribute, tofile or todir can be used. If you use nested fileset elements and if the number of files is more than 1 or if only the dir attribute is specified in the fileset, then only todir is allowed.	
tofile	Specifies the file you want to copy to.	If you use the file attribute, tofile or todir can be used. If you use nested fileset elements and if the number of files is more than 1 or if only the dir attribute is specified in the fileset, then only todir is allowed.	
verbose	Specifies you want to see filenames displayed as the files are being copied.	No	false

 By default, files are only copied if the source file is newer than the destination file or when the destination file does not exist. However, you can explicitly overwrite files with the overwrite attribute.

You can use `fileset` elements inside copy elements to create a fileset to copy. If you want to use a fileset, the todir attribute must be set. You can use nested mapper elements, and `filter` set elements and the copy task supports nested FilterChains.

 If you use filters in your copy operation, limit the operation to text files. Binary files will be corrupted by that kind of copy operation. This is true whether the filters are implicitly defined by the filter task or explicitly provided to the copy operation as filter sets.

Moving Files

The move task moves a file (copies and then deletes the original) to a new file or a new directory or it moves sets of files to a new directory. The attributes and nested elements are the same as for copy (see Table 4-11 and related sections).

 By default, the destination file is overwritten if it already exists. When overwrite is turned off, files are only moved if the source file is newer than the destination file, or when the destination file does not exist.

Here's an example that moves a single file (the net result is that the file is renamed):

```
<move file="file.txt" tofile="file.backup"/>
```

Here's how to move a directory to a new directory:

```
<move todir="source">
    <fileset dir="backup"/>
</move>
```

Example 4-4 uses move to deploy the files it creates.

Example 4-4. Moving a file (ch04/move/build.xml)

```
<?xml version="1.0" ?>
<project default="main">

    <property name="message" value="Deploying the .jar file." />
    <property name="src" location="source" />
    <property name="output" location="bin" />
    <property name="dist" location="user" />

    <target name="main" depends="init, compile, compress, deploy">
        <echo>
            ${message}
        </echo>
    </target>

    <target name="init">
        <mkdir dir="${output}" />
        <mkdir dir="${dist}" />
    </target>
```

Example 4-4. Moving a file (ch04/move/build.xml) (continued)

```
    <target name="compile">
        <javac srcdir="${src}" destdir="${output}" />
    </target>

    <target name="compress">
        <jar destfile="${output}/Project.jar" basedir="${output}"
             includes="*.class" />
    </target>

    <target name="deploy">
      <move todir="${dist}">
        <fileset dir="${output}">
          <exclude name="*.java"/>
          <exclude name="*.class"/>
        </fileset>
      </move>
    </target>

</project>
```

For more examples, see the section "Deploying by Copying."

Deploying Remotely Using FTP

The ftp task is handy for remote deployment. This task can send, receive, list, delete files, and create directories. This is one of Ant's optional tasks, so you'll need two JAR files, which you place in the Ant *lib* directory: *jakarta-oro.jar* (available from *http://jakarta.apache.org/oro/*) and *commons-net.jar* (available from *http://jakarta.apache.org/commons/net/index.html*).

If you want to use this task with MS FTP servers, you need a version of *commons-net.jar* and *jakarta-oro.jar* released after 02/01/2004, or a release of *commons-net.jar* after 1.1.0 and *jakarta-oro.jar* after 2.0.8.

Here's an example that deploys the results of a build to the directory */cgi-bin* on a remote server. Since it's a bad idea to hardcode the username and password in build files, I'll set those as properties on the command line (you can use the input task here) using the properties name and password:

```
%ant -Dname=Steve -Dpassword=let_me_in
```

The build file is shown in Example 4-5. Before running the file, supply the IP address of the server by changing the value of the server attribute from "000.000.000.000" to the IP address of your server or use the name of the server, like "ftp.apache.org."

Though you usually supply an action attribute telling ftp what to do, the default action is to send files (action="send"), so you can omit action here.

Example 4-5. Using ftp (ch04/ftp/build.xml)

```xml
<?xml version="1.0" ?>
<project default="main">

    <property name="message" value="Deploying the .jar file." />
    <property name="src" location="source" />
    <property name="output" location="bin" />

    <target name="main" depends="init, compile, compress, deploy">
        <echo>
            ${message}
        </echo>
    </target>

    <target name="init">
        <mkdir dir="${output}" />
    </target>

    <target name="compile">
        <javac srcdir="${src}" destdir="${output}" />
    </target>

    <target name="compress">
        <jar destfile="${output}/Project.jar" basedir="${output}">
            <include name="*.class"/>
            <include name="*.txt"/>
        </jar>
    </target>

    <target name="deploy">
        <ftp server="000.000.000.000" binary="true" verbose="true"
            userid="${name}" password="${password}" remotedir="/cgi-bin">
            <fileset dir="${output}">
                <exclude name="*.java"/>
                <exclude name="*.class"/>
                <exclude name="*.txt"/>
            </fileset>
        </ftp>
    </target>

</project>
```

Here's what running this build file looks like in Windows when uploading the results of a build to a remote server:

```
C:\ant\ch04\ftp>ant -Dname=steven -Dpassword=let_me_in
Buildfile: build.xml

init:
    [mkdir] Created dir: C:\ant\ch04\ftp\bin
```

```
compile:
    [javac] Compiling 1 source file to C:\ant\ch04\ftp\bin

compress:
      [jar] Building jar: C:\ant\ch04\ftp\bin\Project.jar

deploy:
     [ftp] sending files
     [ftp] transferring C:\ant\ch04\ftp\bin\Project.jar
     [ftp] 1 files sent

main:
    [echo]
    [echo]                 Deploying the .jar file.
    [echo]

BUILD SUCCESSFUL
Total time: 10 seconds
```

That's it; you've deployed the results of the build remotely. Very cool!

 If you want to build in delay times to take into account delays in getting responses from a server, use the Ant waitfor task. You can use the sleep task for this purpose.

To retrieve files from the server using ftp, you set action to get, the remotedir attribute to the remote directory, and the dir attribute to the directory you want the retrieved files stored in locally:

```
<ftp action="get"
    server="000.000.000.000"
    remotedir="/cgi-bin"
    userid="${name}"
    password="${password}">
    <fileset dir="docs">
        <include name="**/*.html"/>
    </fileset>
</ftp>
```

To delete files, set action to "del":

```
<ftp action="del"
    server="000.000.000.000"
    remotedir="/cgi-bin"
    userid="${name}"
    password="${password}">
    <fileset>
        <include name="**/*.html"/>
    </fileset>
</ftp>
```

To list files, set action to "list"; here's how to store the listing of files in the remote */cgi-bin* directory in a file named *file.list*:

```
<ftp action="list"
    server="000.000.000.000"
    remotedir="/cgi-bin"
    userid="${name}"
    password="${password}"
    listing="ftp.list">
    <fileset>
        <include name="**"/>
    </fileset>
</ftp>
```

Here's how to create a directory, */cgi-bin*, by setting action to "mkdir";

```
<ftp action="mkdir"
    server="000.000.000.000"
    remotedir="/cgi-bin"
    userid="${name}"
    password="${password}"/>
```

 You can remove directories; set action to rmdir.

You can see the attributes of this task in Table 4-12.

Table 4-12. The ftp task's attributes

Attribute	Description	Required	Default
action	Specifies the ftp action you want to perform. Possible values: put, get, del, list, chmod, mkdir and rmdir.	No	send
binary	Specifies the transfer mode. Possible values: binary-mode (yes) or text-mode (no).	No	yes
chmod	Specifies the file permissions for new or existing files (Unix only).	No	
depends	Specifies you want to transfer only new or changed files. Set to yes/no.	No	no
ignoreNoncriticalErrors	Specifies you want to allow the task to continue despite some non-fatal error codes.	No	false
listing	Specifies a file to write output from the "list" action.	Required for the "list" action, but ignored otherwise.	
newer	The same as the depends attribute.	No	
passive	Specifies you want to use passive transfers.	No	no
password	Specifies the login password for the FTP server.	Yes	

Table 4-12. The ftp task's attributes (continued)

Attribute	Description	Required	Default
port	Specifies the port of the FTP server.	No	21
preservelastmodified	Specifies whether you want to give downloaded files the same modified time as the original files.	No	false
remotedir	Specifies a directory on the FTP server you want to use.	No	
separator	Specifies the directory separator used on the target FTP server.	No	/
server	Specifies the address of the FTP server.	Yes	
skipFailedTransfers	Specifies unsuccessful transfers should be skipped (with a warning).	No	false
timediffauto	Specifies if to make this task calculate the time difference between you and server. Available in Ant 1.6 or later.	No	
timediffmillis	Specifies the number of milliseconds between times on the target machine compared to the local machine. Available since Ant 1.6.	No	
umask	Specifies the default file permission (unix only).	No	
userid	Specifies the login you want to use on the FTP server.	Yes	
verbose	Specifies whether you want to see information on each file as it's transferred. Set to yes/no.	No	no

> The condition task lets you probe if remote systems are available before attempting an FTP operation. You can use two nested elements in condition: http (which can test can probe for remote servers) and socket (which can send messages to remote servers).

The ftp task supports any number of nested fileset elements, which is how you specify the files to be retrieved, deleted, or listed, or whose mode you want to change.

Deploying Remotely Using Telnet

Ant includes a telnet task that you can use when deploying remotely. For security reasons, Telnet is losing popularity (in favor of SSH), but I'll take a look at telnet, followed by the sshexec task. This is one of Ant's optional tasks, so you'll need *commons-net.jar* (available from *http://jakarta.apache.org/commons/net/index.html*) in the Ant *lib* directory.

This task uses nested read elements to indicate strings to wait for and write elements to specify text to send. Here's an example that connects to a server, and asks for a listing of the directory */home/steven*:

```
<telnet userid="steven" password="let_me_in" server="000.000.000.000">
    <read>/home/steven</read>
    <write>ls</write>
</telnet>
```

You can see the attributes of this task in Table 4-13.

Table 4-13. The telnet task's attributes

Attribute	Values	Required	Default
initialCR	Specifies that you want to send a carriage return after connecting to the server	No	no
password	Specifies the login password you want to use on the Telnet server	Yes, if userid is specified.	
port	Specifies the port on the Telnet server to use	No	23
server	Specifies the address of the remote Telnet server you want to use	Yes	
timeout	Specifies a default timeout for Telnet actions (in seconds)	No	No timeout
userid	Specifies the username to use to log into the Telnet server	Yes, if password is specified.	

Deploying Remotely Using SSH

The more secure SSH protocol is replacing Telnet in general use, and Ant 1.6 added the sshexec task to execute SSH commands on a remote system. This is an optional task, so you'll need *jsch.jar* (which you can get at *http://www.jcraft.com/jsch/index.html*) in the Ant *lib* directory. Here's an example that runs a command, touch, on a remote machine, using sshexec:

```
<sshexec host="000.000.000.000"
    username="${name}"
    password="${password}"
    command="touch index.html"/>
```

You can find the attributes of this task in Table 4-14.

 See the scp task for copying files for deployment to web servers using SSH in Chapter 8.

Table 4-14. The sshexec task's attributes

Attribute	Description	Required	Default
append	Specifies if you want the output file to be appended to or overwritten.	No	false
command	Specifies the command to run remotely.	Yes	
failonerror	Specifies whether you want to stop the build if there are errors.	No	true
host	Specifies the host you want to work with.	Yes	
keyfile	Specifies the name of a file holding a private key.	Yes, if you are using key-based authentication.	
knownhosts	Specifies the known hosts file. Used to check the identity of remote hosts. Must be an SSH2 format file.	No	${user.home}/.ssh/ known_hostswn_hostts
output	Specifies the name of a file in which you want output written.	No	
outputproperty	Specifies the name of a property in which you want output written.	No	
passphrase	Specifies a passphrase you want to use for your private key.	No	" "
password	Specifies the password to use for SSH.	No	
port	Specifies the port to connect to.	No	22
timeout	Specifies whether you want the operation stopped if it timed out (in milliseconds).	No	0 (wait forever)
trust	Specifies if to trust all unknown hosts if set to yes.	No	no
username	Specifies the username you want to use.	Yes	

Deploying Remotely Through Email

You can deploy using email with the `mail` task, attaching files you want to deploy (attachments can be sent using the `files` attribute or nested `fileset` elements). You'll need access to an SMTP server, which you specify in the mailhost attribute and need two JAR files in the Ant *lib* directory: *mail.jar* (which you can get from *http://java.sun.com/products/javamail/*) and *activation.jar* (which you can get from *http://java.sun.com/products/javabeans/glasgow/jaf.html*).

Here's an example, where the results of a build are deployed as an attachment to an email message. This email has the subject "New Build", the message body "Here is the new build.", and has the build's newly created *.tar.gz* files attached:

```
<target name="deploy">
    <mail mailhost="smtp.isp.com" mailport="1025" subject="New Build">
        <from address="developer@isp.com"/>
        <replyto address="developer@isp.com"/>
        <to address="list@xyz.com"/>
        <message>Here is the new build.</message>
        <fileset dir="dist">
            <includes name="**/*.tar.gz"/>
        </fileset>
    </mail>
</target>
```

Now you're deploying via email using Ant. You can see the attributes of the `mail` task in Table 4-15.

Table 4-15. The mailTask's attributes

Attribute	Description	Required	Default
bcclist	List of addresses to send a blind copy of the email to. A comma-separated list.	At least one of tolist, cclist, bcclist, or the equivalent elements (to, cc, or bcc).	
cclist	List of addresses to send a copy of the email to. A comma-separated list.	At least one of tolist, cclist, bcclist, or the equivalent elements (to, cc, or bcc).	
charset	Specifies the character set you want to use in the email.	No	
encoding	Specifies the encoding to use. Possible values are mime, uu, plain, or auto.	No	auto
failonerror	Specifies whether you want to stop the build if there are errors.	No	true
files	Specifies files you want to send as attachments. Use a comma-separated list. You can use nested fileset elements.	No	

Table 4-15. The mailTask's attributes (continued)

Attribute	Description	Required	Default
from	Specifies the email address of the sender.	Either a from attribute or a from element.	
includefilenames	Specifies whether you want to include filename(s) before file contents.	No	false
mailhost	Specifies the hostname of the SMTP server.	No	localhost
mailport	Specifies the TCP port of the SMTP server to use.	No	25
message	Specifies the email's body.	One of message, messagefile, or a message element.	
messagefile	Specifies a file to send as the email's body.	One of message, messagefile, or a message element.	
messagemimetype	Specifies the type of the message's content.	No	text/plain
password	Specifies the password for SMTP authorization.	Yes, if SMTP authorization is required on your SMTP server.	
replyto	Specifies the reply-to address.	No	
ssl	Specifies if you want to use TLS/SSL.	No	
subject	Specifies the email's subject.	No	
tolist	Specifies a list of recipients. A comma-separated list.	At least one of tolist, cclist, bcclist, or the equivalent elements (to, cc, or bcc).	
user	Specifies the username used to log into the SMTP server.	Yes, if SMTP authorization is required on your SMTP server.	

The mail task can take nested to, cc, bcc, from, and replyto elements, which hold email addresses. Here are the attributes of these elements (these attributes are common across all these elements):

address
    Specifies the email address
name
    Specifies the display name for the email address

In addition, the nested `message` element sets the message to include in the email body. Here are the attributes of this element (all are optional):

charset
  Specifies the character set used in the message

mimetype
  Specifies the content type of the message

src
  Specifies the file to use as the message

You can use email to send the results of a build with the mail logger, which is useful if you've set up unattended nightly builds with utilities like at in Windows or crontab in Unix (see Chapter 7 for coverage of both of these). Here's how you use this logger:

```
%ant -logger org.apache.tools.ant.listener.MailLogger
```

You set these properties in the build file to set up the email you want sent:

MailLogger.mailhost
  Specifies the mail server to use (default: localhost)

MailLogger.port
  Specifies the default port for SMTP (default: 25)

MailLogger.from
  Specifies the mail "from" address (required)

MailLogger.failure.notify
  Specifies if to send on failure (default: true)

MailLogger.success.notify
  Specifies if to send on success (default: true)

MailLogger.failure.to
  Specifies the address to send failure messages to (required if failure mail to be sent)

MailLogger.success.toSpecifies
  The address to send success messages to (required if success mail to be sent)

MailLogger.failure.subject
  Specifies the subject of failed build (default: Build Failure)

MailLogger.success.subject
  Specifies the subject of successful build (default: Build Success)

Setting File Protections with chmod

The chmod task changes the permissions of a file or files, and it's useful in deployment after you've got your files deployed in case you need to set file permissions. You set the permissions in Unix style (just as the arguments for the Unix chmod command).

Here's an example that makes *run.sh* readable, writable and executable for the owner on a Unix system, and readable and executable for others:

```
<chmod file="${dist}/run.sh" perm="755"/>
```

This makes all *.sh* files in and below ${dist} readable and executable for anyone on a Unix system:

```
<chmod dir="${dist}" perm="ugo+rx"
    includes="**/*.sh"/>
```

You can see the attributes for this task in Table 4-16.

 At present, the chmod task only works in Unix and the NonStop Kernel (Tandem).

Table 4-16. The chmod task's attributes

Attribute	Description	Required	Default
defaultexcludes	Specifies if you want to use default excludes. Set to yes/no.	No	Default excludes are used.
dir	Specifies the directory holding the files to work on.	One of file, dir, or nested fileset/list elements.	
excludes	Specifies the patterns matching files to exclude, as a comma- or space-separated list.	No	
file	Specifies the file or single directory where you want permissions to be changed.	One of file, dir, or nested fileset/list elements.	
includes	Specifies the patterns matching files to include, as a comma- or space-separated list.	No	
maxparallel	Specifies limits on how many files to pass at once. Set this attribute to 0 or negative values for unlimited parallelism. Available in Ant 1.6 or later.	No	unlimited
parallel	Specifies the task should process multiple files using a single chmod command.	No	true
perm	Specifies the new permissions you want.	Yes	
type	Specifies the target type. Possible values: file, dir, or both.	No	file
verbose	Specifies whether the task should display what it's doing as it does it. Available in Ant 1.6 or later.	No	false

This task holds an implicit FileSet and supports all of FileSet's attributes and nested elements directly. Since Ant 1.6, you can specify nested fileset or dirset elements, and you can use nested filelists.

Scheduling Automatic Builds

It's time to add some automation to the build process. When you're working alone, you probably won't need to automate nightly builds, but as part of a team, it's a good idea. Larger projects typically have nightly builds posted to a web site, and using various automation tools and tasks like ftp, that's no problem. I'll take a look at various options here.

Unix

You can schedule recurring builds with Unix utilies like crontab, which you use to configure the cron daemon. For example, say you have a shell script that runs your nightly build, *dobuild.sh*, something like this:

```
export ANT_HOME=/usr/local/ant
export JAVA_HOME=/usr/local/jdk1.4
export PATH=${PATH}:${ANT_HOME}/bin
cd /home/work
ant -f nightlybuild.xml
```

You can schedule that build to happen at various times with crontab by starting its editing mode:

```
-bash-2.05b$ crontab -e
```

Edit the crontab file to include this line:

```
run at 00:01 every day 30 0 * * * $HOME/work/dobuild.sh
```

That makes your build run every night at 12:01 A.M. Easy enough.

Windows

The Windows at command schedules commands to run in Windows at specific times. For example, say you had a batch file, *dobuild.bat*, which runs your nightly build:

```
set ANT_HOME=C:\ant\apache-ant-1.6.1
set JAVA_HOME=C:\jdk1.4
set PATH=%PATH%;%ANT_HOME%\bin
cd C:\work
call %ANT_HOME%\bin\ant.bat -f nightlybuild.xml
```

You can schedule that build for every night with the Windows at command:

```
C:\ant>at 00:01 /every:M,T,W,Th,F "C:\work\dobuild.bat"
Added a new job with job ID = 1
```

To list scheduled at jobs, enter at:

```
C:\ant>at
Status ID   Day                     Time          Command Line
----------------------------------------------------------------------
         1  Each M T W Th F         12:01 AM      C:\work\dobuild.bat
```

 Want to get the results of your nightly build emailed to you? Use the Ant mail logger, covered earlier in this chapter.

The crontab and at commands are basic ways to get your builds to run automatically, but they're still basic. There are more advanced and powerful tools available.

Anthill

In my opinion, Anthill is the easist of the automatic build tools to use as well as the easiest to install. It's a software build management server that can handle most of your build needs, from individual up to the corporate. The web site is *http://www.urbancode.com/default.jsp*, and this is how Anthill describes itself:

> Anthill ensures a controlled build process and promotes the sharing of knowledge within an organization. Anthill performs a checkout from the source repository of the latest version of a project before every build and tags the repository with a unique build number after every build. It supports many repository adapters including: Concurrent Version System (CVS), Visual Source Safe, Perforce, Clearcase, PVCS, StarTeam, MKSIntegrity and FileSystem. Anthill automatically updates a project intranet site with artifacts from the latest build.

Anthill comes in two versions: Anthill Pro (fairly expensive) and Anthill OS (free). To install Anthill, download the binary distribution you want and expand it. Copy *anthill.war* from the expanded *dist* directory to a web server's application deployment directory, such as the *webapps* directory of a Tomcat server installation.

Anthill is designed to be used with a web server that can execute Java code, like Tomcat, and you can get Tomcat free from *http://jakarta.apache.org/tomcat/*. (Anthill was developed and has only been tested using the Tomcat server, though it's supposed to work with any servlet container.)

Anthill gives you a servlet-based console, hosted by Tomcat or similar server, that lets you configure your automatic build process. Anthill is designed to check source code out of a code repository automatically and build that code.

For example, you can test your Anthill installation by logging into the Anthill CVS server to retrieve the code for a project named anthill-test, using the password "anthill-example":

```
%cvs -d :pserver:anthill-example@cvs2.urbancode.com:/usr/local/anthill-test login
Logging in to :pserver:anthill-example@cvs2.urbancode.com:2401:/usr/local/anthill-test
CVS password: **************
```

In the same command-prompt session, start Tomcat and navigate to *http://localhost:8080/anthill* to open the Anthill console, as shown in Figure 4-1. This is the console that lets you schedule and configure your builds. Successfully built projects are marked with a green box in the right column of the console.

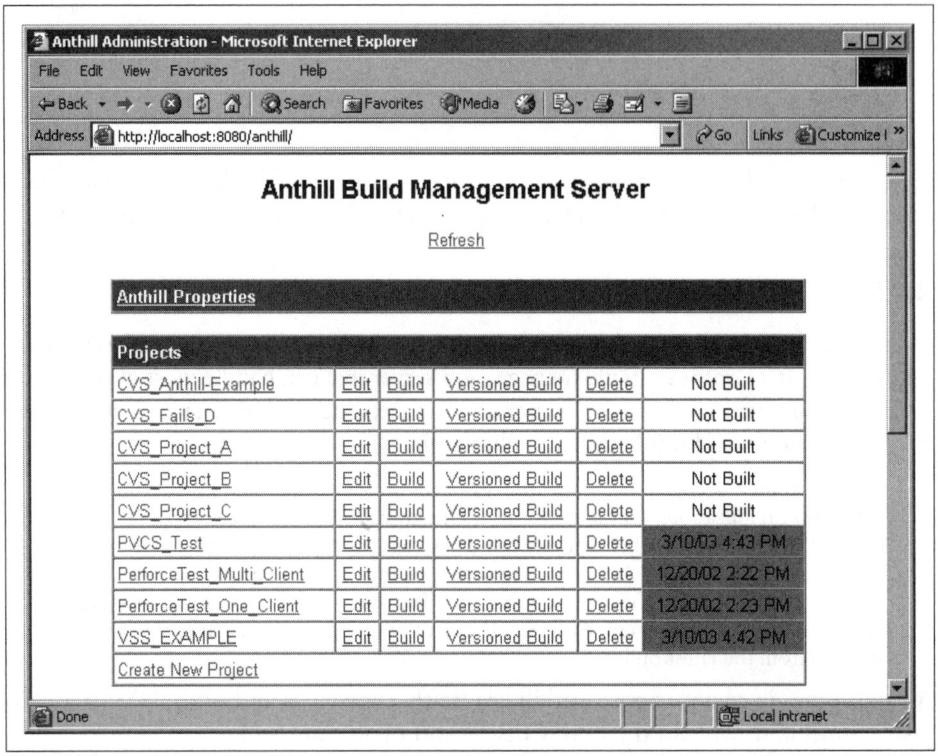

Figure 4-1. The Anthill build management server

Having logged into the Anthill CVS server, click the *Build* hyperlink in the top line of the table shown in Figure 4-1, which will build the CVS_Anthill example. This opens the Build Project page shown in Figure 4-2. Click the Force Build checkbox, enter a build version such as 1.1, and click the Build button.

Anthill will download the code for this project from the Anthill CVS server and build it. The Anthill console page will reappear; click Refresh to verify that the project has been built. A green box should appear at right in the CVS Anthill-Example line in the console table, as shown in Figure 4-3, if the build was successful.

If you click the *CVS_Anthill-Example* hyperlink in the console now, you'll get access to the results of the build, as shown in Figure 4-4.

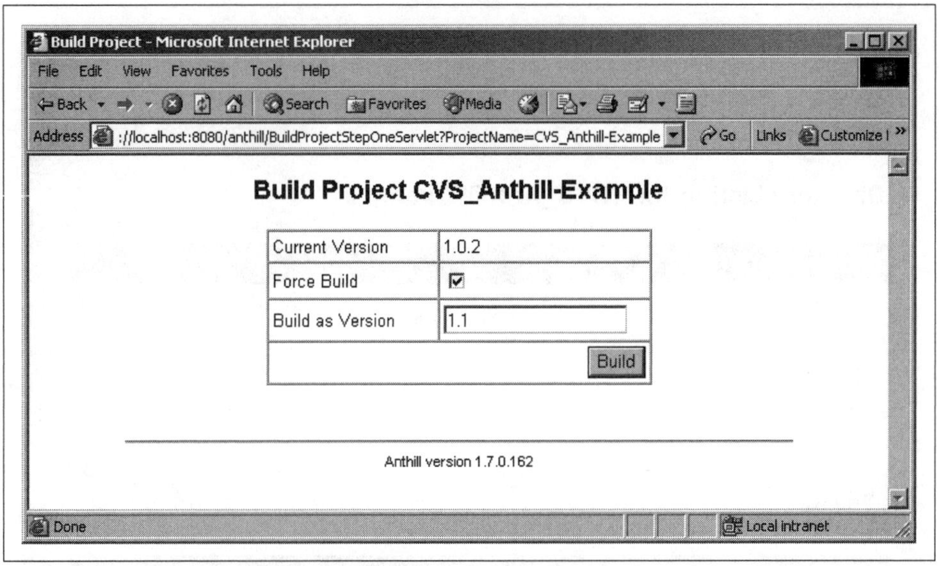

Figure 4-2. Forcing a build

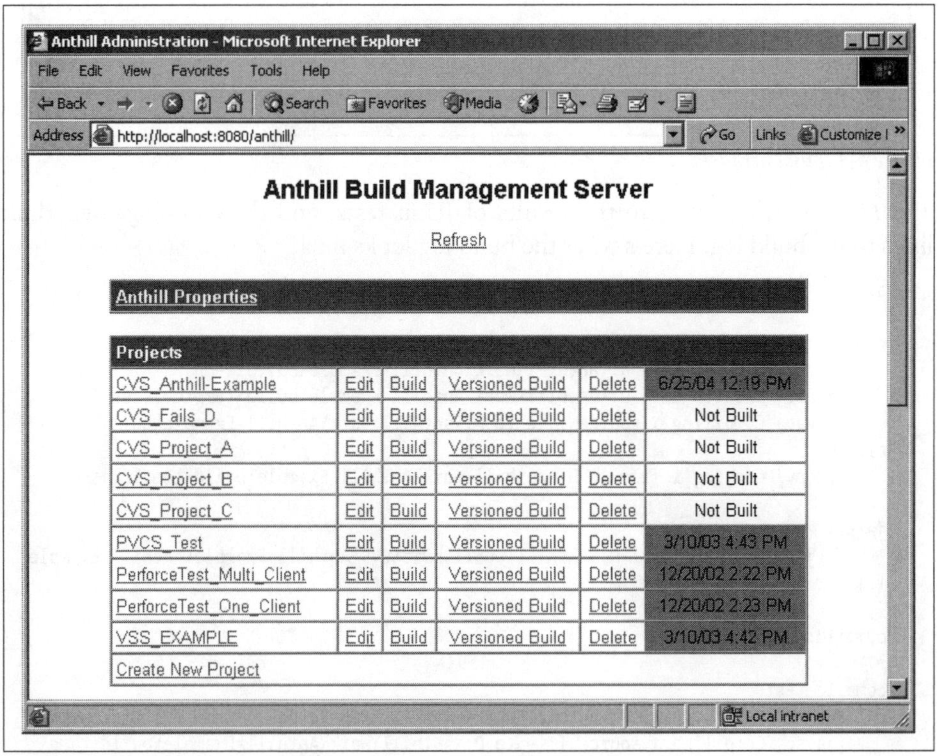

Figure 4-3. Running a new build

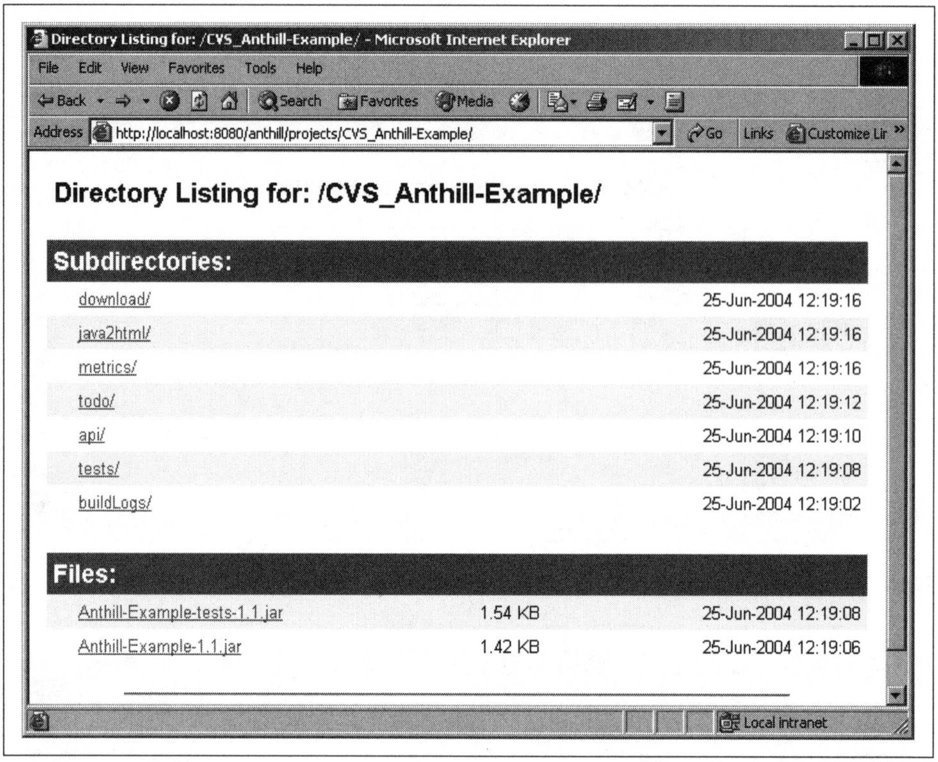

Figure 4-4. Build artifacts

The *tests* hyperlink links to the results of JUnit tests, and the *buildLogs* hyperlink links to the build log. Here's what the build log looks like:

```
all:

compile:
    [mkdir] Created dir: D:\anthill\work\Anthill-Example\build\temp
    [mkdir] Created dir: D:\anthill\work\Anthill-Example\build\temp\classes
    [javac] Compiling 1 source file to D:\anthill\work\Anthill-Example\build\temp\
classes
     [copy] Copying 1 file to D:\anthill\work\Anthill-Example\build\temp\classes

jars:
      [jar] Building jar: D:\anthill\publishDir\CVS_Anthill-Example\Anthill-Example-
1.1.jar

compile:

compile-tests:
    [mkdir] Created dir: D:\anthill\work\Anthill-Example\build\temp\tests\classes
    [javac] Compiling 1 source file to D:\anthill\work\Anthill-Example\build\temp\
tests\classes
```

```
    [jar] Building jar: D:\anthill\publishDir\CVS_Anthill-Example\Anthill-Example-
tests-1.1.jar

run-tests:
    [mkdir] Created dir: D:\anthill\work\Anthill-Example\build\temp\tests\data
    [mkdir] Created dir: D:\anthill\publishDir\CVS_Anthill-Example\tests
    [junit] Running example.WidgetTestCase
    [junit] Tests run: 2, Failures: 0, Errors: 0, Time elapsed: 0.651 sec
    [junit] Testsuite: example.WidgetTestCase
    [junit] Tests run: 2, Failures: 0, Errors: 0, Time elapsed: 0.651 sec

[junitreport] Using Xalan version: Xalan Java 2.2.D11
[junitreport] Transform time: 1051ms

doc:

javadoc:
    [mkdir] Created dir: D:\anthill\publishDir\CVS_Anthill-Example\api
  [javadoc] Generating Javadoc
  [javadoc] Javadoc execution
  [javadoc] Loading source files for package example...
  [javadoc] Constructing Javadoc information...
  [javadoc] Standard Doclet version 1.4.0

  [javadoc] Building tree for all the packages and classes...
  [javadoc] Building index for all the packages and classes...
  [javadoc] D:\anthill\work\Anthill-Example\source\java\example\Widget.java:12:
warning - @author tag has no arguments.
  [javadoc] Building index for all classes...
  [javadoc] Generating D:\anthill\publishDir\CVS_Anthill-Example\api\stylesheet.css..
  .
  [javadoc] 1 warning

        .
        .
        .

clean:
    [delete] Deleting directory D:\anthill\work\Anthill-Example\build\temp

BUILD SUCCESSFUL
Total time: 15 seconds
```

You schedule builds from the console page, *http://localhost:8080/anthill/*, if you're using Tomcat. Click Create New Schedule in the Schedule box, configure the new schedule as shown in Figure 4-5, and click Update to update the scheduler.

All in all, Anthill is a great automated build tool: easy to set up, easy to use.

Cruise Control and Gump

Cruise Control and Gump are two other Ant automated build tools for use with Ant. You can get Cruise Control at *http://cruisecontrol.sourceforge.net/*. It's an extensive build management tool, but it takes some effort to install. To configure a build, you

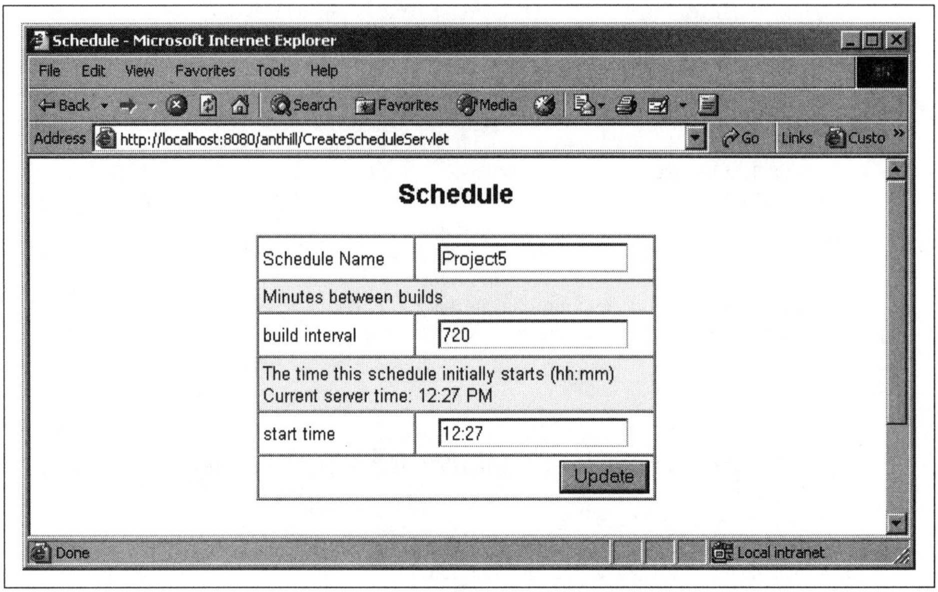

Figure 4-5. Setting up a schedule

work with a *modification set*. Cruise Control supports an Ant task named modificationset that contains nested tasks you can use to configure your build.

After setting up the build as you want it, you start the Cruise Control runner using *.sh* and *.bat* scripts, depending on your operating system, and Cruise Control takes it from there.

An alternative automated build tool is Gump. You can get Gump from the Jakarta CVS repository, using the password anoncvs:

```
%cvs -d :pserver:anoncvs@cvs.apache.org:home/cvspublic login
Logging in to pserver:anoncvs@cvs.apache.org:home/cvspublic
CVS password: *******

%cvs -d :pserver:anoncvs@cvs.apache.org:home/cvspublic checkuot jakarta-alexandria
```

You can read all about Gump and how it works at *http://gump.apache.org/*. Using Gump, project definitions are converted from XML to scripts native to the platform on which you are running. These scripts execute CVS or SVN update commands for every module which contains a project being built, and then builds each of those projects.

CHAPTER 5

Testing Builds with JUnit

This chapter is about a crucial aspect of the build process: testing build results before deploying them. It doesn't make sense to deploy a build that has been broken, and using the JUnit framework with Ant, you can run tests on your code and deploy a build only if it satisfies those tests. This is a great way to make sure changes to your code haven't broken anything.

To test the results of a build automatically, you'll need to use one of Ant's most powerful optional tasks: junit. This task is part of the repertoire of every serious Ant developer, especially those working in teams. If someone else on your project has broken your code, you should know about it before you deploy or upload to a shared code repository, and junit will let you know about these problems automatically.

To demonstrate how JUnit works with Ant in this chapter, we're going to use *Project.java*, shown in Example 5-1, as a guinea pig.

Example 5-1. A simple Project file

```
package org.antbook;

public class Project
{
    public Project (String name)
    {

    }

    public boolean returnTrue( )
    {
        return true;
    }

    public int return4( )
    {
        return 2 + 2;
    }
```

Example 5-1. A simple Project file (continued)

```
public Object returnObject( )
{
    return new Integer(1);
}

public static void main(String args[])
{
    Project project = new Project("project");
    System.out.println(project.returnTrue( ));
    System.out.println(project.return4( ));
    System.out.println(project.returnObject( ));
}
}
```

This application, *Project.java*, has three simple methods, each of which returns a value:

returnTrue( )
> Returns a boolean value of true

return4( )
> Returns an integer value of 4

returnObject( )
> Returns an Integer object containing a value of 1

When you compile *Project.java* and run it, each of these methods are executed. Now you can use the junit task to make sure that alterations to this application's code doesn't break the expected operation of these methods.

You can see the original build file that builds and deploys the *Project.java* application in Example 5-2. Note the section where the JUnit tests will be added. Break the build if those tests don't pass.

Example 5-2. Using Junit ch05/junit/build.xml

```xml
<?xml version="1.0" ?>
<project default="main">

    <property name="message" value="Building the project...." />
    <property name="testsOK" value="Tested OK...." />
    <property name="src" location="source" />
    <property name="output" location="." />
    <property name="results" location="results" />
    <property name="jars" location="jars" />
    <property name="dist" location="user" />
    <property name="junit.fork" value="true"/>

    <target name="main" depends="init, compile, test, compress, deploy">
        <echo>
        ${message}
```

Example 5-2. Using Junit ch05/junit/build.xml (continued)

```
            </echo>
    </target>

    <target name="init">
        <mkdir dir="${output}" />
        <mkdir dir="${results}" />
        <mkdir dir="${jars}" />
    </target>

    <target name="compile">
        <javac srcdir="${src}" destdir="${output}" />
    </target>

    <target name="test" depends="test1, test2, test3, test4, test5">
        <echo>
    ${testsOK}
        </echo>
    </target>
        .
        .
        .
    <!-- [TESTS GO HERE] -->
        .
        .
        .
    <target name="compress">
        <jar destfile="${jars}/Project.jar" basedir="${output}">
        <include name="**/*.class"/>
        </jar>
    </target>

    <target name="deploy">
        <delete dir="${dist}" />
        <mkdir dir="${dist}" />
        <copy todir="${dist}">
        <fileset dir="${jars}">
            <include name="*.jar"/>
        </fileset>
        </copy>
    </target>

</project>
```

Using JUnit

JUnit is an open source testing framework housed online at *http://www.junit.org/*, where you'll find downloads and documentation. Using JUnit, you can construct a set of standard tests for everyone working on an application, and if they change the application's code, all they'll need is to run the build file to verify that the application still passes the standard set of tests.

JUnit is primarily made up of a set of assertion methods that can test various conditions. Here they are:

assertEquals(a, b)

Tests if a is equal to b (a and b are primitive values or must have an equals method for comparison purposes)

assertFalse(a)

Tests if a is false, where a is a boolean value

assertNotNull(a)

Tests if a is not null, where a is an object or null

assertNotSame(a, b)

Tests if a and b do not refer to the identical object

assertNull(a)

Tests if a is null, where a is an object or null

assertSame(a, b)

Tests if a and b refer to the identical object

assertTrue(a)

Tests if a is frue, where a is a boolean value

To work with JUnit, you modify your code to extend the junit.framework.TestCase class, which in turn extends the junit.framework.Assert class. After subclassing the TestCase class, you can use the various assertXXX( ) methods to test the results from your newly compiled code. Each of these methods, along with their various versions, are listed in Table 5-1.

 Though your code extends the TestCase class, these methods are part of TestCase's base class, the Assert class.

Table 5-1. The junit.framework.Assert methods

Method	Does this
static void assertEquals(boolean expected, boolean actual)	Tests if two booleans are equal
static void assertEquals(byte expected, byte actual)	Tests if two bytes are equal
static void assertEquals(char expected, char actual)	Tests if two chars are equal
static void assertEquals(double expected, double actual, double delta)	Tests if two doubles are equal within a value named delta
static void assertEquals(float expected, float actual, float delta)	Tests if two floats are equal within a value named delta
static void assertEquals(int expected, int actual)	Tests if two ints are equal

Table 5-1. The junit.framework.Assert methods (continued)

Method	Does this
`static void assertEquals(long expected, long actual)`	Tests if two longs are equal
`static void assertEquals(java.lang.Object expected, java.lang.Object actual)`	Tests if two objects are equal
`static void assertEquals(short expected, short actual)`	Tests if two shorts are equal
`static void assertEquals(java.lang.String message, boolean expected, boolean actual)`	Tests if two booleans are equal
`static void assertEquals(java.lang.String message, byte expected, byte actual)`	Tests if two bytes are equal
`static void assertEquals(java.lang.String message, char expected, char actual)`	Tests if two chars are equal
`static void assertEquals(java.lang.String message, double expected, double actual, double delta)`	Tests if two doubles are equal within a value given by delta
`static void assertEquals(java.lang.String message, float expected, float actual, float delta)`	Tests if two floats are equal within a value given by delta
`static void assertEquals(java.lang.String message, int expected, int actual)`	Tests if two ints are equal
`static void assertEquals(java.lang.String message, long expected, long actual)`	Tests if two longs are equal
`static void assertEquals(java.lang.String message, java.lang.Object expected, java.lang.Object actual)`	Tests if two objects are equal
`static void assertEquals(java.lang.String message, short expected, short actual)`	Tests if two shorts are equal
`static void assertEquals(java.lang.String expected, java.lang.String actual)`	Tests if two Strings are equal
`static void assertEquals(java.lang.String message, java.lang.String expected, java.lang.String actual)`	Tests if two Strings are equal
`static void assertFalse(boolean condition)`	Tests if a condition is false
`static void assertFalse(java.lang.String message, boolean condition)`	Tests if a condition is false
`static void assertNotNull(java.lang.Object object)`	Tests if an object isn't null
`static void assertNotNull(java.lang.String message, java.lang.Object object)`	Tests if an object isn't null
`static void assertNotSame(java.lang.Object expected, java.lang.Object actual)`	Tests if two objects do not refer to the same object

Table 5-1. The junit.framework.Assert methods (continued)

Method	Does this
`static void assertNotSame(java.lang.String message, java.lang.Object expected, java.lang. Object actual)`	Tests if two objects do not refer to the same object
`static void assertNull(java.lang.Object object)`	Tests if an object is null
`static void assertNull(java.lang.String message, java.lang.Object object)`	Tests if an object is null
`static void assertSame(java.lang.Object expected, java.lang.Object actual)`	Tests if two objects refer to the same object
`static void assertSame(java.lang.String message, java.lang.Object expected, java.lang. Object actual)`	Tests if two objects refer to the same object
`static void assertTrue(boolean condition)`	Tests if a condition is true
`static void assertTrue(java.lang.String message, boolean condition)`	Tests if a condition is true
`static void fail()`	Makes a test fail
`static void fail(java.lang.String message)`	Makes a test fail with the specified message

Table 5-2 lists the methods specific to the JUnit TestCase method.

Table 5-2. The junit.framework.TestCase methods

Method	Does this
`int countTestCases()`	Counts how many test cases are executed
`protected TestResult createResult()`	Creates a default `TestResult` object
`java.lang.String getName()`	Gets the name of a `TestCase` and returns it
`TestResult run()`	Runs a test, storing results in a `TestResult` object
`void run(TestResult result)`	Runs a test case and stores the results in `TestResult`
`void runBare()`	Executes a bare test
`void setName(java.lang.String name)`	Specifies the name of a test case
`protected void setUp()`	Lets you perform initialization operations
`protected void tearDown()`	Lets you clean up after your tests, such as closing a network connection
`java.lang.String toString()`	Returns a string representation of a case

Writing the Tests

To add JUnit test cases to your code, you import `junit.framework.TestCase`, base your application's class on it, and write *test cases*. Test cases are methods whose name begins with "test," which means JUnit will call them automatically. In this example, there are three test cases: testTrue( ) to test the return value of the returnTrue( ) method, testEquals( ) to test the results of the return4( ) method, and testNotNull( ) to test the results of the returnObject( ) method. All three of these test cases will be called automatically by the JUnit framework. Inside test cases, you can use the JUnit methods like assertTrue( ), assertEquals( ), and so on, to make sure the build didn't break your application.

To make this work, import junit.framework.TestCase, extend that class, and add three test cases to test the three methods in your code. The JUnit framework will call all three test cases automatically because their names start with "test":

```
package org.antbook;

import junit.framework.TestCase;

public class Project extends TestCase
{
    public Project (String name)
    {

    }

    public void testTrue( )
    {
        .
        .
        .
    }

    public void testEquals( )
    {
        .
        .
        .
    }

    public void testNotNull( )
    {
        .
        .
        .
    }

    public boolean returnTrue( )
    {
        return true;
    }

    public int return4( )
    {
        return 2 + 2;
    }
```

```
public Object returnObject()
{
    return new Integer(1);
}

public static void main(String args[])
{
    Project project = new Project("project");
    System.out.println(project.returnTrue());
    System.out.println(project.return4());
    System.out.println(project.returnObject());
}
}
```

Use the JUnit methods assertTrue( ), assertEquals( ), and assertNotNull( ) to test the results from the three methods in *Project.java*—for example, testing if the return value of return4 really is 4, as it should be. If any of these assertions don't work, an exception is thrown, and that exception causes the build to fail:

```
package org.antbook;

import junit.framework.TestCase;

public class Project extends TestCase
{
    public Project (String name)
    {

    }

    public void testTrue()
    {
        assertTrue("assertTrue test", returnTrue());
    }

    public void testEquals()
    {
        assertEquals("assertEquals test", 4, return4());
    }

    public void testNotNull()
    {
        assertNotNull("assertNotNull test", returnObject());
    }

    public boolean returnTrue()
    {
        return true;
    }

    public int return4()
    {
        return 2 + 2;
    }
```

```
    public Object returnObject( )
    {
        return new Integer(1);
    }

    public static void main(String args[])
    {
        Project project = new Project("project");
        System.out.println(project.returnTrue( ));
        System.out.println(project.return4( ));
        System.out.println(project.returnObject( ));
    }
}
```

Besides writing test cases like these, you can add two additional methods, setUp( ) and tearDown( ), to your code. These methods act much like constructors and destructors for your tests:

protected void setUp( )

Lets you perform initialization, for example, opening a network connection

protected void tearDown( )

Lets you clean up after the tests are complete—for example, closing a network connection

 For further details on how JUnit works, see the JUnit site at *http:// www.junit.org/index.htm.*

Performing Tests with the junit Task

The Ant junit task lets you run JUnit tests from Ant. It's an optional task, so you'll need need to install *junit.jar*, which you get from *http://www.junit.org/œin* the Ant *lib* directory. Using junit, you can tell Ant which *.class* files you want tested, and JUnit will run the test cases in those files. The attributes of the junit task appear in Table 5-3.

Table 5-3. The junit attributes

Attribute	Description	Required	Default
dir	Specifies the directory where you want to run the JVM. Ignored if fork is disabled.	No	
errorproperty	Specifies the name of a property you want set in case there was an error.	No	
failureproperty	Specifies the name of a property in case the task failed.	No	
filtertrace	Removes Junit and Ant stack frames from error stack traces.	No	on
fork	Specifies that you want to run tests in a new JVM.	No	off

Table 5-3. The junit attributes (continued)

Attribute	Description	Required	Default
haltonerror	Specifies you want to stop the build if there are errors.	No	off
haltonfailure	Specifies you want to stop the build if the test fails.	No	off
includeantruntime	Specifies you want to add the Ant classes and JUnit to the classpath in a forked JVM.	No	true
jvm	Specifies the command used to start the Java Virtual Machine. Ignored if fork is disabled.	No	java
maxmemory	Specifies the maximum amount of memory to give to the forked JVM. Ignored if fork is disabled.	No	
newenvironment	Specifies you don't want to copy the old environment when new environment variables are specified. Ignored if fork is disabled.	No	false
printsummary	Specifies you want statistics for each test case. Possible values: on, off, and withOutAndErr (which is the same as on but also writes output of the test as written to System.out and System.err).	No	off
reloading	Specifies whether you want a new classloader to be started for each test case. Since Ant 1.6.	No	true
showoutput	Sends any output to Ant's logging system and to the formatters you specify.	No	Only the formatters receive the output.
tempdir	Specifies where you want this task to place temporary files. Since Ant 1.6.	No	The project's base directory.
timeout	Specifies you want to stop a test if it doesn't finish in time. Time is measured in milliseconds. Ignored if fork is disabled.	No	

The junit task supports a nested classpath element that represents a path-like structure, and which you can use to set the classpath used while the tests are running.

A number of other elements may be nested inside the junit element. If you're using fork, you can pass additional parameters to the new JVM with nested jvmarg elements:

```
<junit fork="yes">
    <jvmarg value="-Djava.compiler=NONE"/>
    .
    .
    .
</junit>
```

You can specify environment variables to pass to a forked JVM with nested env elements. I'll look at this element, including its attributes, in Chapter 7.

Nested sysproperty elements can specify system properties required by the class you're testing. These properties will be made available to the JVM during the execution of the test. You can use the same attributes as the env task here; for example, you can use the key and value attributes to specifies properties and property values, as in this example:

```
<junit>
    <sysproperty key="basedir" value="${basedir}"/>
        .
        .
        .
</junit>
```

Formatting test results

Test results can be printed in various formats, and you use the formatter nested element to specify which format to use (by default, the output of the tests will be sent to a file unless you set the usefile attribute to false). There are three predefined formatters:

- The XML formatter prints the test results in XML format.
- The plain formatter prints plain text.
- The brief formatter will give only brief details, only printing in-depth information for test cases that failed.

I'll look at formatting the results of JUnit tests using these formatters in this chapter. The attributes of the formatter element appear in Table 5-4.

Table 5-4. The formatter task's attributes

Attribute	Description	Required	Default
classname	Specifies the name of the custom formatter class you want to use.	Exactly one of type or classname	
extension	Specifies the extension for the output filename.	Yes, if classname has been used	
if	Specifies JUnit will only use this formatter if a specified property is set.	No	true
type	Specifies a predefined formatter you want to use. Possible values are xml, plain, or brief.	Exactly one of type or classname	
unless	Specifies JUnit should use the formatter if a specified property is not set.	No	true
usefile	Specifies if you want to send output to a file.	No	true

Specifying the test class

You use the test nested element to specify a class to test. The attributes of this element appear in Table 5-5.

Table 5-5. The test task's attributes

Attribute	Description	Required	Default
errorproperty	Specifies the the name of a property you want to have set if there is an error	No	
failureproperty	Specifies the name of a property in case the task fails	No	
filtertrace	Removes Junit and Ant stack frames from error stack traces	No	on
fork	Specifies you want to run tests in a new JVM	No	
haltonerror	Specifies you want to stop the build if there are errors	No	
haltonfailure	Specifies you want to stop the build if the test fails	No	
If	Specifies this test should run only if a specified property is set	No	
name	Specifies the name of the test class you want to use	Yes	
outfile	Sets the filename where the test results should go	No	TEST-*name*, where *name* is the name of the test specified in the name attribute
todir	Specifies the directory you want the reports written to	No	The current directory
unless	Specifies this test should run only if a specified property is not set	No	

Running tests in batches

Another nested element, batchtest, lets you set up a number of tests at once. The batchtest element collects the included files from any number of nested filesets, and generates a test class name for each file that ends in *.java* or *.class*. You'll use this element later in this chapter. The attributes for batchtest appear in Table 5-6.

Table 5-6. The batchtest element's attributes

Attribute	Description	Required	Default
errorproperty	Specifies the name of a property you want set in case there is an error	No	
failureproperty	Specifies the name of a property in case the task fails	No	
filtertrace	Removes Junit and Ant stack frames from error stack traces	No	on
fork	Specifies you want to run tests in a new JVM	No	
haltonerror	Specifies you want to stop the build if there are errors	No	
haltonfailure	Specifies you want to stop the build if the test fails	No	
if	Specifies this test should run only if a specified property is set	No	
todir	Specifies the directory where you want reports written to	No	The current directory
unless	Specifies this test should run only if a specified property is not set	No	

Other nested elements are available since Ant 1.6. You can specify a set of properties to be used as system properties with syspropertysets. If you're forking a new JVM, you can specify the location of bootstrap class files using the bootclasspath path-like structure inside the junit task. You can revoke or grant security permissions during the execution of a class with a nested permissions element. And you can even control Java 1.4 assertions with an assertions subelement.

Running Test Cases

To run the JUnit test cases, add a test target to the build file introduced at the beginning of the chapter, and make the main target depend on the test target as part of the build process:

```
<target name="main" depends="init, compile, test, compress, deploy">
    <echo>
        ${message}
    </echo>
</target>
```

The test target will run the six targets you're going to create in this chapter:

```
<property name="testsOK" value="Tested OK...." />
    .
    .
    .
<target name="test" depends="test1, test2, test3, test4, test5, test6">
    <echo>
        ${testsOK}
    </echo>
</target>
```

If you're not using Ant or a Java IDE, you usually run JUnit tests from the command line and use the junit.textui.TestRunner class like this, testing the example class created earlier in the chapter, org.antbook.Project:

```
%java junit.textui.TestRunner org.antbook.Project
```

You can do essentially the same thing in Ant using the java task, and that looks like this in the build file for the first test task, test1. Note that I'm adding *junit.jar* to the classpath:

```
<target name="test1" depends="compile">
    <java fork="true"
        classname="junit.textui.TestRunner"
        classpath="${ant.home}/lib/junit.jar;.">
        <arg value="org.antbook.Project"/>
    </java>
</target>
```

Here's what this task looks like when it's running:

```
test1:
    [java] ...
    [java] Time: 0.01

    [java] OK (3 tests)
```

Each dot (.) indicates a test case that's running, and three test cases are in the example. As you can see from the last line, the tests all passed OK, but this isn't exciting and it doesn't stop a build if there's a problem.

Using the Plain Formatter for Reports

The second test, test2, will use junit to run the test. No results are printed out by successful JUnit tests unless you use a formatter, so the plain formatter is used here, set by a formatter element. classpath is used to specify where junit should search for the class to test, and the test nested element sets up the test, giving the name of the class to test and the directory in which to store the formatted results of the test:

```
<target name="test2" depends="compile">
    <junit
        printsummary="yes"
        errorProperty="test.failed"
        failureProperty="test.failed"
        haltonfailure="yes">
        <formatter type="plain"/>
        <classpath path="."/>
        <test todir="${results}" name="org.antbook.Project"/>
    </junit>
    <fail message="Tests failed!" if="test.failed"/>
</target>
```

Note that if you set haltonfailure to true, the build will halt if the test fails—what to do if you want to avoid deploying a defective build.

 You can use attributes like errorProperty instead of haltonfailure to set properties indicating the build had problems. That's useful if you want to clean up after the partial build with other tasks instead of failing immediately in the junit task.

Here's the output you see when this task runs:

```
test2:
    [junit] Running org.antbook.Project
    [junit] Tests run: 3, Failures: 0, Errors: 0, Time elapsed: 0.011 sec
```

The plain formatter creates the output file *TEST-org.antbook.Project.txt*, which holds these contents:

```
Testsuite: org.antbook.Project
Tests run: 3, Failures: 0, Errors: 0, Time elapsed: 0.01 sec
```

```
Testcase: testTrue took 0 sec
Testcase: testEquals took 0 sec
Testcase: testNotNull took 0 sec
```

All the tests succeeded, and the results look good. But what if you changed a test so the return4 method is supposed to return 5 rather than 4:

```
public void testEquals()
{
    assertEquals("assertEquals test", 5, return4());
}
```

In that case, you'd see this in the build:

```
test2:
    [junit] Running org.antbook.Project
    [junit] Tests run: 2, Failures: 1, Errors: 0, Time elapsed: 0.02 sec
```

You could read all about the problems in the output file *TEST-org.antbook.Project.txt*, which indicates the problem:

```
Testsuite: org.antbook.Project
Tests run: 2, Failures: 1, Errors: 0, Time elapsed: 0.02 sec


Testcase: testTrue took 0.01 sec
Testcase: testEquals took 0 sec
    FAILED
assertEquals test expected:<5> but was:<4>
junit.framework.AssertionFailedError: assertEquals test expected:<5> but was:<4>
    at org.antbook.Project.testEquals(Unknown Source)
    at sun.reflect.NativeMethodAccessorImpl.invoke0(Native Method)
    at sun.reflect.NativeMethodAccessorImpl.invoke(Unknown Source)
    at sun.reflect.DelegatingMethodAccessorImpl.invoke(Unknown Source)
```

If there's a problem, you can use the formatter's output to track it down.

Using the Brief Formatter for Reports

The brief formatter prints little unless there's been an error. Here's how to use it in a new test, test3:

```
<target name="test3" depends="compile">
    <junit printsummary="yes" fork="yes" haltonfailure="yes">
        <formatter type="brief" usefile="true"/>
        <classpath path="."/>
        <test todir="${results}" name="org.antbook.Project"/>
    </junit>
</target>
```

If everything goes well, this formatter displays a brief message during the build:

```
test3:
    [junit] Running org.antbook.Project
    [junit] Tests run: 2, Failures: 1, Errors: 0, Time elapsed: 0.01 sec
```

And it puts a brief message in *TEST-org.antbook.Project.txt*:

```
Testsuite: org.antbook.Project
Tests run: 3, Failures: 0, Errors: 0, Time elapsed: 0.01 sec
TEST-org.antbook.Project.txt:
```

On the other hand, if you reproduce an error as in test2 (changing the expected value from 4 to 5), you'll see more information in *TEST-org.antbook.Project.txt*:

```
Testsuite: org.antbook.Project
Tests run: 2, Failures: 1, Errors: 0, Time elapsed: 0.01 sec

Testcase: testEquals(org.antbook.Project):FAILED
assertEquals test expected:<5> but was:<4>
junit.framework.AssertionFailedError: assertEquals test expected:<5> but was:<4>
    at org.antbook.Project.testEquals(Unknown Source)
    at sun.reflect.NativeMethodAccessorImpl.invoke0(Native Method)
    at sun.reflect.NativeMethodAccessorImpl.invoke(Unknown Source)
    at sun.reflect.DelegatingMethodAccessorImpl.invoke(Unknown Source)
```

Using the XML Formatter for Reports

The XML formatter gives you the most information of all formatters. Here's how you use it in a new task, test4:

```
<target name="test4" depends="compile">
    <junit printsummary="yes" fork="yes" haltonfailure="yes">
        <formatter type="xml"/>
        <classpath path="."/>
        <test todir="${results}" name="org.antbook.Project"/>
    </junit>
</target>
```

This task creates a new file, *TEST-org.antbook.Project.xml*, which contains a tremendous amount of information, including the names and values of all properties, as well as the results of the tests:

```
<?xml version="1.0" encoding="UTF-8" ?>
<testsuite name="org.antbook.Project" tests="3" failures="0" errors="0" time="0.04">
  <properties>
    <property name="java.runtime.name" value="Java(TM) 2 Runtime Environment,
        Standard Edition"></property>
    <property name="ant.java.version" value="1.4"></property>
    <property name="java.vm.vendor" value="Sun Microsystems Inc."></property>
    <property name="java.vendor.url" value="http://java.sun.com/"></property>
    <property name="path.separator" value=";"></property>
    <property name="java.vm.name" value="Java HotSpot(TM) Client VM"></property>
    <property name="file.encoding.pkg" value="sun.io"></property>
    <property name="user.country" value="US"></property>
    <property name="sun.os.patch.level" value="Service Pack 3"></property>
        .
        .
        .
  </properties>
```

```
<testcase name="testTrue" classname="org.antbook.Project" time="0.0"></testcase>
<testcase name="testEquals" classname="org.antbook.Project"
    time="0.0"></testcase>
<testcase name="testNotNull" classname="org.antbook.Project"
    time="0.0"></testcase>
<system-out><![CDATA[]]></system-out>
<system-err><![CDATA[]]></system-err>
</testsuite>
```

This kind of output is primarily designed to be used with the junitreport task.

Creating Reports with the junitreport Task

You can use the junitreport task to merge XML files generated by the JUnit task's XML formatter and apply a stylesheet on the resulting merged document to create a browseable report of results. This is an optional Ant task, and you need *xalan.jar*, version 2+, in the Ant *lib* directory to run it. You can get *xalan.jar* from *http://xml.apache.org/xalan-j/*.

The attributes for this task appear in Table 5-7.

Table 5-7. The junitreport task's attributes

Attribute	Description	Required	Default
todir	Specifies the directory where you want XML-formatted reports to be written	No	The current directory
tofile	Specifies the name of the report file	No	TESTS-TestSuites.xml

The junitreport task can contain nested fileset elements. junitreport collects XML files generated by the JUnit task as specified in the nested fileset elements.

The junitreport task can contain nested report elements. These elements are the ones that generate the browseable report based on the merged XML documents. The attributes of the report element appear in Table 5-8.

Table 5-8. The report task's attributes

Attribute	Description	Required	Default
format	Specifies the format you want to use in the report. Must be noframes or frames.	No	frames
styledir	Specifies the directory where the task should look for stylesheets. If you're using frames format, the stylesheet must be named *junit-frames.xsl*. If you're using noframes format, the stylesheet must be named *junit-noframes.xsl*.	No	Embedded stylesheets
todir	Specifies the directory where output should be written.	No	The current directory

In the build file's test5 target, create an XML-formatted report for the JUnit tests:

```
<target name="test5" depends="compile">
    <junit printsummary="yes" fork="yes" haltonfailure="yes">
        <formatter type="xml"/>
        <classpath path="."/>
        <test todir="${results}" name="org.antbook.Project"/>
    </junit>
    .
    .
    .
```

Then use junitreport to merge and translate any XML reports into something you can look at in a browser. Here's what it looks like in the build file:

```
<target name="test5" depends="compile">
    <junit printsummary="yes" fork="yes" haltonfailure="yes">
        <formatter type="xml"/>
        <classpath path="."/>
        <test todir="${results}" name="org.antbook.Project"/>
    </junit>

    <junitreport todir="${results}">
        <fileset dir="${results}">
            <include name="TEST-*.xml"/>
        </fileset>
        <report format="frames" todir="${results}"/>
    </junitreport>
</target>
```

The junit task creates *TEST-org.antbook.Project.xml*, and the junitreport task creates *TESTS-TestSuites.xml* and the browseable report. To see the report, open the created *index.html*, shown in Figure 5-1.

You can browse through the results of your tests by clicking the Project link in the frame labeled Classes, opening the page you see in Figure 5-2, which reports on each test case.

Clicking the Properties link displays a page showing all property names and values.

Testing in Batches

When you're working with JUnit, you can set up *test suites*, which run multiple tests, by extending the TestSuite class:

```
import junit.framework.TestCase;
import junit.framework.TestSuite;
    .
    .
    .
public class NewSuite extends TestSuite
{
```

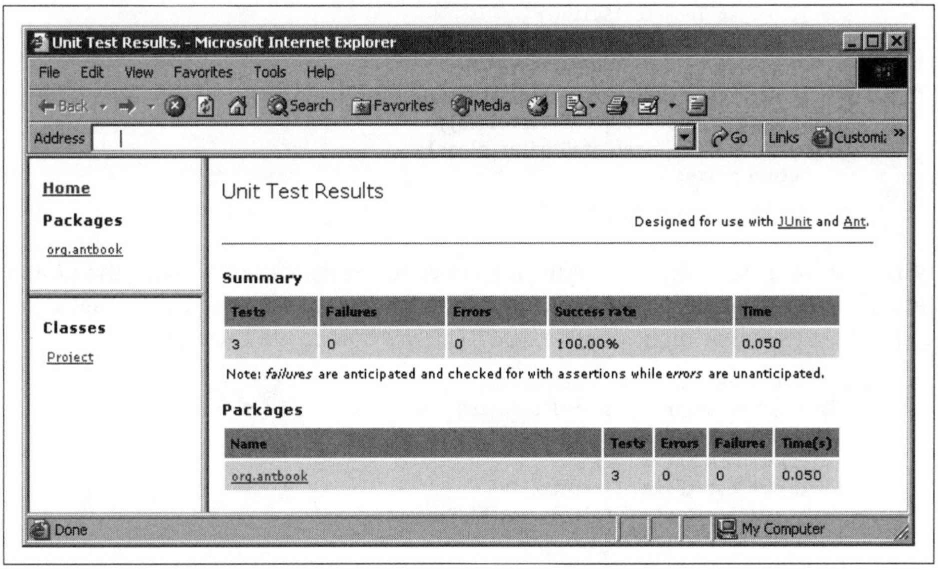

Figure 5-1. A JUnit report

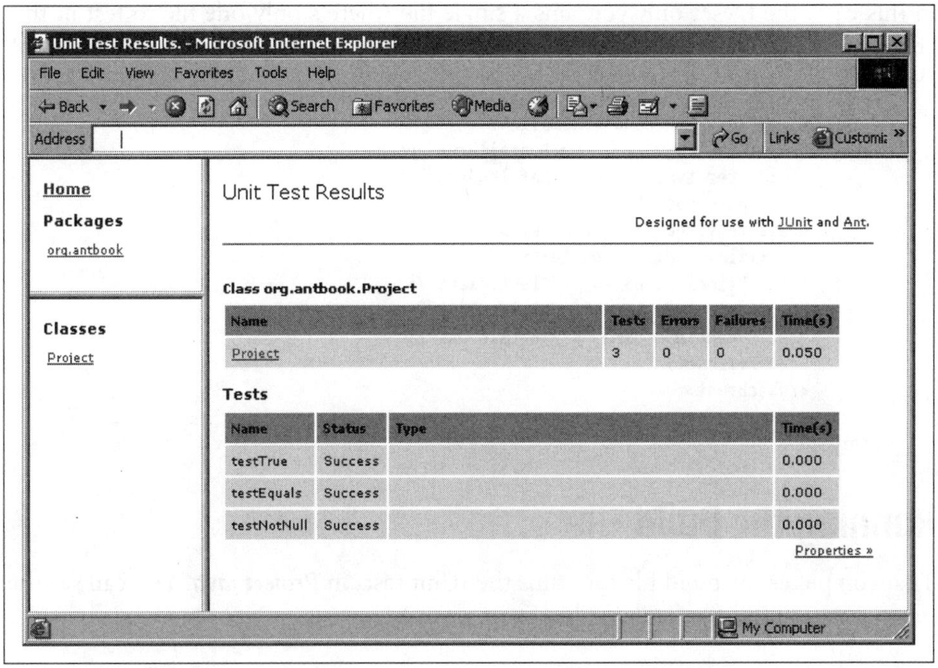

Figure 5-2. Browsing test case results

```
    static public Test testSuite()
    {
        TestSuite suite = new TestSuite();
        suite.addTestSuite(Project.class);
        suite.addTestSuite(Connector.class);
        suite.addTestSuite(DataHandler.class);
        return suite;
    }
}
```

When you're using JUnit from Ant, it's easier to use *batch testing* with the nested
batchtest task. This task lets you specify whole filesets to test using the fileset type,
and the results will be merged into a report. Here's how to use batchtest:

```
<target name="test6" depends="compile">
    <junit printsummary="yes" haltonfailure="yes">
        <formatter type="brief" usefile="true"/>
        <classpath path="."/>
        <batchtest todir="${results}">
            <fileset dir="." includes="**/Project.class"/>
        </batchtest>
    </junit>
</target>
```

In this case, the fileset only contains a single file (there's only one file to test in this
chapter's example), but you can include as multiple files in your nested fileset
element:

```
<target name="test6" depends="compile">
    <junit printsummary="yes" haltonfailure="yes">
        <formatter type="brief" usefile="true"/>
        <classpath path="."/>
        <batchtest todir="${results}">
            <fileset dir="${build}">
                <include name="**/*Test.class"/>
                <include name="**/*Gold.class"/>
                <exclude name="**/*Beta.class"/>
            </fileset>
        </batchtest>
    </junit>
</target>
```

Running the Build File

That completes the build file that runs the JUnit tests in *Project.java*. You can see the
final version of this file, *build.xml* in Example 5-3.

Example 5-3. Using Junit ch05/junit/build.xml

```
<?xml version="1.0" ?>
<project default="main">
```

Example 5-3. Using Junit ch05/junit/build.xml (continued)

```xml
<property name="message" value="Building the project...." />
<property name="testsOK" value="Tested OK...." />
<property name="src" location="source" />
<property name="output" location="." />
<property name="results" location="results" />
<property name="jars" location="jars" />
<property name="dist" location="user" />
<property name="junit.fork" value="true"/>

<target name="main" depends="init, compile, test, compress, deploy">
    <echo>
        ${message}
    </echo>
</target>

<target name="init">
    <mkdir dir="${output}" />
    <mkdir dir="${results}" />
    <mkdir dir="${jars}" />
</target>

<target name="compile">
    <javac srcdir="${src}" destdir="${output}" />
</target>

<target name="test" depends="test1, test2, test3, test4, test5, test6">
    <echo>
        ${testsOK}
    </echo>
</target>

<target name="test1" depends="compile">
    <java fork="true"
        classname="junit.textui.TestRunner"
        classpath="${ant.home}/lib/junit.jar;.">
        <arg value="org.antbook.Project"/>
    </java>
</target>

<target name="test2" depends="compile">
    <junit
        printsummary="yes"
        errorProperty="test.failed"
        failureProperty="test.failed"
        fork="${junit.fork}"
        haltonfailure="yes">
        <formatter type="plain"/>
        <classpath path="."/>
        <test todir="${results}" name="org.antbook.Project"/>
    </junit>
    <fail message="Tests failed!" if="test.failed"/>
</target>
```

Example 5-3. Using Junit ch05/junit/build.xml (continued)

```xml
<target name="test3" depends="compile">
    <junit printsummary="yes" fork="yes" haltonfailure="yes">
        <formatter type="brief" usefile="true"/>
        <classpath path="."/>
        <test todir="${results}" name="org.antbook.Project"/>
    </junit>
</target>

<target name="test4" depends="compile">
    <junit printsummary="yes" fork="yes" haltonfailure="yes">
        <formatter type="xml"/>
        <classpath path="."/>
        <test todir="${results}" name="org.antbook.Project"/>
    </junit>
</target>

<target name="test5" depends="compile">
    <junit printsummary="yes" fork="yes" haltonfailure="yes">
        <formatter type="xml"/>
        <classpath path="."/>
        <test todir="${results}" name="org.antbook.Project"/>
    </junit>

    <junitreport todir="${results}">
        <fileset dir="${results}">
            <include name="TEST-*.xml"/>
        </fileset>
        <report format="frames" todir="${results}"/>
    </junitreport>
</target>

<target name="test6" depends="compile">
    <junit printsummary="yes" haltonfailure="yes">
        <formatter type="brief" usefile="true"/>
        <classpath path="."/>
        <batchtest todir="${results}">
            <fileset dir="." includes="**/Project.class"/>
        </batchtest>
    </junit>
</target>

<target name="compress">
    <jar destfile="${jars}/Project.jar" basedir="${output}">
        <include name="**/*.class"/>
    </jar>
</target>

<target name="deploy">
    <delete dir="${dist}" />
    <mkdir dir="${dist}" />
    <copy todir="${dist}">
        <fileset dir="${jars}">
```

Example 5-3. Using Junit ch05/junit/build.xml (continued)

```
            <include name="*.jar"/>
        </fileset>
    </copy>
</target>
```

```
</project>
```

Here's what you see when you run the build file:

```
%ant
Buildfile: build.xml

init:
    [mkdir] Created dir: /home/ant/ch05/junit/results
    [mkdir] Created dir: /home/ant/ch05/junit/jars

compile:
    [javac] Compiling 1 source file to /home/ant/ch05/junit

test1:
     [java] ...
     [java] Time: 0

     [java] OK (3 tests)



test2:
    [junit] Running org.antbook.Project
    [junit] Tests run: 3, Failures: 0, Errors: 0, Time elapsed: 0.01 sec


test3:
    [junit] Running org.antbook.Project
    [junit] Tests run: 3, Failures: 0, Errors: 0, Time elapsed: 0.01 sec



test4:
    [junit] Running org.antbook.Project
    [junit] Tests run: 3, Failures: 0, Errors: 0, Time elapsed: 0.04 sec



test5:
    [junit] Running org.antbook.Project
    [junit] Tests run: 3, Failures: 0, Errors: 0, Time elapsed: 0.04 sec
```

```
test6:
    [junit] Running org.antbook.Project
    [junit] Tests run: 3, Failures: 0, Errors: 0, Time elapsed: 0.01 sec


[junitreport] Using Xalan version: Xalan Java 2.4.1
[junitreport] Transform time: 1191ms

test:
    [echo]
    [echo]    Tested OK....
    [echo]

compress:
    [jar] Building jar: /home/ant/ch05/junit/jars\Project.jar

deploy:
    [mkdir] Created dir: /home/ant/ch05/junit/user
    [copy] Copying 1 file to /home/ant/ch05/junit/user

main:
    [echo]
    [echo]    Building the project....
    [echo]

BUILD SUCCESSFUL
Total time: 7 seconds
```

Because all tests ran successfully, the build was allowed to continue on to deployment.

Extending JUnit

There are many extensions for JUnit designed to help test specific types of builds, such as web applications. You can find many extensions on the JUnit site, at *http://www.junit.org/news/extension/index.htm*. Here's a starter list of JUnit extensions:

- Abbot is a scripted Java GUI testing framework.
- dbUnit is a database testing framework, which sets up your database before executing your tests.
- HtmlUnit is a Java unit testing framework for testing web-based applications.
- HttpUnit is a framework for accessing websites from a Java program, with support for following links, submitting forms, handling cookies, and so on.
- JavaBean Tester is a tool to automate the testing of JavaBeans.
- Jemmy is a Java library that is used to create automated tests for Java GUI applications.
- Jenerator generates Unit Tests for all types of EJB for JUnit and Cactus.
- JFCUnit enables you to execute unit tests against Swing-based code.

- JUnit JNDI DataSource helper package can simulate JNDI lookups for database connections.
- JUnitDoclet generates TestSuites, TestCase skeletons, and default tests from Java sources.
- JUnitPerf is a collection of JUnit test decorators to test scalability.
- JUnitX provides access to private and protected classes, methods, and variables between different packages for testing purposes.
- jWebUnit provides a high-level API for navigating a web application combined with a set of assertions to verify the application's correctness.
- Log4Unit is a JUnit extension combining JUnit with Log4J.
- Schema Unit Test (SUT) is a framework for testing XML Schema.
- SQLUnit is a regression and unit testing harness for testing procedures stored in a database.

CHAPTER 6

Getting Source Code from CVS Repositories

Up to this point, you've been working solo with Ant, but—as with any major build tool—Ant can be used in team environments. There's a lot of support built in for the Concurrent Version System (CVS) in Ant, and this chapter is all about making code sharing in teams with CVS happen.

Source Control and Ant

When you work in teams, you have to coordinate your efforts. That means discussing and planning, but even with the best of intentions, you can still end up with unintentional conflicts. You may have made some brilliant changes to the code, only to find them wiped out by mistake when another programmer uploads his own version of the same file.

Source control helps prevent these problems by controlling access to code and by maintaining a history of the changes made so things aren't destroyed unintentionally. Storing a history of your code is powerful; you can compare a new (buggy) file against an older one, and you can revert to a previous version in case things have gone bad.

Ant has several source control tasks, shown in Table 6-1.

Table 6-1. Source control tasks

Task name	Description
clearcase	Tasks for ClearCase cleartool checkin, checkout, uncheckout, update, lock, unlock, mklbtype, rmtype, mklabel, mkattr, mkdir, mkelem, and mkbl commands
Continuus/Synergy tasks	Tasks for Continuus ccmcheckin, ccmcheckout, ccmcheckintask, ccmreconfigure, and ccmcreateTask commands
cvs	Specifies how to work with packages and modules retrieved from a CVS repository

Table 6-1. Source control tasks (continued)

Task name	Description
cvschangelog	Creates change reports from a CVS repository
cvspass	Adds entries to a *.cvspass* file
cvstagdiff	Creates an XML-formatted report of the changes between two tags or dates recorded in a CVS repository
Microsoft Visual Sourcesafe tasks	Tasks for Visual SourceSafe vssget, vsslabel, vsshistory, vsscheckin, vsscheckout, vssadd, vsscp, and vsscreate commands
perforce	Tasks for Perforce p4sync, p4change, p4edit, p4submit, p4have, p4label, p4counter, p4reopen, p4revert, and p4add commands
pvcs	Retrieves and handles source code from a PVCS repository
sourceoffsite	Tasks for SourceOffSite sosget, soslabel, soscheckin, and soscheckout commands
starteam	Tasks for StarTeam stcheckout, stcheckin, stlabel, and stlist commands

Though Ant lets you work with various source control systems, most of its support revolves around CVS, which is used throughout this chapter. CVS is an open source project that started as a set of Unix shell scripts in 1986 and came into its own with dedicated software in 1989. Support for CVS is available on many operating systems: Unix, Linux, Windows, Mac, and others. For the full CVS story, look at *http://www.cvshome.org*.

> To work with CVS using Ant, you need access to a CVS server. Most Linux and Unix installations come with a built-in CVS server. To test if you have a working CVS installation, type **cvs --help** at the prompt; you should see a list of help items. If you can't find a CVS server, you can download what you need from *http://www.cvshome.org*. Many CVS servers are available for Windows, such as CVSNT, available for free from *http://www.cvsnt.org*. To install CVSNT, download the executable file and run it.

The idea behind CVS, as with any repository software, is to manage and record changes to source code. What corresponds to a project for Ant is a *module* in CVS. Modules are represented by directories in CVS; the files you share are stored in the CVS *repository*. When you retrieve a file from the repository, you *check the file out*. After you've modified the file, you *commit* the file, checking it back in and sending those changes to the repository. If you want to refresh your own copy of a file, you *update* it from the repository.

Because each file must be independently tracked, CVS gives the individual files a version number automatically. Each time a file is committed, its version number is incremented. When you commit files to the repository, they'll get a new version number as well.

Using the cvs task, you communicate with the CVS server using CVS commands, which appear in Table 6-2.

 Read more about these commands in the CVS guide at *https://www. cvshome.org/docs/manual/cvs-1.11.7/cvs_16.html.*

Table 6-2. CVS commands

CVS command	Does this
add	Specifies you want to add a new file or directory to the CVS repository
admin	Lets you work with administrative commands
annotate	Specifies the revision where each line was modified
authserver	Specifies authentication mode for the server
chacl	Specifies the access list for a directory
checkout	Checks out source code from the repository
chown	Changes the owner of a directory in the repository
commit	Checks source code files into the repository
diff	Displays the differences between source code revisions
edit	Specifies you want to edit a file
editors	Specifies you want to watch who has been editing a particular file
export	Exports source code from a CVS repository (similar to checkout)
history	Displays the CVS repository access history
import	Imports source code into a CVS repository
info	Displays information about the CVS repository and its supported protocols
init	Creates a CVS repository and initializes it
log	Displays information on file history
login	Asks for a password, if needed
logout	Logs out of a server
ls	Lists the files in the CVS repository
lsacl	Lists the CVS directories access control list
passwd	Sets a user's CVS password
rannotate	Displays the revision in which source lines were modified
rdiff	Creates patch files by comparing two files and outputting a file that be used to update one into the other
release	Specifies that a module will not be used anymore
remove	Removes an item from a CVS repository
rlog	Displays CVS history information for a module

Table 6-2. *CVS commands (continued)*

CVS command	Does this
rtag	Adds a tag to a CVS module
server	Lets you set server modes for access
status	Displays checked-out file information
tag	Adds a tag to checked-out files
unedit	Undoes an edit command that's been executed
update	Updates local copies of a file with those in the CVS repository
version	Shows the CVS version
watch	Watches a file or files
watchers	Displays which users are watching a file or files

The first step in working with CVS is to log into the CVS server, typically done with the cvspass task.

Logging In

You use the cvspass task to log into a CVS server to get access to the code stored in the CVS repository. This task adds entries to a *.cvspass* file, which has the same affect as a CVS login command. When a *.cvspass* file has been created, subsequent logins will get the needed data from this file, and you won't have to supply a password again.

The values you assign to the attribute named cvsroot use the same format of strings that appear in a CVS *.cvspass* file, which specifies the protocol type, username, server, and repository location. For example, using the pserver protocol with a user named Steven, a server named STEVE, and a repository location of */home/steven/ repository*, cvspass would look like:

```
<?xml version="1.0"?>

<project default="main" basedir=".">

    <property name="cvs.dir" value="project" />

    <target name="main" >
        <cvspass cvsroot=":pserver:steven@STEVE:/home/steven/repository"
            password="opensesame" />
        .
        .
        .
    </target>

</project>
```

The CVS-related tasks can read the CVS root value from the cvsroot attribute, if they support that attribute, or from the CVSROOT environment variable.

In Windows, when your username includes a space or spaces, you might run into problems with the cvsroot attribute. In that case, assign a value to the CVSROOT environment variable instead (e.g., C:\ant\ch06>set CVSROOT=:pserver:Steven Holzner@STEVE:/home/steven/repository) and then use cvspass or other CVS-related tasks in your build file normally.

The attributes of the cvspass task appear in Table 6-3.

Table 6-3. Attributes for the cvspass task

Attribute	Description	Required	Default
cvsroot	Specifies the CVS repository you want to add an entry for	Yes	
passfile	Specifies the password file you want to add the entry to	No	~/.cvspass
password	Specifies the password you want to be added to the password file	Yes	

Working with the Server

The cvs task lets you interact with the CVS server after you've logged in. The attributes of this task appear in Table 6-4; to use this task, the cvs command must work on the command line (i.e., the cvs binary must be in your path).

Table 6-4. The cvs attributes

Attribute	Description	Required	Default
append	Specifies whether you want to append output when redirecting text to a file.	No	false
command	Specifies the CVS command you want to execute.	No	checkout
compression	The same as compressionlevel="3".	No	false
compressionlevel	Specifies the compression level you want to use, via a number between 1 and 9. Any other value sets compression="false".	No	false
cvsRoot	Specifies the CVSROOT variable.	No	
cvsRsh	Specifies the CVS_RSH variable.	No	
date	Specifies that you want to use the most recent revision, as long as it is no later than the given date.	No	
dest	Specifies the directory where you want checked-out files to be placed.	No	The project's basedir.
error	Specifies the file where you want error messages stored.	No	Sends errors to the Ant Log as MSG_WARN.
failonerror	Stops the build if the task encounters an error.	No	false
noexec	Specifies that CVS actions should report only, without changing any files.	No	false

Table 6-4. The cvs attributes (continued)

Attribute	Description	Required	Default
output	Specifies the file to which standard output should be directed.	No	Sends output to the Ant Log as MSG_INFO.
package	Specifies the module you want to check out.	No	
passfile	Specifies a password file you want to have the task read passwords from.	No	~/.cvspass.
port	Specifies the port used by the task to communicate with the CVS server.	No	2401
quiet	Suppresses messages. This is the same as using -q on the command line.	No	false
reallyquiet	Suppresses all messages. This is the same as using -Q on the command line. Since Ant 1.6.	No	false
tag	Specifies the module to check out by tag name.	No	

This task is designed to pass commands on to CVS verbatim. For example, here's how you'd pass a CVS diff command to the CVS server:

```
<cvs command="diff -u -N" output="diff.txt"/>
```

You can nest commandline elements and use the value attribute of argument elements to pass arguments to the CVS server; you can pass the diff command this way:

```
<cvs output="patch">
    <commandline>
        <argument value="diff"/>
        <argument value="-u"/>
        <argument value="-N"/>
    </commandline>
</cvs>
```

or this way, using the argument element's line attribute:

```
<cvs output="patch">
    <commandline>
        <argument line="-q diff -u -N"/>
    </commandline>
</cvs>
```

Checking Out Modules

To check out a module from the CVS server, you can use the cvs task without specifying a CVS command; the default for the command attribute is checkout. In Example 6-1, a module named GreetingApp is checked out and stored in a directory named *project*.

In this and the following CVS-related build files, you can omit the cvspass task if you've stored your password in the *.cvspass* file (which is what cvspass does). If you omit cvspass, set the cvsroot attribute in the cvs task, or set the CVSROOT environment variable.

Example 6-1. Checking out a CVS module (ch06/checkout/build.xml)

```
<?xml version="1.0"?>

<project default="checkout" basedir=".">

    <property name="cvs.dir" value="project" />

    <target name="checkout" >
        <cvspass cvsroot=":pserver:steven@STEVE:/home/steven/repository"
            password="opensesame" />
        <cvs package="GreetingApp" dest="${cvs.dir}" />
    </target>

</project>
```

Here's what this build file looks like in action:

```
%ant
Buildfile: build.xml

checkout:
    [cvs] Using cvs passfile: /home/.cvspasss
    [cvs] cvs server: Updating GreetingApp
    [cvs] U GreetingApp/.classpath
    [cvs] U GreetingApp/.project
    [cvs] cvs server: Updating GreetingApp/org
    [cvs] cvs server: Updating GreetingApp/org/antbook
    [cvs] cvs server: Updating GreetingApp/org/antbook/ch06
    [cvs] U GreetingApp/org/antbook/ch06/GreetingClass.java


BUILD SUCCESSFUL
Total time: 2 seconds
```

Before using the build files for this chapter in the downloadable code, make sure you replace the cvsroot attribute value or the CVSROOT environment variable with an appropriate value for your CVS server.

After running this build file, the project directory will hold the checked-out module, including a CVS *.project* file and a *CVS* directory, which holds logging and tracking information. You're free to work with the code that's been downloaded, and when you want to commit the project back to the CVS server, specify the same directory you downloaded the project to.

Updating Shared Code

When you want to update your local copy of a module from the CVS repository, you can use the update command. You can see how that works in Example 6-2; as before, you can omit the cvspass task if your password is in the *.cvspass* file though it causes no harm to leave it in.

Example 6-2. Updating a CVS module ch06/update/build.xml

```xml
<?xml version="1.0"?>

<project default="main" basedir=".">

    <property name="cvs.dir" value="project" />

    <target name="main" depends="login, update">
        <echo>
            Updating....
        </echo>
    </target>

    <target name="login">
        <cvspass cvsroot=":pserver:steven@STEVE:/home/steven/repository"
            password="opensesame" />
    </target>

    <target name="update" depends="login">
        <cvs dest="${cvs.dir}" command="update"/>
    </target>

</project>
```

Here's what you see when running this build file:

```
%ant
Buildfile: build.xml

login:
        [cvs] Using cvs passfile: /home/.cvspass


update:
        [cvs] Using cvs passfile: /home/.cvspass
        [cvs] cvs server: Updating GreetingApp
        [cvs] cvs server: Updating GreetingApp/org
        [cvs] cvs server: Updating GreetingApp/org/antbook
        [cvs] cvs server: Updating GreetingApp/org/antbook/ch06


main:
        [echo]
```

```
    [echo]            Updating....
    [echo]

BUILD SUCCESSFUL
Total time: 3 seconds
```

This updates your local copy of a module with what's currently in the CVS repository.

Committing Source Code

After you've made changes to the code in a checked-out module, you can send the revised module back to the CVS repository by setting the command attribute to commit, as shown in Example 6-3. In this example, the build file commits a new version of a checked-out module, adding the comment "New Version."

Example 6-3. Committing a CVS module ch06/commit/build.xml

```xml
<?xml version="1.0"?>

<project default="main" basedir=".">

    <property name="cvs.dir" value="project" />

    <target name="main" depends="login, commit">
        <echo>
            Committing....
        </echo>
    </target>

    <target name="login">
        <cvspass cvsroot=":pserver:steven@STEVE:/home/steven/repository"
            password="opensesame" />
    </target>

    <target name="commit" depends="login">
        <cvs dest="${cvs.dir}/GreetingApp" command="commit -m 'New Version'"/>
    </target>

</project>
```

Here's what this build file gives you when you run it and the CVS server commits the new code:

```
%ant
Buildfile: build.xml

login:

commit:
        [cvs] Using cvs passfile: /home/.cvspass
        [cvs] cvs commit: Examining .
        [cvs] cvs commit: Examining org
```

```
[cvs] cvs commit: Examining org/antbook
[cvs] cvs commit: Examining org/antbook/ch06
[cvs] Checking in org/antbook/ch06/GreetingClass.java;
[cvs] /home/steven/repository/GreetingApp/org
/antbook/ch06/GreetingClass.java,v
<-- GreetingClass.java
[cvs] new revision: 1.5; previous revision: 1.4
[cvs] done


main:
    [echo]
    [echo]                 Committing....
    [echo]

BUILD SUCCESSFUL
Total time: 1 second
```

Comparing Files

You can compare local files to those in the CVS repository with the CVS `diff` command. For example, say that the module you've been working with, `GreetingApp`, contains *GreetingClass.java*, which holds these contents (presumably committed earlier by you or another developer):

```
package org.antbook.ch06;

public class GreetingClass
{
    public static void main(String[] args)
    {
        System.out.println("No problems here.");
    }
}
```

Then suppose you change the displayed message from "No problems here." to "No problems at all." in the local version of the file:

```
package org.antbook.ch06;

public class GreetingClass
{
    public static void main(String[] args)
    {
        System.out.println("No problems at all.");
    }
}
```

The CVS `diff` command finds the difference between your local copy and the server's version. You can see a build file using this command in Example 6-4; in this case, the differences are written to a file named *patch.txt*.

Example 6-4. Finding differences in a CVS module ch06/diff/build.xml

```
<?xml version="1.0"?>

<project default="main" basedir=".">

    <property name="cvs.dir" value="project" />

    <target name="main" >
        <cvspass cvsroot=":pserver:steven@STEVE:/home/steven/repository"
            password="opensesame" />
        <cvs command="diff" dest="${cvs.dir}/GreetingApp" output="patch.txt"/>
    </target>

</project>
```

Here's what the build process looks like at work:

```
%ant
Buildfile: build.xml

main:
        [cvs] Using cvs passfile: /home/.cvspass
        [cvs] cvs server: Diffing .
        [cvs] cvs server: Diffing org
        [cvs] cvs server: Diffing org/antbook
        [cvs] cvs server: Diffing org/antbook/ch06


BUILD SUCCESSFUL
Total time: 1 second
```

In *patch.txt*, the diff command caught the difference between the local copy of the file and the version in the CVS repository:

```
Index: org/antbook/ch06/GreetingClass.java
=====================================================================
RCS file: /home/steven/repository/GreetingApp/org/antbook/ch06/GreetingClass.java,v
retrieving revision 1.6
diff -r1.6 GreetingClass.java
20c20
<           System.out.println("No problems at all.");
---
>           System.out.println("No problems here.");
```

> If you want to create a patch file that you can, with the patch utility, update code files with, use the CVS rdiff command, not diff.

That's how the cvs task works; you pass the CVS command, along with any command-line options, in the command attribute or a commandline element. You can extrapolate from the CVS examples given here to other CVS commands easily.

Getting Version Data

The cvsversion task retrieves the version of the CVS client and server. For example, this cvsversion element stores the server's version number in the property cvsServerVersion, and the client's version in cvsClientVersion:

```
<cvsversion cvsroot=":pserver:steven@STEVE:/home/steven/repository"
    password="opensesame"
    cvsserverproperty="cvsServerVersion"
    cvsclientproperty="cvsClientVersion"
/>
```

The attributes for this task appear in Table 6-5.

Table 6-5. The cvsversion task's attributes

Attribute	Description	Required	Default
cvsclientproperty	Specifies the name of the property in which you want the version of the cvsclient to be placed	No	
cvsroot	Specifies the CVSROOT variable you want to use	No	
cvsrsh	Specifies the CVS_RSH variable you want to use	No	
cvsserverproperty	Specifies the name of a property where you want the CVS server version to be placed	No	
dest	Specifies the directory which holds, or will hold, a checked-out project	No	Project's basedir
failonerror	Makes the build fail if this task encounters an error	No	false
package	Specifies the module you want to check out	No	
passfile	Specifies the password file you want the task to read passwords from	No	~/.cvspass
port	Specifies the port used to communicate with the CVS server	No	2401

Creating Change Logs

This task creates an XML-formatted report file of the change logs in a CVS repository. If you want to track what's been happening with a module, this is the way to do it. For example, take a look at the build file in Example 6-5, which creates a change log, *changelog.xml*, for the GreetingApp module:

Example 6-5. Getting a CVS change log (ch06/changelog/build.xml)

```
<?xml version="1.0"?>

<project default="main" basedir=".">

    <property name="cvs.dir" value="project" />
```

Example 6-5. Getting a CVS change log (ch06/changelog/build.xml) (continued)

```
<target name="main" >
    <cvspass cvsroot=":pserver:steven@STEVE:/home/steven/repository"
        password="opensesame" />
    <cvschangelog dir="${cvs.dir}/GreetingApp" destfile="changelog.xml" />
</target>

</project>
```

Here's the resulting change log, *changelog.xml*:

```
<?xml version="1.0" encoding="UTF-8"?>
<changelog>
    <entry>
        <date>2005-02-24</date>
        <time>16:18</time>
        <author><![CDATA[steven]]></author>
        <file>
            <name>org/antbook/ch06/GreetingClass.java</name>
            <revision>1.1</revision>
        </file>
        <msg><![CDATA[The Greeting App]]></msg>
    </entry>
    <entry>
        <date>2005-06-22</date>
        <time>16:25</time>
        <author><![CDATA[steven]]></author>
        <file>
            <name>org/antbook/ch06/GreetingClass.java</name>
            <revision>1.3</revision>
            <prevrevision>1.2</prevrevision>
        </file>
        <msg><![CDATA[*** empty log message ***]]></msg>
    </entry>
    <entry>
        <date>2005-02-25</date>
        <time>16:24</time>
        <author><![CDATA[steven]]></author>
        <file>
            <name>.classpath</name>
            <revision>1.1</revision>
        </file>
        <file>
            <name>.project</name>
            <revision>1.1</revision>
        </file>
        <msg><![CDATA[The Greeting App]]></msg>
    </entry>
    <entry>
        <date>2005-02-25</date>
        <time>16:34</time>
        <author><![CDATA[steven]]></author>
        <file>
            <name>org/antbook/ch06/GreetingClass.java</name>
```

```
            <revision>1.2</revision>
            <prevrevision>1.1</prevrevision>
        </file>
        <msg><![CDATA[*** empty log message ***]]></msg>
    </entry>
    <entry>
        <date>2005-06-22</date>
        <time>16:27</time>
        <author><![CDATA[steven]]></author>
        <file>
            <name>org/antbook/ch06/GreetingClass.java</name>
            <revision>1.4</revision>
            <prevrevision>1.3</prevrevision>
        </file>
        <msg><![CDATA[OK]]></msg>
    </entry>
    <entry>
        <date>2005-06-22</date>
        <time>16:29</time>
        <author><![CDATA[steven]]></author>
        <file>
            <name>org/antbook/ch06/GreetingClass.java</name>
            <revision>1.5</revision>
            <prevrevision>1.4</prevrevision>
        </file>
        <msg><![CDATA[New Version]]></msg>
    </entry>
</changelog>
```

The attributes for this task appear in Table 6-6.

Table 6-6. The cvschangelog task's attributes

Attribute	Description	Required	Default
cvsroot	Specifies the CVSROOT variable you want to use	No	
cvsrsh	Specifies the CVS_RSH variable you want to use	No	
daysinpast	Specifies for how many days in the past you want change log information	No	
destfile	Specifies the file in which you want the change log report written	Yes	
dir	Specifies the directory from which to run the CVS log command	No	${basedir}
end	Specifies the latest date for which you want to include change logs	No	
failonerror	Specifies that you want the task to fail if it encounters an error	No	false
package	Specifies the module you want to check out	No	
passfile	Specifies the password file you want the task to read passwords from	No	~/.cvspass
port	Specifies the port the task should use to communicate with the CVS server	No	2401
start	Specifies the earliest date for which you want to include change logs	No	

Table 6-6. The cvschangelog task's attributes (continued)

Attribute	Description	Required	Default
tag	Lets you access change logs by tag	No	
usersfile	Specifies a property file holding name/value pairs connecting user IDs and names, allowing the task to report names inctead of IDs	No	

The nested user element allows you to specify a mapping between a user ID (as it appears to the CVS server) and a name to include in the formatted report. The attributes of the user element appear in Table 6-7.

Table 6-7. The user element's attributes

Attribute	Description	Required
displayname	Specifies the name you want used in the CVS change log report	Yes
userid	Specifies the user ID of the person as far as the CVS server is concerned	Yes

Finding Changes Between Versions

The cvstagdiff task generates an XML-formatted report file of the changes between two tags or dates recorded in a CVS repository. Here's an example that creates a report, *datediff.xml*, for all the changes that have been made in the GreetingApp module in January 2005:

```
<cvstagdiff
    destfile="datediff.xml"
    package="GreetingApp"
    startDate="2005-01-01"
    endDate="2005-31-01"
/>
```

You can see the attributes of this task in Table 6-8.

Table 6-8. The cvstagdiff task's attributes

Attribute	Description	Required	Default
compression	Specifies the compression you want to use. Set to true, false, or a number (1–9) for compression level.	No	No compression
cvsroot	Specifies the CVSROOT variable you want to use.	No	
cvsrsh	Specifies the CVS_RSH variable you want to use.	No	
destfile	Specifies the file where the report should be stored.	Yes	
enddate	Sets the latest date for differences to still be included in the report.	One of endtag or enddate	

Table 6-8. The cvstagdiff task's attributes (continued)

Attribute	Description	Required	Default
endtag	Sets the latest tag for differences to still be included in the report.	One of endtag or enddate	
failonerror	Makes the build fail if this task encounters an error.	No	false
package	Specifies the module you want to analyze. Since Ant 1.6, multiple modules can be separated by spaces.	Yes	
passfile	Specifies the password file you want the task to read passwords from.	No	~/.cvspass
port	Specifies the port used to communicate with the CVS server.	No	2401
quiet	Specifies that you want to suppress displayed messages.	No	false
startdate	Sets the earliest date for differences to still be included in the report.	One of starttag or startdate	
starttag	Sets the earliest tag for differences to still be included in the report.	One of starttag or startdate	

 Here's something useful to know: Ant comes with an XSLT stylesheet, *${ant.home}/etc/tagdiff.xsl*, that you can use to generate a HTML report based on this task's XML output. Here's an example:

```
<style in="datediff.xml"
    out="datediff.html"
    style="${ant.home}/etc/tagdiff.xsl">
  <param name="title" expression="Date Differences"/>
  <param name="module" expression="GreetingApp"/>
</style>
```

Creating Patches

This task applies a patch file to local source code, updating the local code. You can create a patch file with the CVS rdiff command, which lets you compare two files. Here's an example, which applies *patch.txt* to the module in the current directory:

```
<patch patchfile="patch.txt"/>
```

The attributes for this task appear in Table 6-9.

 To use this task, the patch utility must be in your path.

Table 6-9. The patch task's attributes

Attribute	Description	Required	Default
backups	Specifies you want to keep backups of unpatched files.	No	
destfile	Specifies the file you want to send the output to. Since Ant 1.6.	No	
dir	Specifies the directory where you want to run the patch command.	No	The project's basedir
ignorewhitespace	Specifies that you want to ignore whitespace differences.	No	
originalfile	Specifies the file you want to patch.	No	
patchfile	Specifies the file that contains the patch.	Yes	
quiet	Specifies you want to supress messages unless an error occurs.	No	
reverse	Specifies you want to create the patch with old and new files in reverse order (swapped).	No	

CHAPTER 7

Executing External Programs

Part of the build process involves testing what you've built, and an obvious way of doing that is to run the results of a build. Doing so from Ant involves using the tasks detailed in this chapter: java, exec, and apply. You can check the return code from your build to ensure things worked out; if not, you can halt the build before you deploy faulty build results.

Executing code to test it is a fundamental part of the build process, and this chapter covers that aspect of Ant. Besides running your code, you can start and stop external programs needed to test your code, such as when you want to run a JUnit test on a web application and need to start a web server. The tasks in this chapter do more than the usual internal Ant tasks, and because they're designed to deal with the external run-time environment, so they're a little more involved than usual.

Executing Java Code

The java task is part of Ant's core functionality; it executes a Java class in the current JVM, or forks another JVM and runs the class in the new JVM. You can recover the exit code of the Java class and stop the build if the build results you're testing create an error.

Here's an example using this task. Say you have this code, *Project.java*, which reads what the user enters on the command line and displays it:

```
public class Project
{
    public static void main(String args[])
    {
        System.out.println("You said: " + args[0]);
        System.exit(0);
    }
}
```

After compiling this code you can run it with the java task by setting up the class-path with a classpath element and passing a command-line argument, "OK", in a nested arg element. The build file appears in Example 7-1.

Example 7-1. Using the java task (ch07/java/build.xml)

```xml
<?xml version="1.0" ?>
<project default="main">

    <property name="src" location="source" />
    <property name="output" location="bin" />
    <property environment="env" />

    <target name="main" depends="init, compile, run">
        <echo>
            Building and running....
        </echo>
    </target>

    <target name="init">
        <mkdir dir="${output}" />
    </target>

    <target name="compile">
        <javac srcdir="${src}" destdir="${output}" />
    </target>

    <target name="run" failonerror="true">
        <java classname="Project"
            fork="true" >
            <classpath>
                <pathelement location="${output}"/>
            </classpath>
            <arg value="OK" />
        </java>
    </target>
</project>
```

Here's what you see when you run this build file; the code ran without problem and recovered the command-line argument passed to it:

```
%ant
Buildfile: build.xml

init:
    [mkdir] Created dir: /home/steven/ch07/bin

compile:
    [javac] Compiling 1 source file to /home/steven/ch07/bin

run:
    [java] You said: OK
```

```
main:
     [echo]
     [echo]                    Building and running....
     [echo]

BUILD SUCCESSFUL
Total time: 4 seconds
```

The many attributes for this task appear in Table 7-1.

 If things go wrong when you run this task, there may be a conflict with the current JVM, which is running Ant. In that case, set fork="true" to use a new JVM.

Table 7-1. The java task's attributes

Attribute	Description	Required	Default
Append	Specifies whether you want to append to output and error files.	No	false
args	Deprecated. Use nested arg elements. Specifies the arguments for the class that you want to run.	No	
classname	Specifies the Java class you want to run.	One of either jar or classname	
classpath	Specifies the classpath you want to use when the class is run.	No	
classpathref	Specifies the classpath you want to use, as a reference, when the class is run.	No	
dir	Specifies the directory where you want to run Java.	No	
error	Specifies the file where standard error output should be stored.	No	
errorproperty	Specifies the name of a property where you want to store errors.	No	
failonerror	Specifies the build should be stopped if the task encounters errors.	No	false
fork	Specifies you want to run the class in a forked JVM.	No	false
input	Specifies the file where the task should take input to run the class with.	No	
inputstring	Specifies a string holding the input stream for the class to run.	No	
jar	Specifies the location of the *.jar* file to run. The *.jar* file must have a Main-Class entry in the manifest.	jar or classname	
jvm	Specifies the command used to start Java.	No	java
jvmargs	Deprecated. Use nested jvmarg elements. Specifies arguments to pass to the forked Java Virtual Machine.	No	
logError	Specifies you want to send error output to Ant's log.	No	
maxmemory	Specifies the maximum amount of memory you want to give a forked JVM.	No	
newenvironment	Specifies old environment variables should not be passed as new environment variables to a forked JVM.	No	false

Table 7-1. The java task's attributes (continued)

Attribute	Description	Required	Default
output	Specifies the name of a file in which to store the output.	No	
outputproperty	Specifies the name of a property in which you want the output of the task to be placed.	No	
resultproperty	Specifies the name of the property that you want to hold the return code. Use this only if failonerror is false and if fork is true.	No	
spawn	Specifies you want to spawn a new process in which to run the class. To use this attribute, set fork to true.	No	
timeout	Specifies you want the task to quit if it doesn't finish in the given time. Set the time in milliseconds. You should only use this if fork is true.	No	

The java task supports a number of nested elements, many of which are the same as the javac task. You can use arg elements to pass arguments to Java and jvmarg elements to specify arguments to a forked JVM. Nested sysproperty elements specify system properties required by the class you're running. As of Ant 1.6, you can use syspropertyset elements, which specify a set of properties to be used as system properties.

The java task supports nested classpath elements, which you can use to specify a classpath to use when Java runs, and supports as bootclasspath elements (since Ant 1.6) to set the location of bootstrap class files. You can use env elements (see Table 7-3) to specify environment variables to pass to the forked JVM and nested permissions elements. As with the javac task, permissions represents a set of security permissions granted to the code in the JVM where Ant is running. Since Ant 1.6, you can use nested assertions elements to support Java 1.4 assertions.

Handling Errors and Return Codes

By default, the return code of the java task is ignored. If you want to check the return code, you can set the resultproperty attribute to the name of a property and have the result code assigned to it. For example, say your code returned a non-zero value:

```
public class Project
{
    public static void main(String args[])
    {
        System.out.println("You said: " + args[0]);
        System.exit(1);
    }
}
```

You can test the return code from a forked JVM and explicitly fail unless it's 0 this way:

```
<target name="run">
    <java classname="Project"
        fork="true" resultproperty="return.code">
        <classpath>
            <pathelement location="${output}"/>
        </classpath>
        <arg value="OK" />
    </java>
    <condition property="problem">
        <not>
            <equals arg1="${return.code}" arg2="0"/>
        </not>
    </condition>
    <fail if="problem" message="Failed: ${return.code}" />
</target>
```

Here's the result. The java task indicates a nonzero return code and the build was terminated by the fail task:

```
%ant build.xml
Buildfile: build.xml

init:
    [mkdir] Created dir: /home/steven/ch07/bin

compile:
    [javac] Compiling 1 source file to /home/steven/ch07/bin

run:
    [java] You said: OK


    [java] Java Result: 1

BUILD FAILED
/home/steven/ch07/build2.xml:35: Failed: 1

Total time: 4 seconds
```

You can set failonerror="true" in the java task, in which case the only possible value for resultproperty is 0, or the build will terminate. That's how the example in the previous topic was written:

```
<target name="run" failonerror="true">
    <java classname="Project"
        fork="true" >
        <classpath>
            <pathelement location="${output}"/>
        </classpath>
        <arg value="OK" />
    </java>
</target>
```

If failonerror="false" and fork="false", the java task *must* return a value of 0 or the build will exit because the code was run by the build JVM.

Making a build fail if there's an error when you run the build's output is a perfect way to test the results of a build; if the output doesn't run as it should, there's no sense in deploying it. Setting failonerror to true in the java task ensures your build will halt before deployment if the results don't work.

Here's another example using the java task, which forks a JVM and runs a *.jar* file in 512 MB of memory, using the entry point indicated by the manifest:

```
<java jar="${bin}/connect.jar"
    fork="true"
    failonerror="true"
    maxmemory="512m"
    >
    <arg value="-q"/>
    <classpath>
        <pathelement location="${bin}/connect.jar"/>
        <pathelement path="${java.class.path}"/>
    </classpath>
</java>
```

This example passes on a system property and an argument to the JVM:

```
<java classname="Project.main" fork="true" >
    <sysproperty key="DEBUG" value="true"/>
    <arg value="-z"/>
    <jvmarg value="-enableassertions"/>
    <classpath>
        <pathelement location="${bin}/**"/>
    </classpath>
</java>
```

As you can see, there are a great many options when running Java code.

Executing External Programs

The exec task executes a system command or external program. The attributes for this task appear in Table 7-2.

Table 7-2. The exec task's attributes

Attribute	Description	Required	Default
append	Specifies whether you want to append to output and error files.	No	false
command	Deprecated. Use executable and nested arg elements. Specifies the command you want to run.	Exactly one of command or executable	

Table 7-2. The exec task's attributes (continued)

Attribute	Description	Required	Default
dir	Specifies the directory where you want to run the command.	No	
error	Specifies the file where standard error output should be stored.	No	
errorproperty	Specifies the name of a property where you want to store errors.	No	
executable	Specifies the command you want to run (without any command-line arguments).	Exactly one of command or executable	
failifexecutionfails	Specifies the build should be stopped if the executable can't start.	No	true
failonerror	Specifies the build should be stopped if the task encounters errors.	No	false
input	Specifies the file where the task should take input to run the executable with.	No	
inputstring	Specifies a string holding the input stream for the executable to run.	No	
logError	Specifies you want to send error output to Ant's log.	No	
newenvironment	Specifies old environment variables should not be passed as new environment variables to a forked JVM.	No	false
os	Specifies the operating systems in which the executable can be run.	No	
output	Specifies the name of a file in which to store the output.	No	
outputproperty	Specifies the name of a property in which you want the output of the task to be placed.	No	
resolveExecutable	Specifies the name of the executable should be resolved using the project's base directory, then using the execution directory if that doesn't work. Available since Ant 1.6.	No	false
resultproperty	Specifies the name of the property that you want to hold the return code. Use this only if failonerror is false and if fork is true.	No	
spawn	Specifies you want to spawn a new process in which to run the command. To use this attribute, set fork to true.	No	false

Table 7-2. The exec task's attributes (continued)

Attribute	Description	Required	Default
timeout	Specifies you want the task to quit if it doesn't finish in the given time. Set the time in milliseconds.	No	
vmlauncher	Specifies you want to run the executable using the JVM's execution facilities.	No	false

 If you're running a mixed Unix/Windows environment, such as Cygwin, exec task will not understand paths like */bin/release* for the executable attribute because the JVM in which Ant is running is a Windows executable, which means it's unaware of the conventions used in Cygwin.

How you execute general code like this varies by operating system, so you can specify the operating system with the os attribute; operating system names are strings such as "Linux", "Windows 2000", and so on. When you specify a target operating system, the command or program is only executed when the OS matches one of the operating systems you specify.

 If you want to check the OS name for a target platform, use Java to display the value of the os.name system property.

You can nest arg elements in the exec task to pass command-line arguments. And you can set the values of environment variables using nested env elements. The attributes of this element appear in Table 7-3.

 You can send input to a program using the input and inputstring attributes.

Table 7-3. The env element's attributes

Attribute	Description	Required
file	Specifies an environment variable that you want to replace with the absolute name of the file.	Exactly one of value, path, or file
key	Specifies the name of the environment variable you want to work with.	Yes
path	Specifies the value for a path-like environment variable. Use ; or : as path separators.	Exactly one of value, path, or file
value	Specifies the value of the environment variable.	Exactly one of value, path, or file

Handling Return Codes

By default the return code of an exec is ignored. However, if you set `failonerror` to true, then any OS-specific return code that indicates failure means the build will fail. If you start an external program and the program fails to execute, the build halts unless `failifexecutionfails` is set to false. You can set the `resultproperty` to the name of a property that will be assigned the return code for testing. Any of these attributes can test if the results of your build functions as they should.

Example 7-2 shows how to execute a C++ compiler, *cpp.exe*, passing it a command line to execute and watching for errors by setting `failonerror` to true, which means the build will quit if there is an error.

Example 7-2. Running a JVM (ch07/exec/build.xml)

```xml
<?xml version="1.0" ?>
<project default="main">

    <property name="src" location="source" />
    <property name="output" location="bin" />

    <target name="main" depends="init, compile">
        <echo>
            Building and running....
        </echo>
    </target>

    <target name="init">
        <mkdir dir="${output}" />
    </target>

    <target name="compile">
        <exec dir="." executable="/bin/cpp.exe"
        failonerror="true">
            <arg line="-c ${src}/*.cpp ${output}"/>
        </exec>
    </target>
</project>
```

You can use this task to run any general program. Here's an example that will launch the Internet Explorer in Windows, assuming a default installation of that browser, and open the exec task's documentation page:

```xml
<?xml version="1.0" ?>
<project default="main">

    <property name="browser" location=
        "C:/Program Files/Internet Explorer/iexplore.exe"/>
    <property name="file" location="${ant.home}/docs/manual/coretasks/exec.html"/>

    <target name="main">
        <exec executable="${browser}" spawn="true">
```

```
            <arg value="${file}"/>
        </exec>
    </target>

</project>
```

This example starts emacs on X Window's display 1:

```
<?xml version="1.0" ?>
<project default="main">

    <target name="main">
        <exec executable="/usr/bin/emacs">
            <env key="DISPLAY" value=":1.0"/>
        </exec>
    </target>

</project>
```

Targeting Operating Systems

The exec task depends on a specific operating system. If you want your build file to work on multiple platforms, use the os attribute to specify which exec task is intended to run on which platform.

In Example 7-3, two platforms are targeted. The build file executes the ls command on Linux, sending the output to *ls.txt*, and works on Windows via the dir command, sending output to *dir.txt*.

Example 7-3. Targeting operationg systems (ch07/targeting/build.xml)

```
<?xml version="1.0" ?>
<project default="main">

    <target name="main">
        <exec dir="." executable="ls" os="Linux" output="ls.txt" />
        <exec dir="." executable="cmd.exe" os="Windows 2000" output="dir.txt">
            <arg line="/c dir"/>
        </exec>
    </target>

</project>
```

Here's what you might see in Linux:

```
-bash-2.05b$ ant
Buildfile: build.xml

main:

BUILD SUCCESSFUL
Total time: 0 seconds
```

```
-bash-2.05b$ cat ls.txt
build.xml
ls.txt
```

Here's what you might see in Windows:

```
C:\ant\ch07\exec>ant
Buildfile: build.xml

main:

BUILD SUCCESSFUL
Total time: 0 seconds

C:\ant\ch07\exec>type dir.txt
 Volume in drive C has no label.
 Volume Serial Number is 1512-1722

 Directory of C:\ant\ch07\exec

06/25/2004  01:06p       <DIR>          .
06/25/2004  01:06p       <DIR>          ..
06/25/2004  02:02p                   311 build.xml
06/25/2004  02:02p                   104 dir.txt
               2 File(s)            455 bytes
               2 Dir(s)  29,627,777,024 bytes free
```

Handling Timeouts

You can limit the amount of time you want to wait for an external program to execute by setting the timeout attribute to a millisecond value. If the timeout is reached and the program hasn't returned, it's killed and the java tasks's return value will be 1. In that case, the build will halt if failonerror is true. Here's an example:

```
<?xml version="1.0" ?>
<project default="main">

    <target name="main">
        <exec dir="." executable="databaseConnect" timeout="100"
             failonerror="true" />
    </target>

</project>
```

Executing Shell Commands

How about shell and batch scripts? In Unix, executing shell scripts is no problem. Assign the executable attribute the name of the script. In Windows, it's a different story. To execute a batch (*.bat*) file, execute the command-line processor, *cmd.exe*, and pass the name of the batch file using an arg nested element and the /c switch:

```
<exec dir="." executable="cmd" os="Windows 2000">
    <arg line="/c backup.bat"/>
</exec>
```

If you're running a Unix-like shell in Windows, execute the command shell, sh, and use the -c switch, which sends the output to a file:

```
<exec executable="/bin/sh">
    <arg value="-c" />
    <arg value="run.sh &gt; results" />
</exec>
```

Checking for External Programs Before Executing Them

When you start launching external programs, ensure the desired programs are available before launching them. Example 7-4 shows how you can do that with the available task, where the existence of *cc* is verified before compiling C code. If *cc* is found, the build file sets a property named cc.ok, which is checked by the compile target before the compilation is attempted.

Example 7-4. Checking for external programs (ch07/checkfirst/build.xml)

```
<?xml version="1.0" ?>
<project default="main">

    <property name="src" location="source" />

    <target name="main" depends="check, compile">
        <echo>
            Compiling....
        </echo>
    </target>

    <target name="check">
        <condition property="cc.ok">
            <or>
                <available file="cc" filepath="/usr" />
                <available file="cc" filepath="/usr/bin" />
                <available file="cc" filepath="/usr/local/bin" />
            </or>
        </condition>
    </target>

    <target name="compile" depends="check" if="cc.ok">
        <exec dir="." executable="cc">
            <arg line="${src}/Project.cc"/>
        </exec>
    </target>

</project>
```

Performing Batch Execution

What if you want to execute a command on multiple files? If you want to pass a set of files to an external command, use the apply task, a version of exec that takes filesets. The files in the fileset are passed as arguments to the command or external program.

This task is a powerful one, letting you batch your executions and work with external programs as if they supported filesets. In Example 7-5, the build file is running the C compiler gcc on a fileset. In this case, the apply task executes the command line gcc -c -o *target source* for each .c file in ${src}, where *source* with the name of each matching .c file in turn, and *target* is replaced with the name of the corresponding .o output file you want created.

Example 7-5. Using the apply task (ch07/apply/build.xml)

```xml
<?xml version="1.0" ?>
<project default="main">

    <property name="src" location="source" />

    <target name="main">
        <apply executable="gcc">
            <arg value="-c"/>
            <arg value="-o"/>
            <targetfile/>
            <srcfile/>
            <fileset dir="${src}" includes="*.c" />
            <mapper from="*.c" to="*.o" type="glob" />
        </apply>
    </target>
</project>
```

You can see this task's attributes in Table 7-4.

Table 7-4. The apply task's attributes

Attribute	Description	Required	Default
addsourcefile	Specifies if you want source filenames to be added to the command automatically. Since Ant 1.6.	No	true
append	Specifies whether you want to append to output and error files.	No	false
dest	Specifies the directory in which files will be stored by the task.	Yes, if you specify a nested mapper	
dir	Specifies the directory where the command should be executed.	No	
error	Specifies the file where standard error output should be stored.	No	

Table 7-4. The apply task's attributes (continued)

Attribute	Description	Required	Default
errorproperty	Specifies the name of a property where you want to store errors.	No	
executable	Specifies the command to execute (without any command-line arguments).	Yes	
failifexecutionfails	Specifies the build should be stopped if the program doesn't start.	No	true
failonerror	Specifies the build should be stopped if the task encounters errors.	No	
forwardslash	Specifies you want filenames to be passed with forward slashes as directory separators.	No	false
input	Specifies the file where the task should take input to run the class with.	No	
inputstring	Specifies a string holding the input stream for the class to run.	No	
logError	Specifies you want to send error output to Ant's log.	No	
maxparallel	Specifies the maximum number of source files to use at once. Set to a value less than or equal to 0 for unlimited parallelism. Available since Ant 1.6.	No	unlimited
newenvironment	Indicates you do not want to pass to the old environment when new environment variables are specified.	No	false
os	Specifies the operating systems in which the executable can be run.	No	
output	Specifies the name of a file in which to store the output.	No	
outputproperty	Specifies the name of a property in which you want the output of the task to be placed.	No	
parallel	Specifies you want to run the command one time only on multiple files.	No	false
relative	Specifies if filenames should be absolute or relative when passed to the command to execute.	No	false
resolveExecutable	Specifies the name of the executable should be resolved using the project's base directory, then using the execution directory if that doesn't work. Since Ant 1.6.	No	false
resultproperty	Specifies the name of the property that you want to hold the return code. Use this one only if failonerror is false and if fork is true.	No	

Table 7-4. The apply task's attributes (continued)

Attribute	Description	Required	Default
skipemptyfilesets	Specifies you don't want to run the command if no source files found or are newer than their corresponding target files.	No	false
spawn	Specifies you want to spawn a new process in which to run the command. To use this attribute, set fork to true.	No	false
timeout	Specifies you want the task to quit if it doesn't finish in the given time. Set the time in milliseconds.	No	
type	Specifies whether you're working with files or directories. Set to dir, file, or both.	No	file
verbose	Specifies whether you want the task to display its progress. Since Ant 1.6.	No	false
Vmlauncher	Specifies you want to run the executable using the JVM's execution facilities.	No	true

You can use any number of nested fileset elements to specify the files you want to use with this task. Since Ant 1.6, you can use any number of nested filelist and/or dirset elements as well. At least one fileset or filelist is required.

You can use one mapper element to specify the target files relative to the dest attribute for dependency checking, as I'll do below. Command-line arguments can be passed with arg elements, as with the exec task, and you can use nested env elements.

How does Ant pass the names of files to the external program? By default, the filenames of the source files are added to the end of the command line. If you want to insert the names of files in a different place, use a nested srcfile element between nested arg elements. Nested targetfile elements are similar to srcfile elements, except they mark the position of the target filename on the command line. You can only use a targetfile element if you define a nested mapper and the dest attribute.

Multithreading Tasks

The parallel task can contain other Ant tasks and execute each nested task in its own thread. While the tasks within the parallel task are being run, the main thread will be blocked waiting for all the child threads to complete.

This task is useful to speed up build-file processing and to launch external tasks that may depend on each other; you may want to launch a server and run tests on build output, for example. The attributes of this task appear in Table 7-5.

Table 7-5. The parallel task's attributes

Attribute	Description	Required	Default
failonany	Specifies you want the task to fail if any nested task fails.	No	
pollInterval	Polls tasks; not implemented at this point.	No	1000
threadCount	Specifies the maximum numbers of threads you want to use.	No	
threadsPerProcessor	Specifies the maximum number of threads you want to use for each processor. Requires JDK 1.4 or later.	No	
timeout	Specifies a timeout, in miiliseconds, before the task fails.	No	

 Be careful when using this task as you would with any parallel task. For example, if you're compiling and two files have the same dependency, you could have file access conflicts.

The parallel task supports a daemons nested element, which is a list of tasks which are to be run in parallel daemon threads. The parallel task will not wait for these tasks to complete. Because they are daemon threads, however, they will not prevent Ant from completing the task.

The parallel task may be combined with the sequential task to define sequences of tasks to be executed on each thread inside the parallel task; for an example using parallel and sequential, see the next topic.

Setting Execution Order

Like parallel, sequential is a container task which can contain other Ant tasks. In this task, the nested tasks are executed in sequence. You use this task primarily to ensure the sequential execution of a subset of tasks in the parallel task.

The sequential task has no attributes and has no nested elements besides the Ant tasks you want to run. Here's an example which uses the wlrun task to start the WebLogic web server, waits for it to start, runs a JUnit test, and then stops WebLogic:

```
<parallel>
    <wlrun taskname="server"
           classpath="${weblogic.boot.classpath}"
           wlclasspath="${weblogic.classes}:${code.jars}"
           name="antserver"
           home="${weblogic.home}"
           properties="antserver/antserver.properties"/>
    <sequential>
        <sleep seconds="60"/>
        <junit printsummary="yes" haltonfailure="yes">
            <formatter type="plain"/>
            <batchtest fork="true" todir="${reports.tests}">
```

```
            .
            .
            .
        </batchtest>
    </junit>
    <wlstop/>
</sequential>
</parallel>
```

CHAPTER 8

Developing for the Web

Developing for the Web is bread and butter for Ant developers. There is a wide spectrum of tasks at your disposal: Chapter 4 introduced packaging and deploying applications—including web applications—with the move, copy, ftp, telnet, sshexec, and mail tasks, but Ant offers more. This chapter covers the tasks specifically designed for packaging web applications, such as war, cab, ear, and jspc, and for deploying them, such as get, serverdeploy, and scp. I'll cover the custom Ant tasks targeted to specific servers such as deploy, reload, and undeploy. And there's more to come: Chapter 9 covers the many optional Enterprise JavaBeans (EJB) tasks Ant supports.

Creating WAR Archives

The war task is an extension of the jar task, and it compresses web applications into *.war* files, with special handling for files that should end up in the *WEB-INF/lib*, *WEB-INF/classes* or *WEB-INF* directories on the server. For example, say you have this directory layout after you build your project:

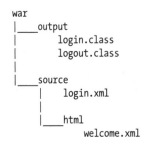

```
war
|____output
|        login.class
|        logout.class
|
|____source
|    |   login.xml
|    |
|    |___html
|            welcome.xml
```

The build file in Example 8-1 will create the *.war* file you need to deploy this application, placing the *.class* files in the *WEB-INF/classes* directory, renaming *login.xml* *web.xml* and placing it in *WEB-INF*, and so on.

Example 8-1. Creating a war file (ch08/war/build.xml)

```xml
<?xml version="1.0" encoding="UTF-8" ?>

<project default="main" basedir=".">

    <property name="bin" value="output" />
    <property name="src" value="source" />

    <target name="main" >
        <war destfile="login.war" webxml="${src}/login.xml">
            <fileset dir="${src}/html"/>
            <classes dir="${bin}"/>
        </war>
    </target>

</project>
```

Here's what this build file looks like at work:

```
%ant
Buildfile: build.xml

main:
       [war] Building war: /home/steven/ant/ch08/war/login.war

BUILD SUCCESSFUL
Total time: 2 seconds
```

That creates the *.war* file. Besides packaging the files specified, Ant supplies a default manifest file, *Manifest.mf*, in the resulting *.war* file, which contains these contents:

```
Manifest-Version: 1.0
Ant-Version: Apache Ant 1.6.1
Created-By: 1.4.2_03-b02 (Sun Microsystems Inc.)
```

After you create your *.war* file, you can deploy it by copying it to your web server's deployment directory, such as to the *webapps* directory in Tomcat.

The attributes of the war task appear in Table 8-1.

 The war task is a shortcut for specifying the particular layout of a *.war* file. The same thing can be accomplished using the prefix and fullpath attributes of zipfilesets in a zip or jar task.

Table 8-1. The war task's attributes

Attribute	Description	Required	Default
basedir	Specifies the source directory for files to include in the compressed file.	No	
compress	Specifies you want to not only store data but compress it.	No	true

Table 8-1. The war task's attributes (continued)

Attribute	Description	Required	Default
defaultexcludes	Specifies if you want to use default excludes or not. Set to yes/no.	No	Default excludes are used.
destfile	Specifies the WAR file you want to create.	Exactly one of destfile or warfile	
duplicate	Specifies what to do if a duplicate file is found. Valid values are add, preserve, and fail.	No	add
encoding	Specifies the character encoding to use for file-names in the WAR file.	No	UTF8
excludes	Specifes the patterns matching files to exclude, as a comma- or space-separated list.	No	
excludesfile	Specifes the name of a file where each line is a pattern matching files to exclude.	No	
filesonly	Specifies you want to store only file entries.	No	false
includes	Specifes the patterns matching files to include, as a comma- or space-separated list.	No	
includesfile	Specifes the name of a file where each line is a pattern matching files to include.	No	
keepcompression	Preserves the compression as it has been in archives you're compressing instead of using the compress attribute. Available since Ant 1.6.	No	false
manifest	Specifies the manifest file to use in the com-pressed file.	No	
update	Specifies whether you want to update or over-write the target file if it exists.	No	false
warfile	Deprecated. Use destfile. Specifies the WAR file you want to create.	Exactly one of destfile or warfile	
webxml	Specifies the deployment descriptor you want to use. Will be deployed to WEB-INF/web.xml.	Yes, unless update is set to true	

The war task can contain elements like fileset and zipfileset to specify what files to include in the .war file. This task can contain these elements to specify where you want various files to go:

- Files contained in the webinf element end up in *WEB-INF*
- Files contained in the classes element end up in *WEB-INF/classes*
- Files contained in the lib element end up in *WEB-INF/lib*
- Files contained in the metainf files end up in *META-INF*

Creating CAB Files

The cab task creates Microsoft *.cab* archive files, and you use this task as you would the jar or zip tasks. The *.cab* files are the .NET equivalent of *.war* files, packaging .NET applications for server deployment. This task works in Windows using the external cabarc tool (this tool comes from Microsoft), which must be in your executable path.

I'm not going to spend much time on this task because the Microsoft Visual Studio IDE has many powerful integrated build tools and wizards that create *.cab* files; most Microsoft developers do not need Ant to solve their build problems. Here's a quick example using the Ant cab task:

```
<cab cabfile="${deploy}/app.cab"
    basedir="${output}"
/>
```

 You can get a free copy of the Microsoft C# command-line compiler, csc, if your version of Windows doesn't have it. Install the .NET Framework's Software Development Kit (SDK), which you can find at *http://msdn.microsoft.com/downloads*. The csc compiler is included.

The attributes of the cab task appear in Table 8-2.

 It's possible to use this task on other platforms besides Windows, but you need to get and compile the libcabinet tool from *http://trill.cis. fordham.edu/~barbacha/cabinet_library/*.

Table 8-2. The cab task's attributes

Attribute	Description	Required	Default
basedir	Specifies the directory to archive files from.	No	
cabfile	Specifies the name of the cab file you want to create.	Yes	
compress	Specifies you want to not only store data but compress it.	No	yes
defaultexcludes	Specifies if you want to use default excludes or not. Set to yes/no.	No	Default excludes are used.
excludes	Specifes the patterns matching files to exclude, as a comma- or space-separated list.	No	
excludesfile	Specifes the name of a file where each line is a pattern matching files to exclude.	No	
includes	Specifes the patterns matching files to include, as a comma- or space-separated list.	No	
includesfile	Specifes the name of a file where each line is a pattern matching files to include.	No	

Table 8-2. The cab task's attributes (continued)

Attribute	Description	Required	Default
options	Specifies any additional command-line options you want to pass to the cabarc tool.	No	
verbose	Specifies you want full (verbose) output. Set to yes or no.	No	no

You can use nested `fileset` elements to specify the files to be included in the archive. As with other Ant tasks, this task forms an implicit FileSet and supports all attributes of the `fileset` element (dir becomes basedir) as well as the nested include, exclude and patternset elements.

Creating Simple Web Deployment

With a WAR file (or CAB file), it's time to turn to the deployment side of the web-development equation. If you're working on the same machine as a web server, deployment can be as easy as copying a *.war* file to the application base directory for the server. Example 8-2 illustrates the point; this build file creates and copies a *.war* file over to the Tomcat *webapps* directory. When you (re)start Tomcat, the *.war* file will expand automatically into a directory of the same name (minus the *.war* extension), and the web application will become available, in this case, at *http://localhost:8080/app*. (If you're deploying a servlet, the URL will reflect the servlet's package, as in *http://localhost:8080/org/antbook/ch08/app* for the servlet class org.antbook.ch08.app.)

Example 8-2. Build file for Tomcat deployment (ch08/simple/build.xml)

```
<?xml version="1.0" encoding = "UTF-8"?>
<project default="main" basedir=".">

    <property name="src" location="source" />
    <property name="wardir" location=
        "c:/tomcat/jakarta-tomcat-5.0.19/webapps"/>
    <property name="warfile" location="${wardir}/app.war"/>

    <target name="main" depends="war">
        <echo message="Deploying the Web app...."/>
    </target>

    <target name="war" >
        <war destfile="${warfile}" webxml="${src}/app.xml" basedir="${bin}" />
    </target>

</project>
```

You can use Ant's ftp task (see Chapter 4) for remote deployment to a web server's base directories.

Deploying with SCP

Another deployment task, available since Ant 1.6, is the scp task, which copies a file or FileSet to or from a remote machine running the SSH daemon. This task is an optional one, and you need *jsch.jar* in the Ant *lib* directory to use it (you can get *jsch.jar* at *http://www.jcraft.com/jsch/index.html*).

This task is handy for deployment. For example, here's how to deploy a single file to a remote host (any host you connect to must be listed in your *knownhosts* file unless you specifically set the trust attribute to yes or true):

```
<scp file="Project.jar"
    todir="user:password@antmegacorp.com:/home/steven/cgi-bin"/>
```

You can use the password attribute explicitly to set the password:

```
<scp file="Project.jar"
    todir="user@antmegacorp.com:/home/steven/cgi-bin""
    password="password"/>
```

Here's how to copy a remote file to a local machine:

```
<scp file="user:password@antmegacorp.com:/home/steven/cgi-bin/Project.jar"
    todir="${archive}"/>
```

Here's how to copy a set of files using a fileset:

```
<scp todir="user:password@antmegacorp.com:/home/steven/source">
    <fileset dir="${src}">
        <include name="**/*.java"/>
    </fileset>
</scp>
```

Example 8-3 gives a complete example build file using the scp task for deployment. (It uses the remote machine's IP address instead of naming the remote server.)

Example 8-3. Using scp (ch08/scp/build.xml)

```
<?xml version="1.0" ?>
<project default="main">

    <property name="message" value="Deploying the .jar file." />
    <property name="src" location="source" />
    <property name="output" location="bin" />

    <target name="main" depends="init, compile, compress, deploy">
        <echo>
            ${message}
        </echo>
    </target>

    <target name="init">
        <mkdir dir="${output}" />
    </target>
```

Example 8-3. Using scp (ch08/scp/build.xml) (continued)

```
<target name="compile">
    <javac srcdir="${src}" destdir="${output}" />
</target>

<target name="compress">
    <jar destfile="${output}/Project.jar" basedir="${output}">
        <include name="*.class"/>
        <include name="*.txt"/>
    </jar>
</target>

<target name="deploy">
    <scp trust="true"
        file="${output}/Project.jar"
        todir="user:password@000.000.000.000:cgi-bin"/>
</target>

</project>
```

Here's what that build file output looks like when run on a Windows machine:

```
%ant
Buildfile: build.xml

init:
    [mkdir] Created dir: C:\ant\ch08\scp\bin

compile:
    [javac] Compiling 1 source file to C:\ant\ch08\scp\bin

compress:
      [jar] Building jar: C:\ant\ch08\scp\bin\Project.jar

deploy:
      [scp] Connecting to 000.000.000.000
      [scp] Sending: Project.jar : 664
      [scp] File transfer time: 1.32 Average Rate: 9502.27 B/s
      [scp] done.

main:
     [echo]
     [echo]                 Deploying the .jar file.
     [echo]

BUILD SUCCESSFUL
Total time: 12 seconds
```

As discussed in Chapter 4, hardcoding passwords and/or usernames in a build file is a bad idea. It's better to use properties like this:

```
<scp todir="${username}:${password}@antmegacorp.com:/home/
steven/source" ...>
```

Pass the username and password to Ant like this:

```
ant -Dusername=steven -Dpassword=opensesame
```

Unix file permissions are not retained when files are copied with the scp task (they get UMASK permissions). If you want to retain Unix permissions, execute the Unix scp command instead (i.e., <exec executable="scp" ... >).

The attributes of this task appear in Table 8-3.

Table 8-3. The scp task's attributes

Attribute	Description	Required	Default
failonerror	Specifies whether you want to stop the build if the task encounters an error.	No	true
file	Specifies the file you want to transfer. You can give a local path or a remote path of the form *user[:password]@host:/directory/path*.	Yes, unless a nested fileset element is used	
keyfile	Specifies the location of a file holding the private key you want to use.	Yes, if you are using key-based authentication	
knownhosts	Specifies the known hosts file, which can be used to validate remote hosts.	No	${user.home}/.ssh/known_hosts.
passphrase	Specifies the passphrase for your private key.	Yes, if you are using key-based authentication	
password	Specifies the password you want to use for logging in.	No, if you are using key-based authentication or the password has been given in the file or todir attribute	
port	Specifies the port you want to connect to on the remote host.	No	22

Table 8-3. The scp task's attributes (continued)

Attribute	Description	Required	Default
todir	Specifies the directory you want to copy to. This can be a local path or a remote path of the form *user[:password]@host:/directory/path*.	Yes	
trust	Specifies you want to trust all unknown hosts if set to yes/true. If set to false (the default), the host you connect to must be listed in your *knownhosts* file.	No	no

You can use `fileset` elements to select sets of files to copy; if you use a fileset, you must assign a value to the `todir` attribute. (The `fileset` element works only when you're copying files from the local machine to a remote machine.)

Deploying to Tomcat

Tomcat (available from *http://jakarta.apache.org/tomcat/*), the reference web server for servlets and JSP, has become more attractive to Ant developers since it comes with custom Ant tasks for deployment. Copy the file *server/lib/catalina-ant.jar* from your Tomcat 5 installation into the *lib* directory of your Ant installation to use these tasks.

The Tomcat deployment tasks are `deploy`, `reload`, and `undeploy`; to use them, add these `taskdef` elements (discussed in Chapter 11) to your build file:

```
<taskdef name="deploy" classname="org.apache.catalina.ant.DeployTask"/>
<taskdef name="reload" classname="org.apache.catalina.ant.ReloadTask"/>
<taskdef name="undeploy" classname="org.apache.catalina.ant.UndeployTask"/>
```

To use these tasks, you'll need manager privileges with Tomcat; edit *conf/tomcat-users.xml* to add manager privileges for a username (admin here) and password such as:

```
<?xml version='1.0' encoding='utf-8'?>
<tomcat-users>
  <role rolename="manager"/>
  <role rolename="role1"/>
  <role rolename="tomcat"/>
  <user username="admin" password="password" roles="manager"/>
  <user username="role1" password="tomcat" roles="role1"/>
  <user username="tomcat" password="tomcat" roles="tomcat"/>
  <user username="both" password="tomcat" roles="tomcat,role1"/>
</tomcat-users>
```

You can use the deploy task to deploy a web application to Tomcat from Ant like this:

```
<target name="install">

    <deploy url="${manager.url}"
        username="${manager.username}"
        password="${manager.password}"
        path="${app.path}"
        localWar="file://${build}"/>

</target>
```

Here, manager.url is the URL of the Tomcat manager servlet. The default name for this servlet is "manager," so this is something like *http://localhost:8080/manager*. The app.path property holds the context path at which this application should be deployed (usually / plus the name of the application as you want to use it in the URL to access the application online). The build property holds the location at which you build the web application as it should be installed in the Tomcat webapps directory.

If you have installed an application and want Tomcat to recognize you have updated Java classes, use the reload task instead:

```
<target name="reload">

    <reload url="${manager.url}"
        username="${manager.username}"
        password="${manager.password}"
        path="${app.path}"/>

</target>
```

To remove a web application, use the undeploy task:

```
<target name="remove">

    <undeploy url="${manager.url}"
        username="${manager.username}"
        password="${manager.password}"
        path="${app.path}"/>

</target>
```

More often than not, you won't be developing your applications on the same server you want to deploy to. You can deploy to a Tomcat installation running on a remote server by contacting the Tomcat manager servlet via URL in a browser. To do that in Ant you use the get task, which gets a file when you pass it a URL. If you're using Java 1.4 or later, this task supports any URL schema, including *http:*, *ftp:*, *jar:*, and *https:*. This task is great if you want to download online content, or, as in this case, issue commands via URLs to online code.

Before getting to deployment, here's an example that uses get to retrieve the Ant home page and stores it in *ant.html*:

```
<get src="http://ant.apache.org/" dest="ant.html"/>
```

You can upload web applications to Tomcat using the manager servlet, passing the local location of the web application to upload. For example, to upload a web application from *C:/ant/ch08/app* in Windows, you'd use this location:

```
file:////C:\ant\ch08\app/
```

To upload a *.war* file, you add an ! at the end of the location to indicate you're uploading a file, not the contents of a directory, like this in Unix:

```
jar:file://///ant/ch08/app.war!/
```

Example 8-3 shows how this works in practice. In this case, the build file deploys a web application from *C:\ant\deploy\app* that consists of a servlet (org.antbook.ch08.Deploy) that displays the message "Project Deployment!" to Tomcat. Here's the URL you pass to the get task to tell the Tomcat manager servlet what you want to do:

```
http://localhost:8080/manager/deploy?path=/deployment&amp;war=file:////c:\ant\deploy\
app/
```

You can see this at work in Example 8-4.

Example 8-4. Deploying with get (ch08/get/build.xml)

```
<?xml version="1.0" encoding="UTF-8" ?>

<project default="main" basedir=".">

  <property name="tomcat.port" value="8080" />
  <property name="tomcat.username" value="admin" />
  <property name="tomcat.password" value="password" />

  <target name="main" >
    <get src="http://localhost:8080/manager/deploy?path=/deployment&amp;war=file:////c:\
ant\deploy\app/"
      dest="deploy.txt"
      username="${tomcat.username}"
      password="${tomcat.password}" />

  </target>

</project>
```

Here's what the build file looks like in action:

```
%ant
Buildfile: build.xml

main:
     [get] Getting: http://localhost:8080/manager/deploy?path=/deployment&war=
file:////c:\ant\ch08\get\app/
```

```
BUILD SUCCESSFUL
Total time: 1 second
```

Here's what Tomcat wrote to the output file, *deploy.txt*:

```
OK - Deployed application at context path /deployment
```

After deployment, navigating to *http://localhost:8080/deployment/org.antbook.ch08. Deploy* shows the deployed servlet, as seen in Figure 8-1.

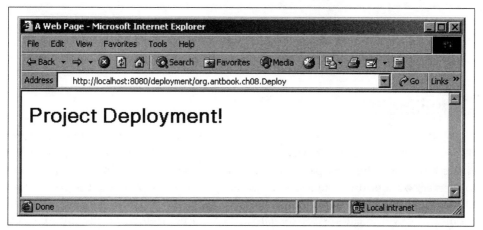

Figure 8-1. Deploying to Tomcat

 For more information on using the Tomcat manager servlet, see *manager/html-manager-howto.html* in your Tomcat installation.

The attributes of the get task appear in Table 8-4.

Table 8-4. The get task's attributes

Attribute	Description	Required	Default
dest	Specifies the file where you want to store the retrieved data.	Yes	
ignoreerrors	Specifies you want to only log errors instead of treating them as fatal.	No	false
password	Specifies the password to use when connecting.	Yes, if username is set	
src	Specifies the URL where the data you want is.	Yes	
username	Specifies the username for BASIC HTTP authentication.	Yes, if password is set	

Table 8-4. The get task's attributes (continued)

Attribute	Description	Required	Default
usetimestamp	Specifies you want to download a file only after checking the timestamp of the local copy to ensure you don't overwrite a more recent version.	No	false
verbose	Specifies you want to see full information as this task executes. Set to true/false.	No	false

 When the verbose option is on, this task will display a dot (.) for every 100 KB received.

Compiling JSPs

When deploying to servers, the jspc task can be useful. This task runs the JavaServer Pages compiler and turns JSP pages into Java source, which you can compile with the javac task. Compiling JSP pages supports fast invocation of JSP pages, deployment on servers without the complete JDK, or lets you check the syntax of pages without deploying them. By default, this task uses the Jasper JSP compiler, which comes with Tomcat. Copy Tomcat's *jasper-compiler.jar* and *jasper-runtime.jar* files into the Ant *lib* directory to use this task. You'll need *servlet.jar*, which comes with Tomcat, in the Ant *lib* directory.

For example, say you have this JSP page, *greeting.jsp*:

```
<HTML>
  <HEAD>
    <TITLE>Creating a Greeting</TITLE>
  </HEAD>

  <BODY>
    <H1>Creating a Greeting</H1>
    <%
        out.println("Hello from JSP!");    //Display the greeting
    %>
  </BODY>
</HTML>
```

Example 8-5 shows how to compile this JSP into *greeting.java*.

Example 8-5. Compiling JSP pages (ch08/jspc/build.xml)

```
<?xml version="1.0" ?>
<project default="main">

    <property name="message" value="Compiling the JSP...." />
    <property name="src" location="source" />
    <property name="output" location="bin" />
```

Example 8-5. Compiling JSP pages (ch08/jspc/build.xml) (continued)

```
<target name="main" depends="init, compile">
    <echo>
        ${message}
    </echo>
</target>

<target name="init">
    <mkdir dir="${output}" />
</target>

<target name="compile">
    <jspc srcdir="${src}"
        destdir="${output}"
        package="org.antbook.jsp"
        verbose="9">
        <include name="**/*.jsp" />
    </jspc>
</target>

</project>
```

Here's what you see when you run the build file:

```
%ant
Buildfile: build.xml

init:

compile:
     [jspc] Compiling 1 source file to
     /home/steven/ant/ch08/jspc/bin/org/antbook/jsp
  [jasperc] 2004-06-30 02:20:09 - Class name is: greeting
  [jasperc] 2004-06-30 02:20:09 - Java filename is:
     /home/steven/ant/ch08/jspc/bin/org/antbook/jsp/greeting.java
  [jasperc] 2004-06-30 02:20:09 - Accepted
    org.apache.jasper.compiler.Parser$Scriptlet at /greeting.jsp(7,4)
  [jasperc] 2004-06-30 02:20:09 - Compiling with: -encoding UTF8

main:
     [echo]
     [echo]                 Compiling the JSP....
     [echo]

BUILD SUCCESSFUL
Total time: 3 seconds
```

And this is what the resulting Java code, *greeting.java*, looks like:

```
package org.antbook.jsp.;

import javax.servlet.*;
import javax.servlet.http.*;
import javax.servlet.jsp.*;
import org.apache.jasper.runtime.*;
```

```java
public class greeting extends HttpJspBase {

    static {
    }
    public greeting( ) {
    }

    private static boolean _jspx_inited = false;

    public final void _jspx_init() throws org.apache.jasper.runtime.JspException {
    }

    public void _jspService(HttpServletRequest request, HttpServletResponse
        response)
        throws java.io.IOException, ServletException {

        JspFactory _jspxFactory = null;
        PageContext pageContext = null;
        HttpSession session = null;
        .
        .
        .
        out.println("Hello from JSP!");     //Display the greeting
        .
        .
        .

    }
}
```

Here's another example, which compiles JSP pages, checks the dependencies, and uses the javac task to create the actual bytecode for this JSP:

```xml
<jspc
    destdir="temp"
    srcdir="${src}"
    package="org.antbook.ch08">
    <include name="**/*.jsp" />
</jspc>

<depend
    srcdir="temp"
    destdir="${bin}"
    classpath="lib/app.jar"/>

<javac
    srcdir="temp"
    destdir="${bin}"
    classpath="lib/app.jar" />
```

You can see the attributes of the jspc task in Table 8-5.

Table 8-5. The jspc task's attributes

Attribute	Description	Required	Default
classpath	Specifies the classpath to use when you're running the JSP compiler. You can specify this by nested classpath elements.	No	
classpathref	Specifies the classpath to use when you're running the JSP compiler, by reference.	No	
compiler	Specifies the classname of a JSP compiler, such as jasper or jasper42.	No	jasper
compilerclasspath	Specifies the classpath that should be used to find the compiler specified by the compiler attribute.	No	
destdir	Specifies where you want to place the compiled files.	Yes	
failonerror	Specifies if the task to fail if it encounters an error.	No	yes
ieplugin	Specifies the Java Plugin class ID for Internet Explorer.	No	
mapped	Specifies you want to generate separate write statements for each HTML line in the JSP. Set to true/false.	No	
package	Specifies the name of the destination package for the generated compiled classes.	No	
srcdir	Specifies where you want the task to look for source JSP files.	Yes	
uribase	Specifies the base URI for relative URI references in JSP pages.	No	
uriroot	Sets the root directory from which URIs should be resolved.	No	
verbose	Specifies you want full (verbose) output. Set to an integer value (0–9).	No	0
webinc	Specifies the filename for the section of *web.xml* that details any servlets.	No	
webxml	Specifies the filename for the generated *web.xml*-type file.	No	

The jspc task is a directory-based task, so the JSP files to be compiled are located the same way as the javac task locates files, which means you can use nested elements, such as includes and excludes. You can use nested classpath and classpathref elements, as well as nested webapp elements. The webapp element, unique to the jspc task, instructs the JSP compiler to build an entire web application. The one attribute of the webapp element is the basedir attribute, which sets the base directory of the application. The base directory must have a *WEB-INF* subdirectory beneath it. If you use this element, the task uses the compiler for all dependency checking. Here's an example using webapp:

```
<jspc
    package="org.antbook.ch08">
    <include name="**/*.jsp" />
    <webapp basedir="${ch08}" />
</jspc>
```

Deploying to EJB Containers

Fundamentally, deploying to Enterprise JavaBean (EJB) application servers is similar to other Ant deployment projects you've seen. You can use the tasks covered to package and deploy EJB applications. For example, you can see a build file developed for the JBoss server in Example 8-6; this build file first creates a *.war* file and then packages it into an *.ear* file for deployment.

Example 8-6. A Jboss EJB build (ch08/ejb/build.xml)

```xml
<?xml version="1.0" ?>
<project default="main" basedir=".">

    <target name="main" depends="init, compile, war, ear"/>

    <target name="init">
        <property name="src" value="${basedir}/src"/>
        <property name="bin" value="${basedir}/output"/>
        <property name="web" value="${basedir}/web"/>
        <property name="descriptors"
            value="${basedir}/output/deploymentdescriptors"/>
        <property name="eardir" value="${basedir}/output/ear"/>
        <property name="wardir" value="${basedir}/output/war"/>
        <property name="warfile" value="app.war"/>
        <property name="earfile" value="app.ear"/>

        <mkdir dir="${wardir}/WEB-INF"/>
        <mkdir dir="${wardir}/WEB-INF/classes"/>
        <mkdir dir="${eardir}/META-INF"/>
    </target>

    <target name="compile">
        <javac destdir="${bin}" srcdir="${src}" includes="**/*.java" />
    </target>

    <target name="war">
        <copy todir="${wardir}">
            <fileset dir="${web}" includes="**/*.*" />
        </copy>

        <copy file="${descriptors}/web.xml" todir="${wardir}/WEB-INF" />

        <copy todir="${wardir}/WEB-INF/classes">
            <fileset dir="${bin}" includes="**/*.class" />
        </copy>

        <jar jarfile="${eardir}/${warfile}" basedir="${wardir}" />
    </target>

    <target name="ear">
        <copy file="${descriptors}/application.xml" todir="${eardir}/META-INF" />
```

Example 8-6. A Jboss EJB build (ch08/ejb/build.xml) (continued)

```
        <jar jarfile="${basedir}/${earfile}" basedir="${eardir}" />
    </target>

</project>
```

That's all it takes. Though this build file gets the job done using standard Ant tasks, tasks built into Ant make it easier to work with EJB applications, starting with the ear task.

Creating EAR Files

The ear task is handy for creating *.ear* files and makes special provisions for the *application.xml* file needed in most EARs. It's not mandatory to use this task to create a *.ear* file, but it can make life easier. You can see the attributes of this task in Table 8-6.

 The ear task is an extension of the Jar task with special treatment for *application.xml*. You can perform the same operation by using the prefix and fullpath attributes of zipfilesets in a zip or jar task.

Table 8-6. The ear task's attributes

Attribute	Description	Required	Default
appxml	Specifies the deployment descriptor you want to use, such as *application.xml*.	Yes, unless update is set to true.	
basedir	Specifies the directory from which to get the files.	No	
compress	Indicates you want to not only store data but compress it.	No	true
defaultexcludes	Specifies if you want to use default excludes or not. Set to yes/no.	No	Default excludes are used.
destfile	Specifies the EAR file you want to create.	Yes	
duplicate	Specifies what to do if a duplicate file is found. Valid values are add, preserve, and fail.	No	add
encoding	Specifies the character encoding to use for filenames in the EAR file.	No	UTF8
excludes	Specifies the patterns matching files to exclude, as a comma- or space-separated list.	No	
excludesfile	Specifies the name of a file where each line is a pattern matching files to exclude.	No	
filesonly	Specifies you want to store only file entries.	No	false
includes	Specifies the patterns matching files to include, as a comma- or space-separated list.	No	
includesfile	Specifies the name of a file where each line is a pattern matching files to include.	No	

Table 8-6. The ear task's attributes (continued)

Attribute	Description	Required	Default
keepcompression	Preserves the compression as it has been in archives you're compressing instead of using the compress attribute. Available since Ant 1.6.	No	
manifest	Specifies the manifest file to use in the compressed file.	No	
update	Specifies whether you want to update or overwrite the target file if it exists.	No	false

The extended `zipfileset` element from the zip task, which supports the attributes prefix, fullpath, and src, is available in the ear task. The nested `metainf` element specifies a fileset; all files included in this fileset will end up in the META-INF directory of the .ear file.

This task lets you specify where to get *application.xml* from, using the appxml attribute. Here's an example that creates an .ear file:

```
<ear destfile="${output}/app.ear" appxml="${src}/application.xml">
    <fileset dir="${wardir}" includes="*.war"/>
</ear>
```

Supporting Hot Deployment

The serverdeploy task is designed to support hot deployment (where you don't have to take the server down before deploying) to EJB-aware servers. You set the action attribute to values you've seen, such as those used for the Tomcat manager servlet: deploy, delete, and undeploy.

 You'll need vendor-specific deployment software to make this one work. Ant provides the build-end, but your server will need to provide a deployment facility that Ant can connect and interact with.

As of this writing, this task only supports WebLogic servers and the JOnAS 2.4 Open Source EJB server, but support for other EJB containers should be added soon. This task has only two attributes, which appear in Table 8-7, and requires some nested elements.

Table 8-7. The serverdeploy task's attributes

Attribute	Description	Required
action	Specifies the action you want to perform, such as deploy, delete, list, undeploy, or update.	Yes
source	Specifies the path and filename of the component you want to deploy. This may be an .ear, .jar, .war, or other file type supported by the server.	Depends on the server

The serverdeploy task supports a nested classpath element to set the classpath. It supports the vendor-specific generic, jonas, and weblogic nested elements.

The generic element

This is the element you use for generic Java-based deployment if you've got deployment code—a Java class—supplied by the server's vendor. If there's a vendor-specific element for serverdeploy, use that, of course, but if not, try the generic element. The attributes of this element appear in Table 8-8.

Table 8-8. The generic element's attributes

Attribute	Description	Required
classname	Specifies the classname of the deployment tool you want to run.	Yes
classpath	Specifies the classpath you want the JVM running the tool to use. May be supplied as a nested element.	Depends on the server
password	Specifies the password you want to use on the server.	Depends on the server
server	Specifies the URL of the server to use.	Depends on the server
username	Specifies the username to log in with.	Depends on the server

The generic element supports nested arg and jvmarg elements. Here's an example using the generic element for deployment that assumes the deployment tool for the target web server is org.steven.j2ee.config.Deploy:

```
<serverdeploy action="deploy" source="${eardir}/app.ear">
    <generic classname="org.steven.j2ee.config.Deploy"
        classpath="${classpath}"
        username="${user.name}"
        password="${user.password}">
        <arg value="-install"/>
        <jvmarg value="-mx512m"/>
    </generic>
</serverdeploy>
```

The weblogic element

The weblogic element is designed to run the weblogic.deploy deployment tool; legal actions for this tool are deploy, undeploy, list, update, and delete. The attributes for this element appear in Table 8-9.

Table 8-9. The weblogic element's attributes

Attribute	Description	Required	Default
application	Specifies the name of the application you want to deploy.	Yes	
classpath	Specifies the classname of the deployment tool you want to run.	No	

Table 8-9. The weblogic element's attributes (continued)

Attribute	Description	Required	Default
component	Specifies the string for deployment targets, of the form: `<component>:<target1>,<target2>.....` In this case, component is the archive name (without a file extension).	No	
debug	Specifies if you want debug information to be displayed during deployment.	No	
password	Specifies the password you want to use on the server.	Yes	
server	Specifies the URL of the server to use.	No	
username	Specifies the username to log in with.	No	`system`

Here's an example using this element inside a serverdeploy element to deploy to a WebLogic server:

```
<serverdeploy action="deploy"
    source="${eardir}/app.ear">
    <weblogic application="app"
        server="ff19://server:7001"
        classpath="${weblogic.home}/lib/weblogic.jar"
        username="${user.name}"
        password="${user.password}"
        component="appserver,productionserver" />
</serverdeploy>
```

The jonas element

The jonas element supports deployment to JOnAS (Java Open Applicaton Server) servers. Valid actions for the JOnAS deployment tool (org.objectweb.jonas.adm. JonasAdmin) are deploy, undeploy, list, and update. The attributes of this element appear in Table 8-10.

Table 8-10. The jonas element's attributes

Attribute	Description	Required	Default
jonasroot	Specifies the root directory for the server.	Yes	
orb	Specifies the orb, such as RMI, JEREMIE, DAVID, and so on. If the orb is DAVID (RMI/IIOP), specifies the davidhost and davidport attributes.	No	The ORB present in the classpath
davidhost	Specifies the value for the property `david.CosNaming.default_host`.	No	
davidport	Specifies the value for the property `david.CosNaming.default_port`.	No	

Table 8-10. The jonas element's attributes (continued)

Attribute	Description	Required	Default
classname	Specifies the classname of the deployment tool you want to run.	No	org.objectweb.jonas.adm.JonasAdmin
classpath	Specifies the classpath you want the JVM running the tool to use. May be supplied as a nested element.	No	
server	Specifies the URL of the server to use.	Yes	

 If you want to build in delay times to take into account delays in getting responses from a server, use the Ant waitfor task. You can use the sleep task for this purpose.

The jonas element supports nested classpath, arg, and jvmarg elements. Here's an example using serverdeploy to deploy to a JOnAS server:

```
<serverdeploy action="deploy" source="${eardir}/app.jar">
    <jonas server="JOnAS5" jonasroot="${jonas.root}">
        <classpath>
            <pathelement path="${jonas.root}/lib/RMI_jonas.jar"/>
        </classpath>
    </jonas>
</serverdeploy>
```

CHAPTER 9

XML and XDoclet

XML support is built into Ant, and not only as far as build files go. You can validate XML documents using XML DTDs and schemas using the xmlvalidate task. You can read properties from an XML document using xmlproperty. You can use the xslt/style task to transform XML documents using XSLT. And you can use the antstructure task to generate an XML DTD for all the tasks Ant knows about.

Besides covering these and other XML tasks, I'm going to discuss XDoclet in this chapter. XDoclet is an open source code generation engine that is designed to run in Ant. Using codes that you embed in Java source code, XDoclet can generate code, deployment descriptors such as *web.xml*, and other artifacts for web and EJB applications.

I'll also round out the discussion of EJB from the previous chapter by discussing the Ant EJB tasks, a specially designed set of optional tasks for developing Enterprise JavaBeans (EJBs).

Validating XML Documents

You use the xmlvalidate task to validate XML documents with Document Type Definitions (DTDs) or XML schema. Your build process may involve generating XML documents, and it can be worthwhile to test those documents for validity before deploying them (for example, see the section on XDoclet in this chapter. You typically use XDoclet to generate XML documents for deploying web applications, such as *web.xml*, *application.xml*, and so on). By default, this task uses the SAX2 parser implementation provided by Sun's JAXP (*http://java.sun.com/xml/jaxp/index.jsp*). The attributes of this task appear in Table 9-1.

Table 9-1. The xmlvalidate task's attributes

Attribute	Description	Required	Default
classname	Specifies the XML parser you want to use.	No	
classpathref	Specifies where to find the XML parser class. Note that you can also use a nested classpath element.	No	

Table 9-1. The xmlvalidate task's attributes (continued)

Attribute	Description	Required	Default
failonerror	Specifies you want this task to fail if it encounters an error.	No	true
file	Specifies the file or files you want to validate. You can use a nested fileset.	No	
lenient	Check only if the XML document is well-formed if true.	No	
warn	Specifies the parser should log warn messages.	No	

This task can contain nested dtd elements, which specify locations for DTD resolution. The attributes of the dtd element appear in Table 9-2.

Table 9-2. The dtd element's attributes

Attribute	Description	Required
location	Specifies the location of the DTD you want to use. Set this to a file, a resource, or a URL.	Yes
publicId	Specifies the public ID of the DTD to resolve.	Yes

You can use nested xmlcatalog elements; an XMLCatalog is a catalog of public resources, such as DTDs or entities, that are referenced in an XML document. The attributes of this element appear in Table 9-3.

Table 9-3. The xmlcatalog element's attributes

Attribute	Description	Required
id	Specifies a unique ID for an XMLCatalog. This ID can be used to reference the XMLCatalog from another XMLCatalog.	No
refid	Specifies the ID of another XMLCatalog whose contents are used in this XMLCatalog.	No

The xmlcatalog element can contain nested dtd, classpath, and catalogpath elements; the catalogpath element is an Ant path-like element, which, as you know, means it can contain nested fileset elements, pathelement elements, and so on.

The xmlvalidate element can contain nested attribute elements, which set SAX Parser features as defined at *http://xml.org/sax/features/*. The attributes of this element appear in Table 9-4.

Table 9-4. The attribute element's attributes

Attribute	Description	Required
name	Specifies the name of the feature to set	Yes
value	Specifies the boolean setting of the feature	Yes

Validating with XML Schema

It's easy enough to use the `xmlvalidate` task to validate XML documents with schema, as shown in Example 9-1, which validates *document.xml*. This example turns on schema validation by setting the parser attribute identified by the URI *http://apache.org/xml/features/validation/schema* to true.

Example 9-1. Valiating with a schema (ch09/schemat/build.xml)

```xml
<?xml version="1.0" encoding="UTF-8" ?>

<project default="main" >

    <target name="main">
        <xmlvalidate
            lenient="no"
            warn="yes"
            file="document.xml"
            classname="org.apache.xerces.parsers.SAXParser">
            <attribute name="http://apache.org/xml/features/validation/schema"
                value="true" />
        </xmlvalidate>
    </target>

</project>
```

Here's *document.xml*, the document to validate, which uses the `xsi:noNamespace SchemaLocation` attribute to specify the name of the schema document, *document.xsd*:

```xml
<?xml version="1.0" encoding="UTF-8" ?>
<document xsi:noNamespaceSchemaLocation="document.xsd"
    xmlns="" xmlns:xsi="http://www.w3.org/2001/XMLSchema-instance" >
    <hello />
</document>
```

Here's the schema, *document.xsd*:

```xml
<?xml version="1.0" encoding="UTF-8" ?>
<xs:schema xmlns:xs="http://www.w3.org/2001/XMLSchema"
    xmlns="" elementFormDefault="qualified" >
    <xs:element name="document">
        <xs:complexType mixed="false">
            <xs:sequence>
                <xs:element name="hello" type="xs:string" />
            </xs:sequence>
        </xs:complexType>
    </xs:element>
</xs:schema>
```

Finally, here's what you see when you execute this build file, showing that the document was successfully validated:

```
%ant
Buildfile: build.xml
```

```
main:
[xmlvalidate] 1 file(s) have been successfully validated.

BUILD SUCCESSFUL
Total time: 1 second
```

Here's what you'd see if there was an error; for example, if "document" had been mispelled "documnt" in the schema:

```
%ant
Buildfile: build.xml

main:
[xmlvalidate] document.xml:4:60: cvc-elt.1 Cannot find the declaration of 'document'.

BUILD FAILED
document.xml is not a valid XML document.
Total time: 1 second
```

Validating with DTDs

Validating documents using DTDs is as easy, as you can see in Example 9-2, which validates a document, *document.xml*, with a DTD.

Example 9-2. Valiating with a DTD ch09/DTD/build.xml

```xml
<?xml version="1.0" encoding="UTF-8" ?>

<project default="main" >

    <target name="main">
        <xmlvalidate
            lenient="no"
            warn="yes"
            file="document.xml"
            classname="org.apache.xerces.parsers.SAXParser">
        </xmlvalidate>
    </target>

</project>
```

Here's the document with a DTD, *document.xml*, to validate:

```xml
<?xml version = "1.0" standalone="yes"?>
<!DOCTYPE document [
<!ELEMENT document (employee)*>
<!ELEMENT employee (name, hiredate, projects)>
<!ELEMENT name (lastname, firstname)>
<!ELEMENT lastname (#PCDATA)>
<!ELEMENT firstname (#PCDATA)>
<!ELEMENT hiredate (#PCDATA)>
<!ELEMENT projects (project)*>
<!ELEMENT project (product,id,price)>
<!ELEMENT product (#PCDATA)>
```

```
<!ELEMENT id (#PCDATA)>
<!ELEMENT price (#PCDATA)>
]>
<document>
    <employee>
        <name>
            <lastname>Kelly</lastname>
            <firstname>Grace</firstname>
        </name>
        <hiredate>October 15, 2005</hiredate>
        <projects>
            <project>
                <product>Printer</product>
                <id>111</id>
                <price>$111.00</price>
            </project>
            <project>
                <product>Laptop</product>
                <id>222</id>
                <price>$989.00</price>
            </project>
        </projects>
    </employee>
    <employee>
        <name>
            <lastname>Grant</lastname>
            <firstname>Cary</firstname>
        </name>
        <hiredate>October 20, 2005</hiredate>
        <projects>
            <project>
                <product>Desktop</product>
                <id>333</id>
                <price>$2995.00</price>
            </project>
            <project>
                <product>Scanner</product>
                <id>444</id>
                <price>$200.00</price>
            </project>
        </projects>
    </employee>
    <employee>
        <name>
            <lastname>Gable</lastname>
            <firstname>Clark</firstname>
        </name>
        <hiredate>October 25, 2005</hiredate>
        <projects>
            <project>
                <product>Keyboard</product>
                <id>555</id>
                <price>$129.00</price>
            </project>
```

```
        <project>
            <product>Mouse</product>
            <id>666</id>
            <price>$25.00</price>
        </project>
    </projects>
</employee>
</document>
```

And here are the results:

```
%ant
Buildfile: build.xml

main:
[xmlvalidate] 1 file(s) have been successfully validated.

BUILD SUCCESSFUL
Total time: 0 seconds
```

Loading Properties from XML Files

The xmlproperty task loads property values from a well-formed XML file. The way you structure the XML document determines the names of the properties it creates.

Say you have this XML document, *properties.xml*, that defines a property named name1, and two nested properties, firstName and lastName, creating the properties name1.firstName and name1.lastName:

```
<name1 language="english">
    <firstName language="german">Stefan</firstName>
    <lastName>Edwards</lastName>
</name1>
```

You can load these properties into a build with the xmlproperty task, as shown in Example 9-3. This build file displays the values of the properties created by *properties.xml*, name1.firstName, and name1.lastName. This example defines attributes for the name1 and firstName properties, creating an attribute named language which can be accessed as name1(language) and as name1.firstName(language). The build file displays the values of these properties.

Example 9-3. Loading XML properties (ch09/xmlproperty/build.xml)

```
<?xml version="1.0" ?>
<project default="main">

    <xmlproperty file="properties.xml" />

    <target name="main">
        <echo>
            ${name1(language)}
            ${name1.firstName}
```

```
            ${name1.firstName(language)}
            ${name1.lastName}
        </echo>
    </target>

</project>
```

Here's what the build file displays when run:

```
%ant
Buildfile: build.xml

main:
    [echo]
    [echo]          english
    [echo]          Stefan
    [echo]          german
    [echo]          Edward
    [echo]


BUILD SUCCESSFUL
Total time: 0 seconds
```

The attributes of this task appear in Table 9-5.

Table 9-5. The xmlproperty task's attributes

Attribute	Description	Required	Default
collapseAttributes	Specifies you want to treat attributes as nested elements	No	false
file	Specifies the XML file you want to parse for properties	Yes	
includeSemanticAttribute	Specifies you want to include the semantic attribute name as part of the property name	No	false
keepRoot	Specifies you want to make the XML root tag the first value in the property name	No	true
prefix	Specifies the prefix to prepend to each property automatically	No	
rootDirectory	Specifies the root directory to search for files	No	${basedir}
semanticAttributes	Specifies you want to use semantic handling of attribute names	No	false
validate	Specifies you want to validate the input file	No	false

Creating Ant Task DTDs

The Ant documentation is useful but at times hard to use if you're looking for the definitions of nested tasks and elements, because they're not listed at the top level. On the other hand, if you can read a DTD and want to know how any Ant task or element is defined, use the `antstructure` task. This task will create a DTD for all Ant tasks that Ant knows about, including optional tasks, with their attributes and nested elements. This task only has one attribute, `output`, which specifies the output file to hold the DTD.

Example 9-4 shows how to use this task, storing the DTD for all Ant tasks in *project.dtd*.

Example 9-4. Using the antstructure task (ch09/antstructure/build.xml)

```xml
<?xml version="1.0" ?>
<project default="main">

    <target name="main">
        <antstructure output="project.dtd"/>
    </target>

</project>
```

Here's part of the DTD, *project.dtd*, generated:

```
<!ELEMENT project (target | %tasks; | %types;)*>
<!ATTLIST project
        name    CDATA #IMPLIED
        default CDATA #IMPLIED
        basedir CDATA #IMPLIED>

<!ELEMENT target (%tasks; | %types;)*>

<!ATTLIST target
        id          ID    #IMPLIED
        name        CDATA #REQUIRED
        if          CDATA #IMPLIED
        unless      CDATA #IMPLIED
        depends     CDATA #IMPLIED
        description CDATA #IMPLIED>

<!ELEMENT patternset (include | patternset | exclude | excludesfile | includesfile)*>
<!ATTLIST patternset
        id ID #IMPLIED
        includes CDATA #IMPLIED
        refid IDREF #IMPLIED
        description CDATA #IMPLIED
        excludesfile CDATA #IMPLIED
```

```
        includesfile CDATA #IMPLIED
        excludes CDATA #IMPLIED>
    .
    .
    .
```

Transforming XML Using XSLT

The xslt task, also called the style task (the two names are interchangeable in Ant), can process a set of documents via XSLT. This is handy for building nicely format- ted views of XML-based documentation in other formats like HTML, or for generat- ing code. How do you use this task to perform XSLT transformations? Example 9-5 shows a build file that puts it to work, transforming *style.xml* into *style.html*, using *style.xsl*.

Example 9-5. Using the xslt/style task ch09/xslt/build.xml

```
<?xml version="1.0" encoding="UTF-8" ?>

<project default="main" >

    <target name="main">
        <xslt basedir="." destdir="." extension=".html" includes="style.xml"
            style="style.xsl"/>
    </target>

</project>
```

Here's *style.xml*, the XML document to transform, which holds data about three U.S. states:

```
<?xml version="1.0" encoding ="UTF-8"?>
<states>

    <state>
        <name>California</name>
        <population units="people">33871648</population><!--2000 census-->
        <capital>Sacramento</capital>
        <bird>Quail</bird>
        <flower>Golden Poppy</flower>
        <area units="square miles">155959</area>
    </state>

    <state>
        <name>Massachusetts</name>
        <population units="people">6349097</population><!--2000 census-->
        <capital>Boston</capital>
        <bird>Chickadee</bird>
        <flower>Mayflower</flower>
        <area units="square miles">7840</area>
    </state>
```

```
<state>
    <name>New York</name>
    <population units="people">18976457</population><!--2000 census-->
    <capital>Albany</capital>
    <bird>Bluebird</bird>
    <flower>Rose</flower>
    <area units="square miles">47214</area>
</state>

</states>
```

In this example, the names of the states are extracted and used to create an HTML document with *style.xsl*:

```
<?xml version="1.0" encoding="UTF-8"?>
<xsl:stylesheet version="1.0" xmlns:xsl="http://www.w3.org/1999/XSL/Transform">

    <xsl:template match="states">
        <HTML>
            <BODY>
                <xsl:apply-templates/>
            </BODY>
        </HTML>
    </xsl:template>

    <xsl:template match="state">
        <P>
            <xsl:value-of select="name"/>
        </P>
    </xsl:template>

</xsl:stylesheet>
```

Here's the resulting HTML document:

```
<HTML>
    <BODY>

        <P>California</P>

        <P>Massachusetts</P>

        <P>New York</P>

    </BODY>
</HTML>
```

The attributes of this task appear in Table 9-6.

 If you are using JDK 1.4 or higher, this task doesn't require external libraries. If you're using an earlier JDK, you'll need Xalan from *http://xml.apache.org/xalan-j/index.html* (or another XSLT processor), and Ant's *optional.jar*.

Table 9-6. The xslt/style task's attributes

Attribute	Description	Required	Default
basedir	Specifies the directory to search for the source XML file.	No	${basedir}
classpath	Specifies the classpath to use when searching for the XSLT processor.	No	
classpathref	Specifies the classpath to use, given as a reference.	No	
defaultexcludes	Specifies if you want to use default excludes or not. Set to yes/no.	No	Default excludes are used.
destdir	Specifies the directory in which you want to store the results.	Yes, unless in and out have been specified	
excludes	Specifies the patterns matching files to exclude, as a comma- or space-separated list.	No	
excludesfile	Specifies the name of a file where each line is a pattern matching files to exclude.	No	
extension	Specifies the file extension to be used for the output files.	No	.html
force	Forces creation of the output files.	No	false
in	Specifies a single XML document to be transformed. This attribute should be used with the out attribute.	No	
includes	Specifies the patterns matching files to include, as a comma- or space-separated list.	No	
includesfile	Specifies the name of a file where each line is a pattern matching files to include.	No	
out	Specifies the output name for the transformed result (specified with the in attribute).	No	

Table 9-6. The xslt/style task's attributes (continued)

Attribute	Description	Required	Default
processor	Specifies the name of the XSLT processor to use. Possible values: `trax` for a TraX compliant processor, `xslp` for the XSL:P processor (note that this value has been deprecated, however), `xalan` for the Apache XML Xalan processor (Version 1; this value has been deprecated), or the name of an arbitrary XSLTLiaison class. The first one found in your class path is the one that is used.	No	Defaults to `trax`, followed by `xalan` and then `xslp` (in that order).
reloadstylesheet	Specifies if the transformer is freshly created for every transformation. Originally introduced to handle a bug in some Xalan-J versions.	No	`false`
scanincludeddirectories	Specifies you want to transform files found in any directories specified by the `include` patterns.	No	`true`
style	Specifies the name of the stylesheet to use for the transformation.	Yes	

This task forms an implicit fileset and so supports all attributes of `fileset` (`dir` becomes `basedir`) as well as the nested `include`, `exclude`, and `patternset` elements. You can use nested `classpath` elements to load the XSLT processor, nested `xmlcatalog` elements (see Table 9-3) for entity and URI resolution, and `attribute` elements (see Table 9-4) to specify settings of the processor factory (the attribute names and values are processor specific). The xslt/style task supports the use of nested `param` elements, whose attributes appear in Table 9-7, to pass values to `xsl:param` declarations in stylesheets.

Table 9-7. The param element's attributes

Attribute	Description	Required
name	Specifies the name of an XSLT parameter you want set	Yes
expression	Specifies the text value to be stored in the parameter	Yes
if	Specifies you want to pass the parameter only if this property is set	No
unless	Specifies you want to pass the parameter only if this property is not set	No

You can use outputproperty elements, whose attributes appear in Table 9-8, with a TraX processor to specify how the result tree should be output.

Table 9-8. *The outputproperty element's attributes*

Attribute	Description	Required
name	Specifies the name of the property to set	Yes
value	Specifies the new value of the property	Yes

TraX processors can accept factory elements to specify factory settings. These elements can contain one attribute, name, which specifies the fully qualified classname of the transformer factory to use.

Using XDoclet

XDoclet is an open source code generation engine designed for use with Ant, and you can pick it up for free at *http://xdoclet.sourceforge.net/*. It'll write code for you, especially deployment descriptors, and is often used for web and EJB development. XDoclet comes with a number of Ant tasks built-in, shown in Table 9-9.

Table 9-9. *The XDoclet Ant tasks*

Ant task	Does this
doclet	Specifies the base class for all XDoclet Ant tasks
ejbdoclet	Specifies which EJB-specific subtasks to execute
hibernatedoclet	Specifies which Hibernate subtasks to execute
jdodoclet	Specifies which JDO-specific subtasks to execute
jmxdoclet	Specifies which JMX-specific subtasks to execute
mockdoclet	Generates mock doclet objects
portletdoclet	Specifies which portlet-specific subtasks to execute
webdoclet	Specifies which web-specific subtasks to execute

XDoclet lets you generate code and deployment descriptors by embedding tags in your code, much like the tags you'd use for Javadoc. There are entire books written about XDoclet because it's an extensive tool. Though there's not room for that level of coverage here—this is a book about Ant, not XDoclet—I'll take a look at several examples creating web and EJB applications here, giving the XDoclet story from Ant's point of view.

Developing Applications

You use the XDoclet webdoclet task to develop web applications. The attributes of this task appear in Table 9-10, and the possible nested elements in Table 9-11.

Table 9-10. The webdoclet Ant tasks

Attribute	Description	Required
addedTags	Specifies you want to add JavaDoc tags to the generated classes	No
destDir	Specifies the destination directory for the generated output	Yes, if destDir is not specified by a subtask
excludedTags	Specifies tags that should not be automatically written to output files	No
force	Specifies you want generation of files to be forced	No
mergeDir	Specifies the directory where subtasks will look for files that they should merged with their generated files	No, but should be set if you want to use the merge feature
verbose	Specifies you want verbose feedback	No

Table 9-11. The webdoclet Ant task's nested elements

Element	Description
configParam	Specifies configuration parameters you want to use
deploymentdescriptor	Specifies you want to generate a *web.xml* deployment descriptor
fileset	Specifies a fileset to indicate the files to parse
jbosswebxml	Specifies you want to generate a *jboss-web.xml* deployment descriptor
jonaswebxml	Specifies you want to generate a web application deployment descriptor for JOnAS
jrunwebxml	Specifies you want to generate a *jrun-web.xml* deployment descriptor
jsptaglib	Specifies you want to generate a *taglib.tld* deployment descriptor for JSP taglibs
packageSubstitution	Substitutes a new package for the package in generated files
resin-web-xml	Specifies you want to generate *web.xml* with Resin extensions
strutsconfigxml	Specifies you want to generate a *struts-config.xml* deployment descriptor
strutsvalidationxml	Specifies you want to generate a Struts Validator *validation.xml* deployment descriptor
subTask	Specifies a subtask for this task
weblogicwebxml	Specifies you want to generate a *weblogic.xml* deployment descriptor for web applications
webspherewebxml	Specifies you want to generate WebSphere-specific deployment descriptors
webworkactiondocs	Specifies you want to generate HTML files containing descriptions of WebWork actions
webworkactionsxml	Specifies you want to generate an *actions.xml* file
webworkconfigproperties	Specifies you want to generate a *views.properties* file

You use tags prefixed with an @ to tell XDoclet what you want it to do. In Example 9-6, in this servlet's code, *ServletApp.java*, I'm telling Ant how to set up the deployment descriptor, *web.xml*.

Example 9-6. The servlet's code ch09/servlet/ServletApp.java

```
package app.web;

import java.io.*;
import javax.servlet.*;
import javax.servlet.http.*;

/**
 * @web.servlet
 *     display-name="Servlet App"
 *     load-on-startup="1"
 *     name="ServletApp"
 *
 * @web.servlet-init-param
 *     name="param1"
 *     value="value1"
 *
 * @web.servlet-init-param
 *     name="param2"
 *     value="value2"
 *
 * @web.servlet-mapping
 *     url-pattern="/app/*"
 *
 * @author Steve
 */

public class ServletApp extends HttpServlet
{
    public void doPost(HttpServletRequest request, HttpServletResponse response)
            throws IOException, ServletException
    {
        response.getWriter( ).println("No worries.");
    }
}
```

To use webdoclet from Ant, you have to use a taskdef task this way to set up the webdoclet task (See Chapter 12):

```
<taskdef
    name="webdoclet"
    classname="xdoclet.modules.web.WebDocletTask"
    classpathref="app.class.path"/>
```

To create *web.xml* for this servlet, you use a deploymentdescriptor element inside the webdoclet element:

```
<deploymentdescriptor
    servletspec="2.3"
    destdir="${app.web-inf.dir}"/>
```

The complete build file appears in Example 9-7. It compiles the code, creates *web.xml*, and is designed to be used from a directory named *build* right under the XDoclet directory (*xdoclet-1.2.1* is the current version as of this writing), while the servlet's code is stored in the directory *build/src/java/app/web*.

Example 9-7. The servlet's build file ch09/servlet/build.xml

```xml
<?xml version="1.0"?>

<project default="main" basedir=".">

    <property name="lib.dir" value="../lib"/>
    <property name="app.dir" value="."/>
    <property name="app.dist.dir" value="${app.dir}/output"/>
    <property name="app.src.dir" value="${app.dir}/src"/>
    <property name="app.java.dir" value="${app.src.dir}/java"/>
    <property name="app.generated-src.dir" value="${app.dist.dir}/generated-src"/>
    <property name="app.web-inf.dir" value="${app.dist.dir}/web-inf"/>
    <property name="app.classes.dir" value="${app.dist.dir}/classes"/>
    <property name="app.xdoclet.force" value="false"/>

    <path id="app.class.path">
        <fileset dir="${lib.dir}">
            <include name="*.jar"/>
        </fileset>
    </path>

    <target name="init">
        <tstamp>
            <format property="TODAY" pattern="d-MM-yy"/>
        </tstamp>

        <taskdef
            name="webdoclet"
            classname="xdoclet.modules.web.WebDocletTask"
            classpathref="app.class.path"/>

        <mkdir dir="${app.classes.dir}"/>
        <mkdir dir="${app.generated-src.dir}"/>
    </target>

    <target name="webdoclet" depends="init">

        <webdoclet
            destdir="${app.generated-src.dir}"
            excludedtags="@version,@author,@todo"
            force="${app.xdoclet.force}"
            verbose="false">

            <fileset dir="${app.java.dir}">
                <include name="**/Servlet*.java"/>
            </fileset>
```

Example 9-7. The servlet's build file ch09/servlet/build.xml (continued)

```
        <deploymentdescriptor
            servletspec="2.3"
            destdir="${app.web-inf.dir}"/>

    </webdoclet>
</target>

<target name="compile" depends="webdoclet">

    <javac
        destdir="${app.classes.dir}"
        classpathref="app.class.path"
        debug="on"
        deprecation="on"
        optimize="off">

        <src path="${app.java.dir}"/>
        <src path="${app.generated-src.dir}"/>

    </javac>

</target>

<target name="main" depends="compile">
    <echo>Using XDoclet....</echo>
</target>

</project>
```

When you run this build file, it'll create a complete *web.xml* for this servlet; here is the crucial part:

```
<servlet>
    <servlet-name>ServletApp</servlet-name>
    <display-name>Servlet App</display-name>
   <servlet-class>app.web.ServletApp</servlet-class>

    <init-param>
        <param-name>param1</param-name>
        <param-value>value1</param-value>
    </init-param>
    <init-param>
        <param-name>param2</param-name>
        <param-value>value2</param-value>
    </init-param>

    <load-on-startup>1</load-on-startup>

</servlet>

<servlet-mapping>
    <servlet-name>ServletApp</servlet-name>
```

```
      <url-pattern>/app/*</url-pattern>
   </servlet-mapping>
```

In this way, XDoclet can write deployment descriptors for you if you remember to put all needed information in your source code files using XDoclet tags.

Working with EJB Containers

This XDoclet Ant task executes EJB-specific sub-tasks to support EJB development. You can see the attributes of this task in Table 9-12. The legal nested elements appear in Table 9-13.

Table 9-12. The ejbdoclet Ant task's attributes

Attribute	Description	Required	Default
addedTags	Specifies you want to add JavaDoc tags to the generated classes.	No	
destDir	Specifies the destination directory to use for output files.	Yes, if destDir is not specified for a subtask.	
ejbClassNameSuffix	Specifies suffixes that should be removed from the bean classname. A comma-separated list.	No	Bean, EJB, Ejb
ejbSpec	Specifies the version of EJB specification ejbdoclet should use. Possible values are 1.1 and 2.0.	No. Default is 2.0.	
excludedTags	Specifies tags that should not be written to output files.	No	
force	Specifies whether you want to force the the generation of files if needed.	No	
mergeDir	Specifies the directory where subtasks will look for files that they should merge with their generated files.	No, but should be set if you use the merge feature.	
verbose	Specifies you want verbose feedback.	No	

Table 9-13. The ejbdoclet Ant task's nested elements

Element	Description
apachesoap	Provides support for Apache SOAP subtasks
axisdeploy	Provides support for axis deployment
axisundeploy	Provides support for axis undeployment
borland	Provides support for Borland code
castormapping	Specifies you want to generate a *mapping.xml* deployment descriptor
configParam	Specifies configuration parameters that will be included as an attribute/value pair
dao	Provides support for DAO
dataobject	Provides support for data objects for Entity EJBs.

Table 9-13. The ejbdoclet Ant task's nested elements (continued)

Element	Description
deploymentdescriptor	Creates a deployment descriptor
easerver	Provides support for configuration files for EJB JAR files in EAServer 4.1+
entitybmp	Creates entity bean classes for BMP entity EJBs
entitycmp	Creates CMP layer code
entityfacade	Provides support for entity facades
entitypk	Creates primary key classes for entity EJBs
fileset	Specifies a fileset of files to parse
homeinterface	Provides support for remote home interfaces for EJBs
hpas	Provides support for an *hp-ejb-jar.xml* deployment descriptor for HPAS
jboss	Provides support for *jboss.xml*, *jaws.xml*, and/or *jbosscmp-jdbc.xml* deployment descriptors for JBoss
jonas	Provides support for the deployment descriptor for JOnAS
jrun	Provides support for jrun.
localhomeinterface	Generates local home interfaces for EJBs
localinterface	Generates local interfaces for EJBs
mvcsoft	Generates MVCSoft's XML
oc4j	Generates OC4J specific deployment descriptor (*orion-ejb-jar.xml*)
openejb	Provides support for *openejb-jar.xml* deployment descriptors for OpenEJB
orion	Provides support for Orion's *orion-ejb-jar.xml*
packageSubstitution	Specifies you want to substitute a new package for the package in generated files
pramati	Provides support for Pramati deployment files
remotefacade	Provides support for stage 2 of remote facade generation
remoteinterface	Provides support for remote interfaces for EJBs
resin-ejb-xml	Provides support for Resin
session	Provides support for sessions
strutsform	Provides support for a Struts ActionForm, based on an entity EJB
subTask	Specifies a subtask for this task
sunone	Provides support for configuration files for EJB jars in iPlanet/SunONE
utilobject	Provides support for util objects
valueobject	Provides support for value objects for Entity EJBs
weblogic	Generates deployment descriptors for WLS 6.0, 6.1, and 7.0
websphere	Generates EJB-related files from one or a set of EJB bean source files that uses custom EJBDoclet JavaDoc tags

The source code for an EJB, *Appbean.java*, appears in Example 9-8 and shows how the ejbdoclet task works. The embedded XDoclet tags hold data for the ejbdoclet task, which will create a deployment descriptor and write code.

Example 9-8. The EJB bean ch09/ejb/Appbean.java

```java
package app.web;

import javax.ejb.*;

/**
 *
 * @ejb.bean name="App"
 *     description="App example bean"
 *     jndi-name="ejb/App"
 *     type="Stateless"
 *
 * @ejb.security-role-ref role-link="Administrator"
 *     role-name="admin"
 *
 * @ejb.permission    role-name="App"
 * @ejb.permission    role-name="Administrator"
 *
 * @ejb.transaction  type="Required"
 * @ejb.transaction-type type="Container"
 *
 * @author Steven
 */

public abstract class AppBean implements SessionBean
{
    /**
     * Add and return values.
     *
     * @ejb.interface-method view-type="remote"
     */
    public double adder(int x, int y)
    {
        return x + y;
    }

    public void ejbActivate()
    {
    }

    public void ejbPassivate()
    {
    }

    public void setSessionContext(SessionContext ctx)
    {
    }

    /**
     * Remove
     *
     * @ejb.transaction
     *     type="Mandatory"
```

Example 9-8. The EJB bean ch09/ejb/Appbean.java (continued)

```
    */
    public void ejbRemove( )
    {
    }
}
```

In the build file, you use `taskdef` to tell Ant about the ejbdoclet task:

```
<taskdef
    name="ejbdoclet"
    classname="xdoclet.modules.ejb.EjbDocletTask"
    classpathref="app.class.path"/>
```

 Include the *.jar* file containing Sun's javax.ejb.* classes on the taskdef task's classpath when creating the ejbdoclet task in a build file.

You can create a deployment descriptor, *ejb-jar.xml*, with the `deploymentdescriptor` element:

```
<deploymentdescriptor
    destdir="${app.meta-inf.dir}"
    description="ejbbean"/>
```

The entire build file appears in Example 9-9. This file is designed to be run from a directory named ejbbuild right under the XDoclet unzip directory with the servlet's code in the directory *build/src/java/app/web*.

Example 9-9. The EJB bean build file ch09/ejb/build.xml

```
<?xml version="1.0" ?>

<project default="main" basedir=".">

    <property name="lib.dir" value="../lib"/>
    <property name="app.dist.dir" value="output"/>
    <property name="app.src.dir" value="src"/>
    <property name="app.java.dir" value="${app.src.dir}/java"/>
    <property name="app.generated-src.dir" value="${app.dist.dir}/generated-src"/>
    <property name="app.web-inf.dir" value="${app.dist.dir}/web-inf"/>
    <property name="app.classes.dir" value="${app.dist.dir}/classes"/>
    <property name="app.lib.dir" value="lib"/>
    <property name="app.meta-inf.dir" value="meta-inf"/>
    <property name="app.xdoclet.force" value="false"/>

    <path id="app.class.path">
        <fileset dir="${lib.dir}">
            <include name="*.jar"/>
        </fileset>
        <fileset dir="${app.lib.dir}">
            <include name="*.jar"/>
```

Example 9-9. The EJB bean build file ch09/ejb/build.xml (continued)

```xml
        </fileset>
    </path>

    <target name="init">
        <tstamp>
            <format property="TODAY" pattern="d-MM-yy"/>
        </tstamp>

        <taskdef
            name="ejbdoclet"
            classname="xdoclet.modules.ejb.EjbDocletTask"
            classpathref="app.class.path"/>

        <mkdir dir="${app.classes.dir}"/>
        <mkdir dir="${app.generated-src.dir}"/>
        <mkdir dir="${app.meta-inf.dir}" />
    </target>

    <target name="ejbdoclet" depends="init">

        <ejbdoclet
            destdir="${app.generated-src.dir}"
            mergedir="parent-fake-to-debug"
            excludedtags="@version,@author,@todo"
            ejbspec="2.0"
            force="${app.xdoclet.force}"
            verbose="false">

            <fileset dir="src/java">
                <include name="**/*.java"/>
            </fileset>

            <remoteinterface/>
            <localinterface/>
            <homeinterface/>
            <localhomeinterface/>

            <entitycmp/>
            <entitybmp/>

            <session/>

            <deploymentdescriptor
                destdir="${app.meta-inf.dir}"
                description="ejbbean"/>

        </ejbdoclet>
    </target>

    <target name="compile" depends="ejbdoclet">
```

Example 9-9. The EJB bean build file ch09/ejb/build.xml (continued)

```
        <javac
            destdir="${app.classes.dir}"
            classpathref="app.class.path"
            debug="on"
            deprecation="on"
            optimize="off">

            <src path="${app.java.dir}"/>
            <src path="${app.generated-src.dir}"/>
        </javac>

    </target>

    <target name="main" depends="compile">
        <echo>Using EJBDoclet....</echo>
    </target>

</project>
```

Running this build file creates EJB interface code and a deployment descriptor, *ejb-jar.xml*. Here is the relevant part of the generated *ejb-jar.xml*:

```
<?xml version="1.0" encoding="UTF-8"?>
<!DOCTYPE ejb-jar PUBLIC "-//Sun Microsystems, Inc.//DTD Enterprise JavaBeans 2.0//
EN" "http://java.sun.com/dtd/ejb-jar_2_0.dtd">

<ejb-jar >

    <description><![CDATA[ejbbean]]></description>
    <display-name>Generated by XDoclet</display-name>

    <enterprise-beans>

        <!-- Session Beans -->
        <session >
            <description><![CDATA[App example bean]]></description>

            <ejb-name>App</ejb-name>

            <home>app.web.AppHome</home>
            <remote>app.web.App</remote>
            <local-home>app.web.AppLocalHome</local-home>
            <local>app.web.AppLocal</local>
            <ejb-class>app.web.AppSession</ejb-class>
            <session-type>Stateless</session-type>
            <transaction-type>Container</transaction-type>

            <security-role-ref>
                <role-name>admin</role-name>
                <role-link>Administrator</role-link>
            </security-role-ref>
```

```
    </session>
         .
         .
         .
<!-- Assembly Descriptor -->
<assembly-descriptor >
  <!--
     To add additional assembly descriptor info here, add a file to your
     XDoclet merge directory called assembly-descriptor.xml that contains
     the <assembly-descriptor></assembly-descriptor> markup.
  -->
  <security-role>
     <role-name>App</role-name>
  </security-role>
  <security-role>
     <role-name>Administrator</role-name>
  </security-role>

  <method-permission >
     <role-name>App</role-name>
     <role-name>Administrator</role-name>
     <method >
        <ejb-name>App</ejb-name>
        <method-name>*</method-name>
     </method>
  </method-permission>
       .
       .
       .
<!-- transactions -->
<container-transaction >
   <method >
      <ejb-name>App</ejb-name>
       <method-name>*</method-name>
    </method>
    <trans-attribute>Required</trans-attribute>
 </container-transaction>
<container-transaction >
   <method >
      <ejb-name>App</ejb-name>
      <method-intf>LocalHome</method-intf>
      <method-name>remove</method-name>
      <method-params>
      </method-params>
   </method>
   <trans-attribute>Mandatory</trans-attribute>
</container-transaction>
<container-transaction >
   <method >
      <ejb-name>App</ejb-name>
      <method-intf>Home</method-intf>
      <method-name>remove</method-name>
      <method-params>
      </method-params>
```

```
        </method>
        <trans-attribute>Mandatory</trans-attribute>
    </container-transaction>
        .
        .
        .
    </ejb-jar>
```

XDoclet is a powerful tool that's still developing. Currently, you can only run it in Ant, but a command-line tool is in the works. Once you get the hang of it, XDoclet helps with web and EJB application development in a way that makes sense; when you modify your code, you modify the deployment descriptors and the EJB code you generate at the same time. It's a tool worth watching.

Developing Enterprise JavaBeans

Ant provides a number of optional tasks for developing EJBs. Generally, these tasks are specific to the particular vendor's EJB Server. Currently, these tasks support these servers:

- Borland Application Server 4.5
- IBM WebSphere 4.0
- iPlanet Application Server 6.0
- JBoss 2.1 and above EJB servers
- JOnAS 2.4.x and 2.5 Open Source EJB server
- WebLogic 4.5.1 to 7.0 EJB servers

The Ant EJB tasks and the servers they target appear in Table 9-14.

Table 9-14. The Ant EJB tasks

Task	Does this	Application servers
blgenclient	Specifies you want to create a client .jar file corresponding to an EJB .jar file	Borland Application Server 4.5 and 5.x
ddcreator	Specifies you want to compile WebLogic text-based deployment descriptors into an EJB deployment descriptor	WebLogic 4.5.1
ejbc	Lets you run WebLogic's ejbc tool	WebLogic 4.5.1
ejbjar	Supports creation of EJB .jar files (EJB 1.1 & 2.0)	Borland Application Server 4.5 and 5.x, iPlanet Application Server 6.0, JBoss, JOnAS 2.4.x and 2.5, WebLogic 5.1 to 7.0, and IBM WebSphere 4.0
iplanet-ejbc	Supports compilation of EJB stubs and skeletons for iPlanet Application Server 6.0	iPlanet Application Server 6.0
wlrun	Lets you start a WebLogic server	WebLogic 4.5.1 to 7.0
wlstop	Lets you stop a WebLogic server	WebLogic 4.5.1 to 7.0

JARing Files

The largest and most general of the EJB tasks is the ejbjar task. This task works by scanning directories; for each deployment descriptor found, ejbjar will parse it to determine the necessary *.class* files which implement the bean. These files are assembled along with the deployment descriptors into a well-formed EJB *.jar* file. (Any support files which should be included in the created *.jar* file can be added with the support nested element.) For each class included in the *.jar* file, ejbjar will scan for any super classes or super interfaces, which will be added to the generated *.jar* file. The attributes of this task appear in Table 9-15.

Table 9-15. The Ant ejbjar task's attribute

Attribute	Description	Required	Default
basejarname	Specifies the base name you want used for the generated *.jar* files.	No	
classpath	Specifies the classpath you wnt used when resolving classes that are to be added to the *.jar*.	No	
cmpversion	Specifies the CMP version. Possible values are 1.0 or 2.0.	No	1.0
dependency	Specifies which classes and interfaces are added to the *.jar*.	No	
descriptordir	Specifies the directory under which the task shoulc scan for EJB deployment descriptors.	No	
destdir	Specifies the directory into which you want generated JAR files to be placed.	Yes, unless you use vendor-specific deployment elements.	
flatdestdir	Specifies you want to store all generated JARs in the root of the destdir, rather than the location specified by the deployment descriptor. Set to true/false.	No	
genericjarsuffix	Specifies a string that you want appended to the deployment descriptor in order to create the filename of a generic EJB JAR file.	No	-generic.jar
naming	Specifies the naming convention you want to use to name generated EJB jars.	No	
srcdir	Specifies the base directory containing the *.class* files that make up the generated bean.	Yes	

You can nest classpath elements to set the classpath in the ejbjar task, and you can use nested dtd elements to specify the local location of DTDs to be used when parsing the EJB deployment descriptor (see Table 9-2 for the dtd element's attributes).

You can use nested support elements to specify additional *.class* files to be included in the generated *.jar* files. The support element is a fileset, so it can reference a fileset declared elsewhere or it can be defined with the appropriate `include` and `exclude` nested elements. The `ejbjar` task supports vendor-specific nested elements, which let you use the vendors' deployment tools.

Vendor-specific nested elements provide support for various vendor deployment tools. (If no nested vendor-specific deployment elements are present, the task will create a generic EJB *.jar* file.) For each nested deployment element, the vendor-specific deployment tool is run to generate a *.jar* file for deployment to that vendor's EJB server. Here are the legal vendor-specific nested elements:

`borland`
> For Borland Application Server 4.5 and 5.x

`iPlanet`
> For iPlanet Application Server 6.0

`jboss`
> For JBoss

`jonas`
> For JOnAS 2.4.x and 2.5

`weblogic`
> For WebLogic 5.1 to 7.0

`websphere`
> For IBM WebSphere 4.0

These vendor-specific elements can become involved. For example, the attributes of the `weblogic` element, used to control the `weblogic.ejbc` compiler for generating WebLogic EJB *.jar* files, appear in Table 9-16.

Table 9-16. The weblogic element's attribute

Attribute	Description	Required	Default
args	Specifies any additional arguments you want to pass to the `weblogic.ejbc` tool.	No	
classpath	Specifies the classpath that should be used when the task runs the `weblogic.ejbc` tool.	No	
compiler	Specifies a different compiler to be used for compiling the generated Java files.	No	
destdir	Specifies the directory where the generated JAR files should be stored.	Yes	
ejbcclass	Specifies the classname of the ejbc compiler. When used with Version 7, this attribute should be set to `weblogic.ejbc` to avoid a deprecation warning.	No	
genericjarsuffix	Specifies the suffix used for the generic JAR file. This JAR file is generated as an intermediate step in building the WebLogic deployment JAR.	No	-generic.jar

Table 9-16. The weblogic element's attribute (continued)

Attribute	Description	Required	Default
jvmargs	Specifies any additional arguments you want passed to the JVM running the `weblogic.ejbc` tool.	No	
jvmdebuglevel	Specifies the debug level for messages. Set to 16 to avoid warnings about EJB Home and Remotes in the classpath.	No	
keepgenerated	Specifies if WebLogic will preserve the Java files it generates.	No	false
keepgeneric	Specifies if you want the generic file used for input to ejbc to be preserved.	No	false
newCMP	Specifies ejbjar should parse the WebLogic deployment descriptor to find the CMP descriptors. Set to true/false.	No	false
noEJBC	Specifies you don't want WebLogic's ejbc to be run on the EJB *.jar* file.	No	
outputdir	Specifies this directory as the output directory instead of a *.jar* file.	No	
rebuild	Specifies if `weblogic.ejbc` should always be used to build the *.jar* file.	No	true
suffix	Specifies the string that should be added to the deployment descriptor to create the WebLogic JAR filename.	No	.jar
wlclasspath	Specifies the classpath for the WebLogic classes to avoid a warning when the home and remote interfaces of a bean are on the classpath used by `weblogic.ejbc`.	No	

The weblogic nested element supports nested `classpath` and `wlclasspath` nested elements; the `wlclasspath` element holds the classpath used by the WebLogic Server as detailed by the `wlclasspath` attribute in Table 9-16, and it takes the same attributes and nested elements as `classpath`. The weblogic element supports nested sysproperty elements to allow Java system properties to be set.

Investigating them all would take us many pages deep into the mechanics of these six EJB servers, and far from Ant. If you're interested, you can find the details for using various vendor-specific tools in the Ant EJB Tasks User Manual at *${ant-home}/docs/manual/OptionalTasks/ejb.html*.

CHAPTER 10

Optional Tasks

A significant number of optional tasks come with Ant (the full list appears in Table 1-5), and you'll see several of them in this chapter. Some of the optional tasks are specialized, but a number are useful in everyday builds. You've seen optional tasks like junit and ftp, and this chapter expands that coverage with a look at tasks like sound, splash, replaceregexp, and depend.

Using Sound

The sound task plays a sound-file at the end of the build according to whether the build failed or succeeded. You can specify one sound file to play, or if you specify a directory, the sound task will randomly select a sound file to play.

 If you're using Java 1.3 or later, you need the Java Media Framework on the classpath (*javax.sound*).

The sound task can contain success and fail elements. The success element specifies the sound you want played if the build succeeds and failures the sound if it fails. Here's an example where the build file specifies the sounds to play depending on if the build succeeded or failed:

```
<target name="sounds">
    <sound>
        <success source="${user.home}/sounds/success.wav"/>
        <fail source="${user.home}/sounds/noway.wav"/>
    </sound>
</target>
```

These success and failure elements support the attributes you see in Table 10-1.

Table 10-1. The success and fail elements' attributes

Attribute	Description	Required	Default
source	Specifies the name of a sound file	Yes	
loops	Specifies the number of times to play the sound file	No	0
duration	Specifies the time (measured in milliseconds) you want to play the sound file	No	

Creating Splash Screens

This task creates a splash screen displayed while the build is progressing. In Example 10-1, I'm using a splash screen that the Apache Jakarta Project makes available at *http://jakarta.apache.org/images/jakarta-logo.gif*, and I'm displaying it for five seconds.

Example 10-1. Using a splash screen (ch10/splash/build.xml)

```xml
<?xml version="1.0"?>

<project default="main" basedir=".">

    <property name="cvs.dir" value="project" />

    <target name="main" depends="splash">
        <echo>
            Checking out and updating....
        </echo>
    </target>

    <target name="splash">
        <splash imageurl="http://jakarta.apache.org/images/jakarta-logo.gif"
        showduration="5000"/>
    </target>

</project>
```

You can see the Apache Jakarta logo that appears when this task executes in Figure 10-1. This task provides a nice touch if you're distributing your build files to a team.

Figure 10-1. Sample build splash logo

The attributes of this task appear in Table 10-2.

Table 10-2. The splash attributes

Attribute	Description	Required	Default
imageurl	Specifies an URL that points to the image you want the splash screen to display.	No	antlogo.gif from the classpath
showduration	Sets the length of time the splash screen should be visible. Set to a value in milliseconds.	No	5000

If you need to retrieve an image from behind a firewall, use the Ant setproxy task.

Substituting Text Using Regular Expressions

The replaceregexp task can replace every occurrence of a given regular expression with a substitution pattern in a selected file or set of files.

The output file is written only if it differs from the existing file.

Example 10-2 uses replaceregexp, where text in the XML comment in the build file matching "Here's a comment." is converted to "Here's an XML comment."

Example 10-2. Using regular expression substitutions (ch10/regexp/build.xml)

```
<?xml version="1.0"?>

<project default="main" basedir=".">

<!--Here's a comment.-->

    <target name="main">
        <replaceregexp
            match="a comment"
            replace="an XML comment">
            <fileset dir="." includes="**/*.xml" />
        </replaceregexp>
    </target>

</project>
```

Here's what the build file looks like after you run it:

```
<?xml version="1.0"?>

<project default="main" basedir=".">

<!--Here's an XML comment.-->
```

```
<target name="main">
    <replaceregexp
        match="a comment"
        replace="an XML comment">
        <fileset dir="." includes="**/*.xml" />
    </replaceregexp>
</target>

</project>
```

Changing the contents of other files this way will be useful if you need to rewrite build files that you're about to call with the ant task. Here's an example of editing build files to convert from a local to an FTP install:

```
<?xml version="1.0"?>

<project default="main" basedir=".">

    <target name="main">
        <replaceregexp
            match="<copy file='Project.jar' todir='dist'/>"
            replace="<ftp server='ftp.isp.com'><fileset dir='bin'/></ftp>"
            <fileset dir="subproject" includes="**/*.xml" />
        </replaceregexp>
    </target>

    <ant dir="subproject"/>

</project>
```

Unless it's unavoidable, editing build files this way is not good programming practice. It's better to pass parameters along with the ant call.

Here's another example, this time of replacing all whitespace in documentation files with spaces:

```
<replaceregexp match="\s+" replace=" " flags="g">
    <fileset dir="docs" includes="**/*.html" />
</replaceregexp>
```

The attributes of this task appear in Table 10-3.

Support exists for the regular expression library built into Java 1.4; you should have *jakarta-oro.jar* in the Ant *lib* directory.

Table 10-3. The replaceregexp attributes

Attribute	Description	Required	Default
byline	Specifies you want to process the file(s) one line at a time, executing the replacement on one line at a time.	No	false
encoding	Specifies the encoding of the file you're using. Available since Ant 1.6.	No	The default JVM encoding
file	Specifies the file in which text matching the regular expression should be replaced.	Yes, if no nested fileset is used	
flags	Specifies flags to use when matching the regular expression. For example, "g" means global replacement, "i" means case insensitive, and so on.	No	
match	Specifies the regular expression pattern you want to use to match text in the source file(s).	Yes, if no nested regexp is used	
replace	Specifies the text to replace matched text with.	Yes, if no nested substitution is used	

This task supports a nested `fileset` element. You can use a nested `regexp` element to specify the regular expression this way:

```
<regexp id="id" pattern="\s+"/>
<regexp refid="id"/>
```

The replaceregexp task supports a nested `substitution` element to specify the substitution pattern; here are some examples:

```
<substitution id="id" expression="beta\1alpha"/>
<substitution refid="id"/>
```

Handling Dependencies

The javac task does a good job of handling dependencies, but it's limited because it only compiles *.java* files if the corresponding *.class* file is older or does not exist. It doesn't check the files those *.java* files might depend on, such as parent or imported classes. The depend task, however, lets you perform this kind of dependency checking.

When this task finds out-of-date classes, it removes the *.class* files of any other classes that depend on them. To determine dependencies, this task analyzes the classes in all files passed to it, using the class references encoded into *.class* files by the compiler. (It does not parse or read source code.)

You typically use the depend task before compiling. Here's an example that uses depend before calling javac:

```
<?xml version="1.0" ?>
<project default="main">

    <property name="message" value="Building..." />
    <property name="src" location="source" />
    <property name="output" location="bin" />
```

```
                <target name="main" depends="init, compile, compress">
                    <echo>
                        ${message}
                    </echo>
                </target>

                <target name="init">
                    <mkdir dir="${output}" />
                </target>

                <target name="compile">
                    <depend srcdir="${src}"
                        destdir="${output}"
                        closure="yes"/>
                    <javac srcdir="${src}" destdir="${output}" />
                </target>

            <target name="compress">
                    <jar destfile="${output}/Project.jar" basedir="${output}"
                        includes="*.class" />
            </target>
        </project>
```

The attributes of this task appear in Table 10-4.

 If you don't want to have to check dependencies, you can wipe all the directories that contain compiled code and rebuild from scratch. When there are a large number of files to compile, that's a less attractive option, and using the depend task can save significant time. (But experience shows that if your dependencies are complex, it can save time to do a wipe and start fresh.)

Table 10-4. The depend attributes

Attribute	Description	Required	Default
cache	Specifies the directory where you want the task to store dependency data	No	
classpath	Specifies the classpath, which should also be checked when checking dependencies	No	
closure	Specifies the task should traverse all class dependencies, deleting all classes that depend on out-of-date material	No	false
destdir	Specifies the root directory containing the class files that you want to check	No	The value of srcdir
dump	Specifies the dependency information should be sent to the debug log	No	
srcdir	Specifies the directory where the source is	Yes	

Like many other Ant tasks, this task forms an implicit FileSet and so supports all attributes of fileset (though dir becomes srcdir) as well as the nested include, exclude, and patternset elements. The depend task's classpath attribute is a path-like structure and can also be set using a nested classpath element. If you specify a classpath, depend will include classes and JARs on the classpath for dependency checking; any classes which depend on an item from the classpath and which are older than that item will be deleted.

 If you're going to include a classpath to check for dependencies, don't end up including the entire Java library structure by mistake; doing so will slow this task down.

Checking dependencies can become involved. For example, what if a class depends on another, which in turn depends on a third? If the third class is out of date, only the second class would normally be rebuilt, even if you use the depend task. But you can ensure the depend task catches *all* dependencies, including indirect ones like this, by setting the closure attribute to true.

 Nonpublic classes can also cause a couple of problems with this task. For example, depend cannot connect the class file containing a non-public class to a source file. depend can't detect when a nonpublic class is missing. If you've set the Java compiler to optimize its compilation, that can also cause problems. Inner classes, on the other hand, are no problem.

Normal Ant processing usually handles dependencies with no problem, but if you've got a complex dependency situation, or indirect dependencies, this task can work wonders. If you can't handle your dependencies with depend, wipe the output directories before compiling to start with a clean slate.

CHAPTER 11

Integrating Ant with Eclipse

Ant is the premiere build tool for Java developers, and Eclipse is the premiere integrated development environment (IDE) for Java programmers. Eclipse is great at visual development, and Ant is great for builds. For that reason, the latest Eclipse version (3.0) comes with Ant 1.6.1 (the version of Ant this book was written with), and there's an extensive Ant interface in Eclipse.

Doesn't Ant have its own IDE? Well, sort of. Antidote, started in 2000, was supposed to have been the Ant IDE; see *http://ant.apache.org/projects/antidote/index.html.* Unfortunately, that project appears to be more or less moribund, largely because the big guys behind Eclipse have been integrating Ant into their IDE now.

Introducing Eclipse

If you're a Java developer, you know how finicky Java can feel at times. Missed import statements, forgotten variable declarations, omitted semi-colons, garbled syntax, and typos will cause the Java command-line compiler, javac, to cough and display pages of error messages.

The error messages tell you that javac knows what the error is, so why doesn't it just fix the problem and let you continue developing? javac can't fix the problem; to do that, you can use an IDE, which will catch errors before you compile and suggest solutions. Java is badly in need of a good IDE, and the premiere Java IDE these days is Eclipse. You can see what it looks like in Figure 11-1.

Eclipse is free for the downloading, like a number of other Java IDEs, but Eclipse has a serious advantage behind it, which is the power of IBM, reportedly spending $40 million developing it. It's now an open source project, largely under IBM's development but part of a software consortium named eclipse.org.

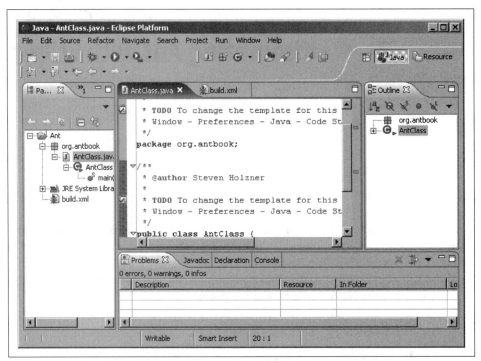

Figure 11-1. Eclipse

Want to read more on Eclipse? See *Eclipse* by yours truly (O'Reilly).

Getting Eclipse

Eclipse is free for the downloading; all you have to do is navigate to *http://www.eclipse.org/downloads*. Select one of the download mirrors available on that page. When you do, you'll be presented with a list of the available downloads of these various types:

Release builds
　　These versions are for general use.

Stable builds
　　These are comparable to beta versions.

Integration builds

These builds are made up of components that have been fairly well tested, but their operation together may still have some issues.

Nightly builds

These are the most experimental of all publicly available Eclipse builds. They're created nightly by the Eclipse team, and there's really no guarantee that things will work well.

 As with other software, you generally want to use the latest release version of Eclipse; I'll use Eclipse 3.0, the most recent release build, in this chapter.

Select the download for your operating system and click the appropriate link to download it. Installing Eclipse is easy; all you've got to do is to unzip or untar it, depending on your operating system. Since you download the version of Eclipse targeted to your operating system, you'll find the executable file ready to run as soon as you uncompress Eclipse. You start Eclipse by running the Eclipse executable. When you first run Eclipse, you should see the Welcome page. To get an overview of Eclipse or to run a tutorial, click the appropriate links. To close this Welcome page, click the X in the page's tab.

Creating an Eclipse Project

If you've installed Eclipse and have got it running, you have access to the Ant/Eclipse interface and no extra work is needed. Development work in Eclipse is based on *projects*, and I'll create a new project to show how to use Ant inside Eclipse. To create a new project, select File → New → Project, opening the New Project dialog. Select the Java Project item and click Next.

On the next page, give this project the name AntExample. Leave the other defaults as they are and click Finish.

This opens the new project in Eclipse; you can see the AntExample project at left in Eclipse's Package Explorer.

This project is empty so far; to add Java code, select the AntExample project in the Package Explorer and select File → New → Class, opening the New Java Class dialog. Give the package name as org.antbook, the name of the new class as AntClass, and select the checkbox marked public static void main(String[] args) to make Eclipse create a main method. Click the Finish button.

This creates the code, *AntClass.java*, you see in the Eclipse editor at the center of Figure 11-2, complete with a main( ) method.

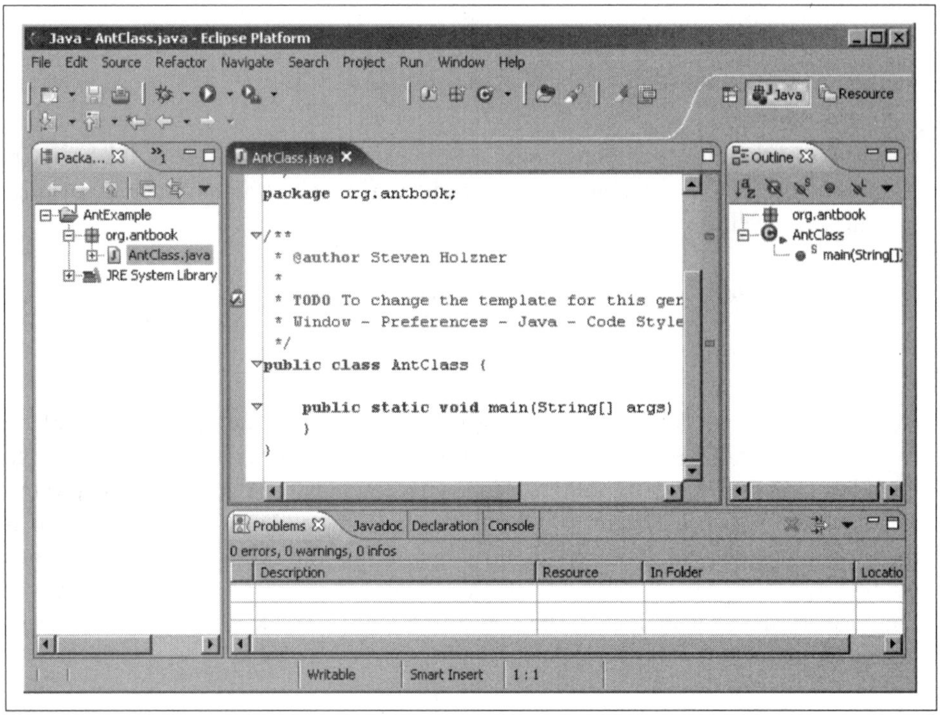

Figure 11-2. A new Java class

Add this code to make this class do something:

```
public static void main(String args[])
{
    System.out.println("No worries.");
}
```

Click the Save icon in the toolbar to save the changes to *AntClass.java*, and select Run → Run As → Java Application. You'll see the output of this code, No worries., in the Console tab at the bottom of Eclipse.

Writing an Ant Build File in Eclipse

To create an Ant build file in Eclipse, right-click the AntExample project in the Package Explorer and select New → File. In the File Name box, enter **build.xml**, and click Finish, adding this new file to the AntExample project. To JAR the output of this project, enter this XML in the build file:

```
<?xml version="1.0" ?>
<project default="main">
    <target name="main" depends="compile, compress" description="Main target">
        <echo>
            Building the .jar file.
        </echo>
    </target>
```

```
    <target name="compile" description="Compilation target">
        <javac srcdir="org/antbook"/>
    </target>

    <target name="compress" description="Compression target">
        <jar jarfile="Project.jar" basedir="org/antbook" includes="*.class" />
    </target>
</project>
```

After entering this XML, save the new build file. The Eclipse support for Ant is evident; *build.xml* appears in the Package Explorer at left with an Ant icon and the syntax in the build file is colored with XML declarations in one color, attribute values in another, and Ant keywords in another, as shown (in glorious black and white) in Figure 11-3. The targets of this build file appear at right, in the Outline view.

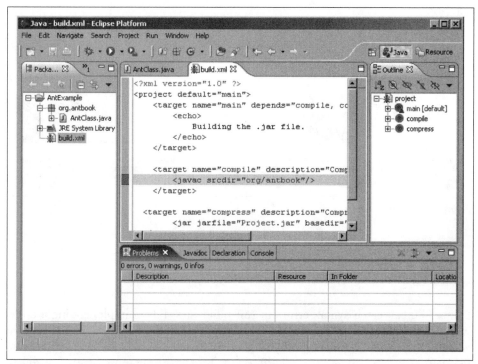

Figure 11-3. An Ant build file in Eclipse

 If you close *build.xml*, you can open it again in the Eclipse Ant editor; double-click it in the Package Explorer. This is different than previous versions of Eclipse, which had no default Ant editor. You had to take extra steps to open Ant build files for editing.

Support for Ant is evident in Eclipse's *code assist* (also called *content assist*), which was added for Ant build files in Eclipse 3.0. When you enter partial text for Ant elements or attributes, you can press Ctrl-Space to open code assist, which will list possible completions of what you've been typing, as shown in Figure 11-4.

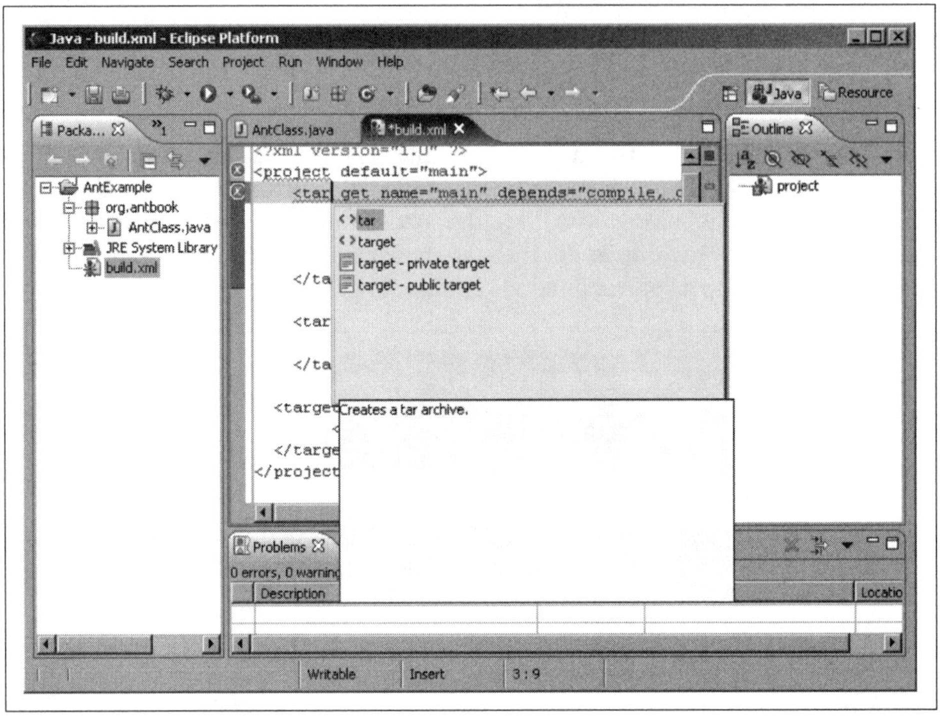

Figure 11-4. Using code assist

> If you enter a $ and use code assist, Eclipse's Ant editor will list all the Ant property names it knows about.

Eclipse 3.0 can catch syntax errors in Ant build files. For example, ending a target with \</targe>, instead of a \</target> tag, is immediately caught by the Eclipse Ant editor, as shown in Figure 11-5. If you let your cursor rest over the circled X icon to the left of the problem line, you'll see Eclipse's explanation of the problem: "Expected '\</target>' to terminate element starting on line 3." This kind of syntax checking and corrections alone are worth the price of admission.

> You can reformat an Ant build file-indenting everything nicely, using the Format command (Ctrl-Shift-F) from the Ant editor's context menu or by selecting Edit → Format.

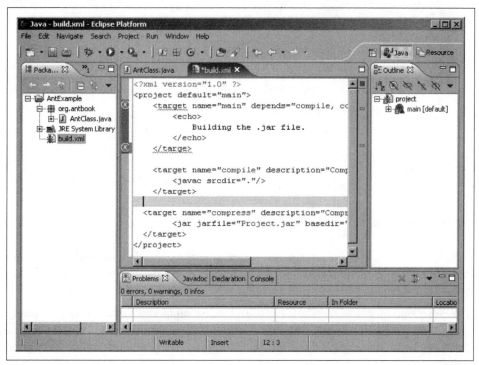

Figure 11-5. Handling syntax errors

Want to see the value of a property? Let the mouse hover over it, and its value will appear in a tooltip.

 Under some circumstances, Eclipse can generate Ant scripts for you. For example, if you're creating an Eclipse plug-in, which extends Eclipse with your own views and editors, you'll use a plug-in manifest file named *plugin.xml*. If you right-click the manifest file and select the Create Ant Build File item, Eclipse will create a build file for you. If you select Project → Generate Javadoc, the Javadoc wizard will create an Ant build file that runs the javadoc tool, which you can edit as needed.

Running Ant Build Files

You have two options to run these build files from within Eclipse. You can right-click *build.xml* in the Package Explorer and select Run → Ant Build. Doing so runs Ant and gives you the results in Eclipse's Console view.

Eclipse 3.0 runs Ant in a separate JVM, solving many problems that used to plague previous versions.

The output in the Console view is the same as you'd see from Ant if you ran the build file on the command line:

```
Buildfile: D:\eclipse3\eclipse\workspace\AntExample\build.xml
compile:
    [javac] Compiling 1 source file
compress:
      [jar] Building jar: D:\eclipse3\eclipse\workspace\AntExample\Project.jar
main:
    [echo] Building the .jar file.
BUILD SUCCESSFUL
Total time: 2 seconds
```

If there are problems, you can see Ant's output in the Console view. Eclipse will give you a summary in the Problems view, which you can see by clicking the Problems tab at the bottom of Eclipse.

The other option to run a build file is to right-click *build.xml* in the Package Explorer and select Run → Ant Build..., this time with an ellipsis (three dots). This opens the Ant launch configuration dialog you see in Figure 11-6. The Ant launch configuration is specific to the current project.

By default, the Targets tab is selected in this dialog, showing a list of the targets in *build.xml*. The default target has been selected; you can click the Run button to run that target, or you can select other targets to run. If you leave the default target selected and click Run, you'll see the same results as before in the Console view.

You can set the execution order of targets, shown in the Target execution order box at the bottom of the page (the order in which you select the items is the order in which they will run). Ant will still run each target's dependencies, but you have to be careful in case your changes mess up the overall build order.

Selecting the Build File and Passing Arguments to Ant

You can get as much use out of Ant in Eclipse as you can from the command line. For example, to pass arguments to Ant, right-click *build.xml* in the Package Explorer and select Run → Ant Build... to open the Ant launch configuration. Click the Main tab shown in Figure 11-7. In this page, you can set the build file you want to use, the base directory for the build, and you can pass arguments to Ant.

The Capture output checkbox at the bottom of this dialog indicates whether you want to capture the Ant output to the Eclipse Console view, as we've been doing by default.

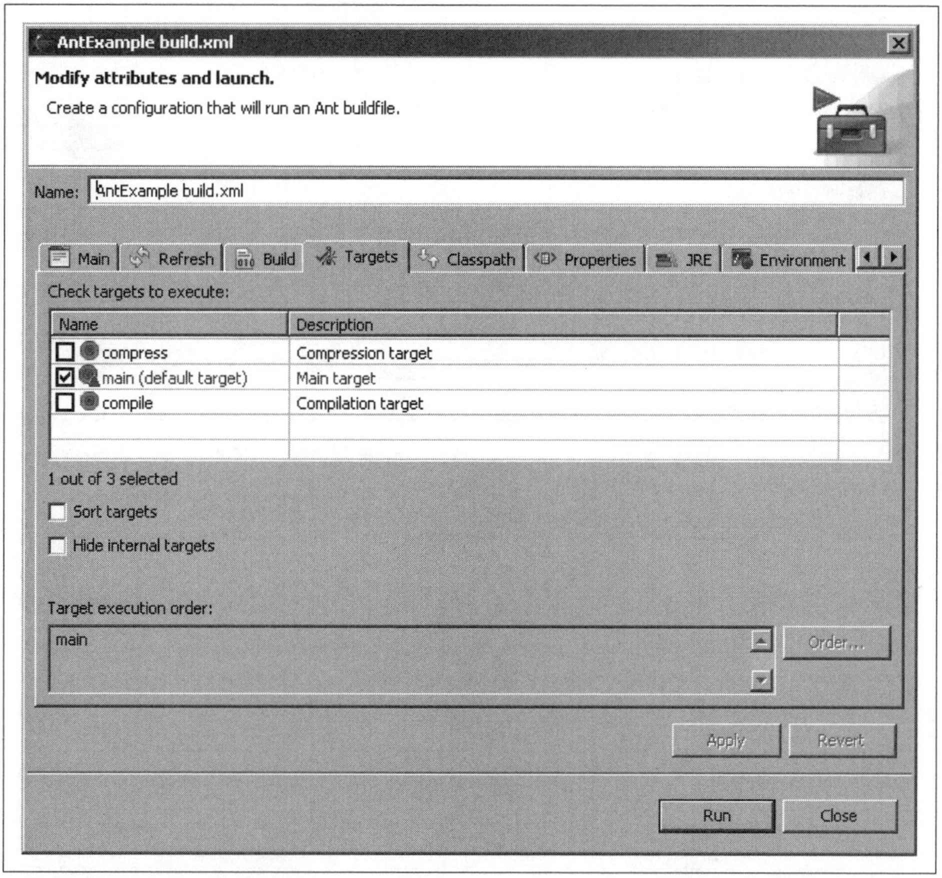

Figure 11-6. Selecting an Ant target

Modifying the Ant Classpath

When using an optional or custom task, adding extra libraries to the classpath may be necessary. The Ant classpath can be modified globally or by using an individual project's launch configuration. To set the Ant classpath for an individual Eclipse project, open the Ant launch configuration for the project and click the Classpath tab. You can add external JARs by clicking the Add External JARs button.

You can modify the Ant classpath globally for all projects. To do that, select Window → Preferences → Ant → Runtime, and click the Classpath tab. You can add JAR files as needed here, and they'll be used globally for all Ant builds.

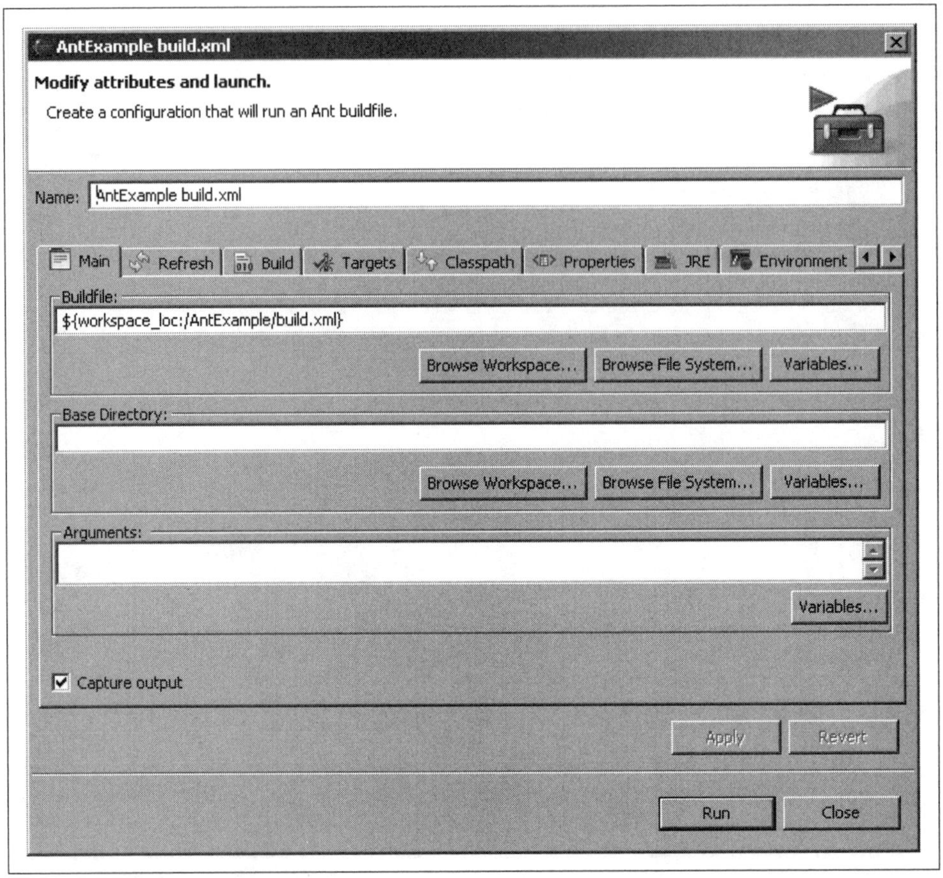

Figure 11-7. Setting the build file and arguments to pass to Ant

Setting Property Values

You can set global Ant properties using the Ant preferences page, which you open by selecting Window → Preferences → Ant → Runtime and clicking the Properties tab. To add a new property, click the Add Property button and fill in the Name and Value fields in the dialog that appears. This will set the global properties for all Ant builds in Eclipse, and since properties are immutable, you will be setting the final value for such properties.

You can set properties on a project-by-project basis by setting the project's Ant launch configuration. Click the Properties tab in the launch configuration (as seen in Figure 11-8), deselect the "Use global properties as specified in the Ant runtime preferences" checkbox, and click the Add Property button to set new properties.

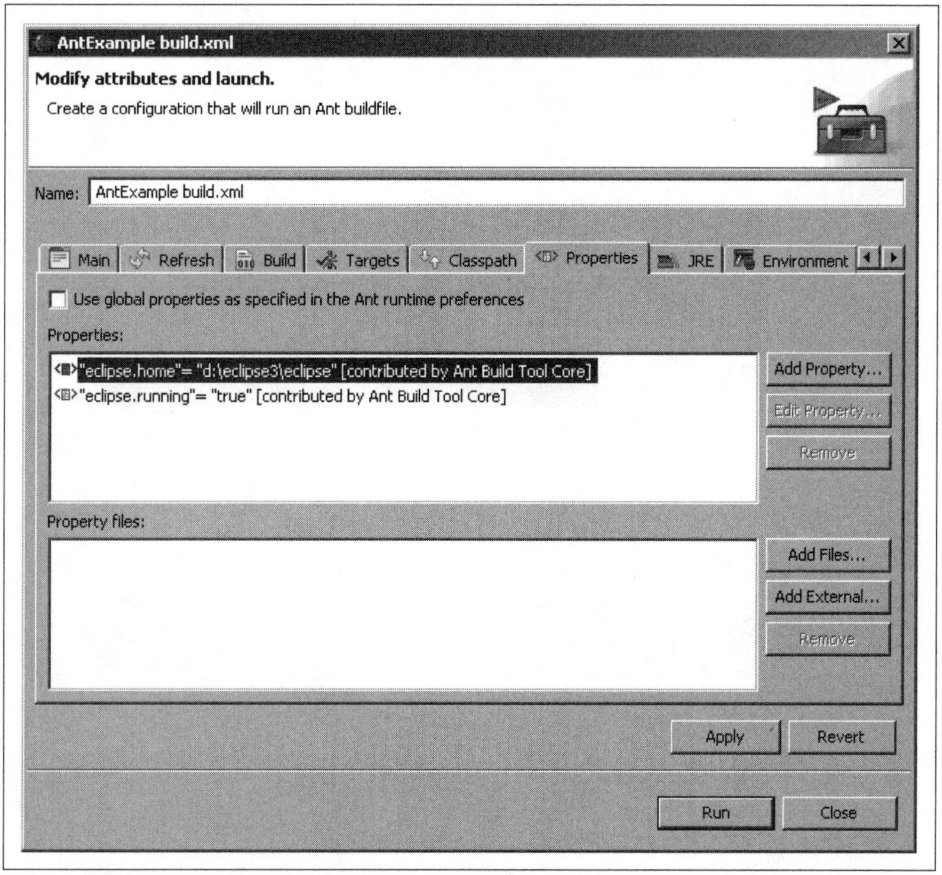

Figure 11-8. Setting properties

Setting Environment Variables

You can set the environment variables you want passed to Ant, but you have to ensure Ant will run in its own JRE (the default). In the project's Ant launch configuration, click the JRE tab and click the Separate JRE radio button. To set environment variables, click the Environment tab, shown in Figure 11-9, and click the New button to create a new environment variable.

When you click the New button, the New Environment Variable dialog appears. Enter the name and value of the environment variable in the appropriate fields and click OK.

Configuring the Ant Editor

You can reformat an Ant build file using the Format command (Ctrl-Shift-F) from the Ant editor's context menu or by selecting Edit → Format. To configure how that

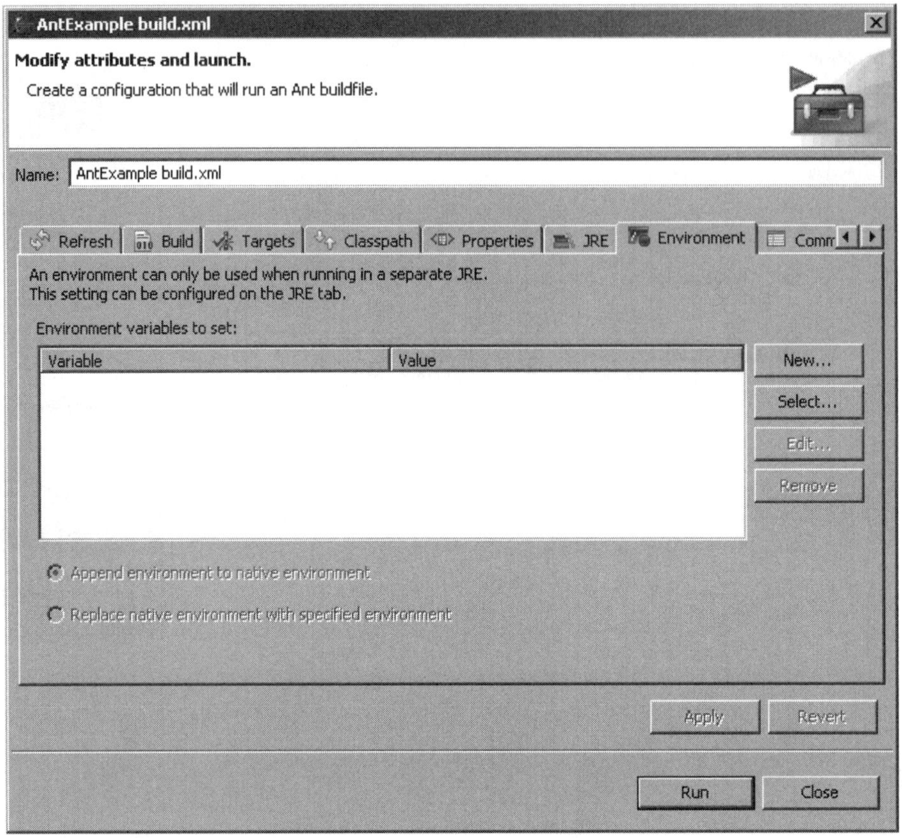

Figure 11-9. Setting environment variables

formatting works, open the Ant preferences page with Window → Preferences → Ant → Editor → Formatter, as shown in Figure 11-10. Any changes you make will be reflected in the Preview box.

Selecting Window → Preferences → Ant → Editor lets you configure the build file editor by setting tab widths, margins, highlighting and more.

Adding New Ant Tasks and Types

You can add new Ant tasks and types (covered in detail in the next chapter) to Eclipse by using the Ant preferences page at Window → Preferences → Ant → Runtime. These tasks and types will be available for build files without having to use the taskdef or typedef tasks, which are normally needed.

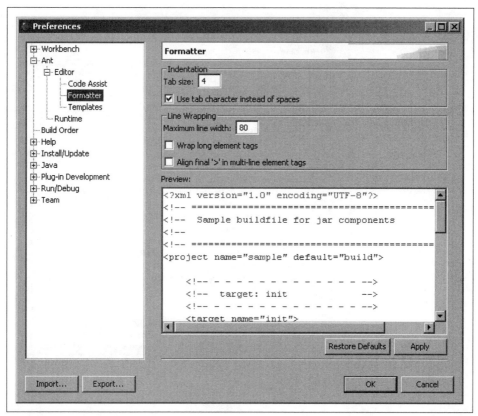

Figure 11-10. Configuring Ant formatting

To add a new task, select the Tasks tab, shown in Figure 11-11, click the Add Task button, and navigate to the JAR file in which the new Ant task is located. To add a new type, click the Types tab and follow the same steps.

 If you can't find the JAR files you need, add them to the Ant classpath first.

Alternatively, you can add additional classes defining tasks and types to the Ant classpath by clicking the Classpath tab.

Using a Different Version of Ant

Eclipse comes with Ant 1.6.1, but it's possible to use a different version. Open the Ant preferences page by selecting Window → Preferences → Ant → Runtime and clicking the Classpath tab.

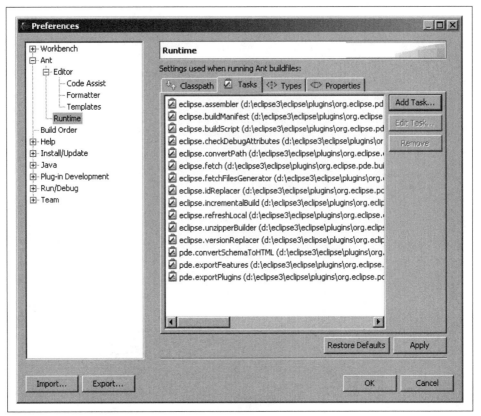

Figure 11-11. Adding Ant tasks

When Eclipse runs Ant, it looks for the appropriate classes on the Ant classpath, as set in the Ant Home Entries item. To change the Ant Home Entries, click the Ant Home button and choose the Ant installation you wish to use.

 If you don't want to change the classpath, you can run Ant as an external tool from Eclipse. To do that, select Run → External Tools → External Tools to open the External Tools dialog. Click the Program item and then the New button. Enter a name for the new tool (such as "Ant 1.8" or whatever is appropriate). Next, to the Location field, click the Browse File System button and navigate to *ant.sh* or *ant.bat*, whichever is right for your operating system, and click Open. The External Tools dialog will reappear; in the Arguments field, enter any arguments you want to pass to Ant. Finally, in the Working Directory field, enter the directory of the build file you want to use and click Run to launch the new version of Ant. The problem with doing this is that you won't have easy access to predefined values that you have while working inside Eclipse. In most cases, it's far better to use Ant from inside Eclipse when building Eclipse projects.

Using the Ant View

Eclipse comes with a dedicated view for working with Ant—called the Ant view—which is a window that gives you an overview of the targets in build files. To open this view, select Window → Show View → Ant; the Ant view appears at right in Figure 11-12.

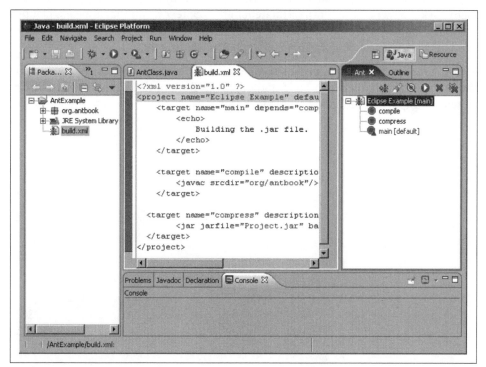

Figure 11-12. The Ant view

The toolbar in this view contains these buttons (from left to right):

- Add Build Files
- Add Build Files with Search
- Hide Internal Targets
- Run the Default Target
- Remove Selected Build File
- Remove All Build Files

To add a build file to the Ant view, click the Add Build Files button, opening the Choose Location dialog. In the left box, select the Eclipse project you want to use, and in the right box, select the build file you want to add to the Ant view. Click OK, adding the build file to the Ant view.

In Windows, you can add build files to the Ant View with drag and drop.

Besides giving you an overview of a build file, the Ant view lets you run build files. Select a build file in the Ant view and click the Run the Default Target button. Or right-click a target and select the Run item in the context menu that appears. Double-clicking a build file in the Ant view opens it in the Ant editor (as does right-clicking the build file and selecting the Open With → Ant Editor item).

Using Ant with Eclipse is a potent combination. Eclipse allows you to develop and debug code, and Ant lets you build and deploy it. Both of these tools are free for the downloading. It's a combination I recommend.

CHAPTER 12

Extending Ant

There's more to Ant than what comes out of the box because you can extend Ant in various ways. The most common way of extending Ant is by creating your own tasks, and this chapter covers how to do that. You'll learn how to create new tasks, handle task attributes, access property values, work with nested text and elements, make builds fail, work with filesets, use custom tasks as wrappers for external programs, and more.

Besides creating new tasks, you can extend Ant in other ways, such as using scripting languages such as JavaScript, which I'll explain. You can even create listeners that respond to build file events by executing Java code, and create loggers that log data as a build progresses. And you can create custom filters and selectors, which you can use with some Ant tasks such as copy.

Creating a Simple Custom Ant Task

Creating new Ant tasks is simple since all you need is an execute( ) method. Example 12-1 is a Java class named Greeting that displays the text "No worries."

Example 12-1. A simple Ant task (ch12/greetingtask/src/Greeting.java)

```
public class Greeting
{
    public void execute( )
    {
        System.out.println("No worries.");
    }
}
```

To install this class as a new Ant task, you compile this code and use the taskdef task to declare it in Ant. The attributes of the taskdef task are shown in Table 12-1.

The taskdef task is based on the typedef task, except that the values of two attributes, adapter and adapto, are preset to fixed values (org.apache.tools.ant.TaskAdapter and org.apache.tools.ant.Task, respectively).

Table 12-1. The taskdef task's attributes

Attribute	Description	Required	Default
adapter	Specifies the adapter, which adapts the defined class to another interface/class.	No	org.apache.tools.ant.TaskAdapter
adaptto	Specifies the interface/class to which to adapt. Used with the adapter attribute.	No	org.apache.tools.ant.Task
classname	Specifies the classname that will support/perform the type or task.	Yes, unless file or resource have been specified.	
classpath	Specifies the classpath you want to use when searching for classname.	No	
file	Specifies the name of the file from which to load definitions, if any.	No	
format	Specifies the format of the file or resource pointed to by the file or resource attributes. Possible values are properties or xml.	No	properties
loaderRef	Specifies the loader that you want to use to load the class.	No	
name	Specifies the name of the data type or task you're creating.	Yes, unless the file or resource type attributes have been specified.	

Table 12-1. The taskdef task's attributes (continued)

Attribute	Description	Required	Default

onerror	Specifies what to do if there is an error while defining a type. Possible values are:
	
	`fail`
	  Causes a build exception
	
	`report`
	  Outputs a warning
	
	`ignore`
	  Does nothing
	
	Since Ant 1.6.
		No	`fail`

resource	Specifies the name of the resource from which you want to load definitions.	No	
uri	Specifies the URI at which this type/task definition should be found. Since Ant 1.6.	No	

The taskdef task's `classpath` attribute is a path-like structure and can be set with a nested `classpath` element.

The build file in Example 12-2 builds the simple Ant task and JARs it in *greeting.jar*. The taskdef task in the same build file retrieves the task from that JARfile and executes the task, which should print out the "No worries." message.

Example 12-2. Build file for a simple Ant task (ch12/greetingtask/build.xml)

```xml
<?xml version="1.0"?>
<project default="main">

    <property name="src" location="src"/>
    <property name="output" location="output"/>

    <target name="main" depends="jar">
        <taskdef name="greeting" classname="Greeting" classpath="greeting.jar"/>
        <greeting/>
    </target>

    <target name="jar" depends="compile">
        <jar destfile="greeting.jar" basedir="${output}"/>
    </target>
```

Example 12-2. Build file for a simple Ant task (ch12/greetingtask/build.xml) (continued)

```
    <target name="compile">
        <mkdir dir="${output}"/>
        <javac srcdir="${src}" destdir="${output}"/>
    </target>

</project>
```

Here's what you see when the build file runs. The execute( ) method of the task's code was indeed called, displaying the expected message:

```
%ant
Buildfile: build.xml

compile:
    [mkdir] Created dir: /home/steven/ant/ch12/greetingtask/output
    [javac] Compiling 2 source files to /home/steven/ant/ch12/greetingtask/output

jar:
      [jar] Building jar: /home/steven/ant/ch12/greetingtask/greeting.jar

main:
 [greeting] No worries.

BUILD SUCCESSFUL
Total time: 3 seconds
```

Extending the Task Class

Usually, you extend an Ant task class like org.apache.tools.ant.Task when you write custom tasks. Ant comes with a selection of task classes meant to be extended:

AbstractCvsTask
> Abstract CVS task class

JDBCTask
> Handles JDBC configuration needed by SQL type tasks

MatchingTask
> Abstract task that should be extended by tasks required to include or exclude files based on pattern matching

Pack
> Abstract base class for pack tasks

Task
> Generic task and the one most commonly extended

Unpack
> Abstract base class for unpacking tasks

The Task class (i.e., org.apache.tools.ant.Task) is used for most of this chapter, though some samples will use MatchingTask. The methods of the Task class appear in Table 12-2.

Table 12-2. The Task class's methods

Method	Does this
void execute( )	Specifies the task should execute.
java.lang.String getDescription( )	Returns the task's description.
Location getLocation( )	Returns the file and location at which the task is supported.
Target getOwningTarget( )	Returns the target that contains this task.
RuntimeConfigurable getRuntimeConfigurableWrapper( )	Returns the wrapper class instance the task uses for runtime configuration.
java.lang.String getTaskName( )	Returns the task name (used when when logging messages from the task).
java.lang.String getTaskType( )	Returns the type of task as a string.
protected RuntimeConfigurable getWrapper( )	Returns the runtime configurable structure for this task as a RuntimeConfigurable object.
protected void handleErrorFlush(java.lang.String output)	Handles errors by logging them with ERR priority.
protected void handleErrorOutput(java.lang.String output)	Handles errors by logging them with WARN priority.
protected void handleFlush(java.lang.String output)	Handles errors by logging them with INFO priority.
protected int handleInput(byte[] buffer, int offset, int length)	Handles input requests using byte buffers.
protected void handleOutput(java.lang.String output)	Handles string output by logging it using INFO priority.
void init( )	Called automatically so the task can be initialized.
protected boolean isInvalid( )	Returns a value of true if this task is invalid.
void log(java.lang.String msg)	Logs a string message, giving it (default) INFO priority.
void log(java.lang.String msg, int msgLevel)	Logs a string message, giving it priority you specify.
void maybeConfigure( )	Configures the task, if it has not already been configured.
void perform( )	Performs this task. If the task is not still valid, a replacement version will be created and the task will be performed with that.

Table 12-2. The Task class's methods (continued)

Method	Does this
void reconfigure()	Reconfigures a task, forcing the reconfiguration if necessary.
void setDescription(java.lang.String desc)	Specifies a string description for this task.
void setLocation(Location location)	Specifies the file and location where this task was first defined.
void setOwningTarget(Target target)	Specifies the target that contains this task.
void setRuntimeConfigurableWrapper(RuntimeConfigurable wrapper)	Sets the wrapper class that should be used for runtime configuration.
void setTaskName(java.lang.String name)	Specifes the task name (use for logging messages).
void setTaskType(java.lang.String type)	Specifies type of task in string format.

The Task Life Cycle

Tasks go through a well-defined life cycle, and here are the specific stages:

1. The task is instantiated using a no-argument constructor.

2. The task's references to its project and location inside the build file are initialized via inherited project and location variables.

3. If the user specified an id attribute in this task, the project registers a reference to this newly created task.

4. The task gets a reference to the target it belongs to through its inherited target variable.

5. The init() method is called to initialize the task.

6. All child elements of the task's element are created through the task's createXXX() methods or instantiated and added to this task with its addXXX() methods.

7. All attributes of this task get set via their corresponding setXXX() methods.

8. The character data sections inside the task's element are added to the task using its addText() method (if there is one).

9. All attributes of all child elements get set using their setXXX() methods.

10. The execute() method is called to run the task.

Accessing the Project and Properties in Code

When you extend the Task class, you have access to a great deal of data about the project. The Task class inherits the getProject() method, which returns a Project object that holds such items as the project's name and properties. You can see selected methods of the Project class in Table 12-3. You can do nearly anything with these methods, from setting a project's default target and logging text to reading property values and setting property values. That's a typical way for custom tasks to perform their work: reading property values with the Project object's getProperty( ) method and setting property values with setProperty( ). After a property has been set, it can be accessed in the build file, letting the custom task communicate with the rest of the build file.

Table 12-3. Selected Project class methods

Method	Does this
void addBuildListener(BuildListener listener)	Adds a build listener to the current project to catch build events.
void addTarget(Target target)	Adds a new target to the project at runtime.
void addTaskDefinition(java.lang.String taskName, java.lang.Class taskClass)	Adds the definition of a new task to the project.
Task createTask(java.lang.String taskType)	Creates a new task instance.
int defaultInput(byte[] buffer, int offset, int length)	Reads input data for the project from the default input stream.
void executeTarget(java.lang.String targetName)	Executes the specified target (and any targets it depends on).
void executeTargets(java.util.Vector targetNames)	Executes the specified targets in the given sequence (and the targets they depend on).
java.io.File getBaseDir( )	Returns the base directory of the project. The directory is returned as a File object.
java.util.Vector getBuildListeners( )	Returns the list of build listeners that have been added to the project.
java.io.InputStream getDefaultInputStream( )	Returns this project's default input stream as an InputStream object.
java.lang.String getDefaultTarget( )	Returns the name of the default target of the project as a string.
java.lang.String getDescription( )	Returns the project description as a string, if one has been specified.
java.lang.String getElementName(java.lang.Object element)	Returns a description of the given element as a string.
java.lang.String getName( )	Returns the name of the project if one has been specified.
java.util.Hashtable getProperties( )	Returns the project's properties table.
java.lang.String getProperty(java.lang.String name)	Returns the value of a property if it has been set in the project.
java.lang.Object getReference(java.lang.String key)	Looks up a reference in the project by ID string.
java.util.Hashtable getReferences( )	Returns a hashtable of the references in the project.
java.util.Hashtable getTargets( )	Returns the hashtable of the targets in the project.

Table 12-3. Selected Project class methods (continued)

Method	Does this
`java.util.Hashtable getTaskDefinitions()`	Returns the current task's definition hashtable.
`java.util.Hashtable getUserProperties()`	Returns the user properties' hashtable.
`java.lang.String getUserProperty(java.lang.String name)`	Returns the value of a user property in the project if it has been set.
`void init()`	Initializes the project, readying it for execution.
`void log(java.lang.String message)`	Writes a string message to the log. Uses the default log level, MSG_INFO.
`void log(java.lang.String message, int msgLevel)`	Writes a project-level message to the log. Uses message level you specify.
`void log(Target target, java.lang.String message, int msgLevel)`	Writes a message-level message to the log. Uses message level you specify.
`void log(Task task, java.lang.String message, int msgLevel)`	Writes a task-level message to the log. Uses message level you specify.
`java.lang.String replaceProperties(java.lang.String value)`	Replaces any occurences of ${ } constructions in the given string with the value of the matching property.
`java.io.File resolveFile(java.lang.String fileName)`	Returns the full form of a filename.
`void setBaseDir(java.io.File baseDir)`	Specifies the base directory you want to use for the project.
`void setBasedir(java.lang.String baseD)`	Specifies the base directory, passed as a string, for the project.
`void setDefault(java.lang.String defaultTarget)`	Specifies the default target of the project, passed as a string.
`void setDefaultInputStream(java.io.InputStream defaultInputStream)`	Specifies the default System input stream as an InputStream object.
`void setDescription(java.lang.String description)`	Specifies the project description in string format.
`void setInheritedProperty(java.lang.String name, java.lang.String value)`	Specifies a user property by name and value.
`void setKeepGoingMode(boolean keepGoingMode)`	Specifies "keep-going" mode. In this mode, all targets that don't depend on failed targets will be executed.
`void setName(java.lang.String name)`	Specifies the name of the project as a string.
`void setNewProperty(java.lang.String name, java.lang.String value)`	Specifies the new value of a property if no value exists.
`void setProjectReference(java.lang.Object obj)`	Specifies a reference to this Project using the specified object.
`void setProperty(java.lang.String name, java.lang.String value)`	Specifies a property, by name and value.

Table 12-3. Selected Project class methods (continued)

Method	Does this
void setUserProperty(java.lang.String name, java.lang.String value)	Specifies a user property, by name and value.
static java.lang.String translatePath(java.lang.String toProcess)	Translates a general path into its OS-specific specific form.

Letting a custom task interact with the rest of the build through the use of properties is an important part of creating custom tasks. Take a look at Example 12-3, which is the code for an Ant task that reports the name of the project using the ant.project.name property, and the current location in the build file with the getLocation( ) method.

Example 12-3. Accessing projects and properties (ch12/projecttask/src/Project.java)

```java
import org.apache.tools.ant.Task;

public class Project extends Task
{
    public void execute( )
    {
        String name = getProject( ).getProperty("ant.project.name");

        System.out.println("Welcome to project " + name
            + " at " + getLocation( ));
    }
}
```

Example 12-4 shows the build file for this custom task.

Example 12-4. Build file for accessing properties (ch12/projecttask/build.xml)

```xml
<?xml version="1.0"?>
<project name="TheTask" basedir="." default="main">

    <property name="src" location="src"/>
    <property name="output" location="output"/>

    <target name="main" depends="jar">
        <taskdef name="project" classname="Project" classpath="project.jar"/>
        <project/>
    </target>

    <target name="jar" depends="compile">
        <jar destfile="project.jar" basedir="${output}"/>
    </target>

    <target name="compile">
        <mkdir dir="${output}"/>
        <javac srcdir="${src}" destdir="${output}"/>
    </target>

</project>
```

The results show that the build file reports the name of the project as set by the project element's name attribute, and the line location in the build file:

```
%ant
Buildfile: build.xml

compile:
    [mkdir] Created dir: /home/steven/ant/ch12/projecttask/output
    [javac] Compiling 1 source file to /home/steven/ant/ch12/projecttask/output

jar:
      [jar] Building jar: /home/steven/ant/ch12/projecttask/project.jar

main:
  [project] Welcome to project TheTask at
  /home/steven/ant/ch12/projecttask/build.xml:9:

BUILD SUCCESSFUL
Total time: 3 seconds
```

Handling Attributes in Custom Tasks

If your custom task supports attributes, Ant will pass the value of the attribute to your code if you have a setter method, much as you'd use in a JavaBean. For example, if you have an attribute named language, define a method—e.g., public void setLanguage(String language). Ant will pass this method the string value (after performing any needed property expansion) of the language attribute.

Strings are the most common attribute values, but you can ask Ant to perform conversions of attribute values to other data types based on the type of the argument in your setter method. Here are the possible data types and how they're handled:

boolean
> Your method will be passed the value true if the value specified in the build file is one of true, yes, or on, and false otherwise.

char (or java.lang.Character)
> Your method will be passed the first character of the attribute value.

Primitive types (int, short, and so forth)
> Ant will convert the value of the attribute into this type and pass it to your setter method.

java.io.File
> Ant will pass you a File object if the attribute value corresponds to a valid filename.

org.apache.tools.ant.types.Path
> Ant will tokenize the value specified in the build file, using : and ; as path separators.

java.lang.Class

Ant will want to interpret the attribute value as a Java class name and load the named class from the system class loader.

Any other type that has a constructor with a single String argument

Ant will use this constructor to create a new instance using the name in the attribute.

A subclass of org.apache.tools.ant.types.EnumeratedAttribute

Ant will invoke this class's setValue( ) method if your task supports enumerated attributes (i.e., attributes with values that must be part of a predefined set of legal values).

> What happens if more than one setter method is present for a given attribute? A method taking a String argument will not be called if more specific methods are available. If Ant could choose from other setters, only one of them will be called—but which one is called is indeterminate, depending on your JVM.

Example 12-5 shows the code to handle a String attribute named language and displays the value assigned to this attribute in the build file. The setLanguage( ) method will be passed the attribute's value.

Example 12-5. Accessing attributes (ch12/attributetask/src/Project.java)

```java
import org.apache.tools.ant.Task;
import org.apache.tools.ant.BuildException;

public class Project extends Task
{
    private String language;

    public void execute( ) throws BuildException
    {
        System.out.println("The language is " + language);
    }

    public void setLanguage(String language)
    {
        this.language = language;
    }
}
```

The build file that builds the custom task in Example 12-5 and then uses it appears in Example 12-6. In this example, Ant builds the code for the new task, project, and uses that task, setting the language attribute to English. The code for this task reads the value of the language attribute and displays it during the build.

Example 12-6. Build file for accessing attributes (ch12/attributetask/build.xml)

```
<?xml version="1.0"?>
<project basedir="." default="main">

    <property name="src" value="src"/>
    <property name="output" value="output"/>

    <target name="main" depends="jar">
        <taskdef name="project" classname="Project" classpath="Project.jar"/>
        <project language="English"/>
    </target>

    <target name="compile">
        <mkdir dir="${output}"/>
        <javac srcdir="${src}" destdir="${output}"/>
    </target>

    <target name="jar" depends="compile">
        <jar destfile="Project.jar" basedir="${output}"/>
    </target>

</project>
```

Here's what the build output looks like:

```
%ant
Buildfile: build.xml

compile:
    [javac] Compiling 1 source file to /home/steven/ant/ch12/attributetask/output

jar:
      [jar] Building jar: /home/steven/ant/ch12/attributetask/Project.jar

main:
  [project] The language is English

BUILD SUCCESSFUL
Total time: 4 seconds
```

Making Builds Fail

Want to make a build fail? Make your task code throw an org.apache.tools.ant.
BuildException. For example, if your custom task supports a failonerror attribute,
you might use code something like this:

```
public void setFailonerror(boolean failOnError)
{
    this.fail = failOnError;
}

public void execute() throws BuildException
{
```

```
        if (fail) {
            if error...
                throw new BuildException("Attribute language is required");
        } else {
            ....
        }
    }
```

Ant will display the text you pass to the BuildException constructor in the fail message.

Handling Nested Text

Ant tasks can support nested text, and custom tasks can support such text as well. Take a look at Example 12-7, which includes a project task that contains the nested text "No worries."

Example 12-7. Build file for accessing nested text (ch12/nestedtext/build.xml)

```xml
<?xml version="1.0"?>
<project basedir="." default="main">

    <property name="src" value="src"/>
    <property name="output" value="output"/>

    <target name="main" depends="jar">
        <taskdef name="project" classname="Project" classpath="Project.jar"/>
        <project>No worries.</project>
    </target>

    <target name="compile">
        <mkdir dir="${output}"/>
        <javac srcdir="${src}" destdir="${output}"/>
    </target>

    <target name="jar" depends="compile">
        <jar destfile="Project.jar" basedir="${output}"/>
    </target>

</project>
```

In your task's code, you can receive access to an element's nested text with the addText( ) method. The text will be passed to this method, and Example 12-8 shows how to retrieve that text and display it.

Example 12-8. Accessing nested text (ch12/nestedtext/src/Project.java)

```java
import org.apache.tools.ant.Task;

public class Project extends Task
{
    String text;
```

Example 12-8. Accessing nested text (ch12/nestedtext/src/Project.java) (continued)

```java
    public void addText(String text)
    {
        this.text = text;
    }

    public void execute( )
    {
        System.out.println(text);
    }
}
```

Here's what you get when you run this build file and the custom task with the nested text "No worries." in Example 12-7:

```
%ant
Buildfile: build.xml

compile:
    [mkdir] Created dir: /home/steven/ant/ch12/nestedtext/output
    [javac] Compiling 1 source file to /home/steven/ant/ch12/nestedtext/output

jar:
      [jar] Building jar: /home/steven/ant/ch12/nestedtext/Project.jar

main:
   [project] No worries.

BUILD SUCCESSFUL
Total time: 7 seconds
```

The supporting code for the custom task recovered the nested text and, in this case, displayed it during the build.

> Want to handle properties in nested text? Use replaceProperties-(java.lang.String value), which replaces ${} style constructions in the given value with the string value of the corresponding data types, and returns the resulting string.

Handling Nested Elements

Nested text is one thing, but what if you have nested *elements* in a custom task? For instance, assume that your custom task has nested elements named nested, as in Example 12-9, and suppose that these elements have an attribute named language. How can you recover the values of the language attributes?

Example 12-9. Nested elements in a custom task (ch12/nestedelement/build.xml)

```xml
<?xml version="1.0"?>
<project basedir="." default="main">
```

Example 12-9. Nested elements in a custom task (ch12/nestedelement/build.xml) (continued)

```xml
    <property name="src" value="src"/>
    <property name="output" value="output"/>

    <target name="main" depends="jar">
        <taskdef name="project" classname="Project" classpath="Project.jar"/>
        <project>
            <nested language="English"/>
            <nested language="German"/>
        </project>
    </target>

    <target name="compile">
        <mkdir dir="${output}"/>
        <javac srcdir="${src}" destdir="${output}"/>
    </target>

    <target name="jar" depends="compile">
        <jar destfile="Project.jar" basedir="${output}"/>
    </target>

</project>
```

In the code supporting this custom task, shown in Example 12-10, you need a class, Nested, representing the nested element, and you can use a method named createNested( ) to handle calls from Ant for each nested element. Each time createNested( ) is called, the code adds the new nested element to a Vector named nesteds. The language attribute of each nested element is passed to the setLanguage( ) method and can be recovered with the getLanguage( ) method. After the Vector is filled, the execute( ) method is called and the code iterates over the Vector, displaying the language attribute value for each nested element.

Example 12-10. Handling nested elements (ch12/nestedelement/src/Project.java)

```java
import java.util.Vector;
import java.util.Iterator;
import org.apache.tools.ant.Task;
import org.apache.tools.ant.BuildException;

public class Project extends Task
{
    public void execute()
    {
        for (Iterator iterator = nesteds.iterator(); iterator.hasNext();){
            Nested element = (Nested)iterator.next();
            System.out.println("The language is " + element.getLanguage());
        }
    }

    Vector nesteds = new Vector();

    public Nested createNested()
```

```
    {
        Nested nested = new Nested( );
        nesteds.add(nested);
        return nested;
    }

    public class Nested
    {
        public Nested( ) {}

        String language;

        public void setLanguage(String language)
        {
            this.language= language;
        }

        public String getLanguage( )
        {
            return language;
        }
    }
}
```

Here's what the build file looks like when running. The support code handled the nested elements and recovered the value of the language attributes:

```
%ant
Buildfile: build.xml

compile:
    [javac] Compiling 1 source file to /home/steven/ant/ch12/nestedelement/output

jar:
      [jar] Building jar: /home/steven/ant/ch12/nestedelement/Project.jar

main:
   [project] The language is English
   [project] The language is German

BUILD SUCCESSFUL
Total time: 3 seconds
```

Using Filesets

You can make your custom tasks support filesets with the right code. Example 12-11 shows a custom task, project, acting as a fileset with an include nested element. In this case, the custom project element will display all the *.java* files in and below the base directory.

Example 12-11. Supporting filesets in a build file (ch12/fileset/src/Project.java)

```xml
<?xml version="1.0"?>
<project basedir="." default="main">

    <property name="src" value="src"/>
    <property name="output" value="output"/>

    <target name="main" depends="jar">
        <taskdef name="project" classname="Project" classpath="Project.jar"/>
        <project dir="${basedir}">
            <include name="**/*.java"/>
        </project>
    </target>

    <target name="compile">
        <mkdir dir="${output}"/>
        <javac srcdir="${src}" destdir="${output}"/>
    </target>

    <target name="jar" depends="compile">
        <jar destfile="Project.jar" basedir="${output}"/>
    </target>

</project>
```

To handle filesets, you extend the `MatchingTask` class. In this example, the code that supports the custom task reads the value assigned to the `dir` attribute and uses the `org.apache.tools.ant.DirectoryScanner` class's `getIncludedFiles( )` method to scan that directory. This method returns an array of filenames, which the code displays. All the support code appears in Example 12-12.

Example 12-12. Supporting filesets (ch12/fileset/src/Project.java)

```java
import java.io.File;
import org.apache.tools.ant.Task;
import org.apache.tools.ant.BuildException;
import org.apache.tools.ant.DirectoryScanner;
import org.apache.tools.ant.taskdefs.MatchingTask;

public class Project extends MatchingTask
{
    private File directory;

    public void setDir (File directory)
    {
        this.directory = directory;
    }

    public void execute( ) throws BuildException
    {
        DirectoryScanner directoryscanner = getDirectoryScanner(directory);
        String[] files = directoryscanner.getIncludedFiles( );
```

Example 12-12. Supporting filesets (ch12/fileset/src/Project.java) (continued)

```
        for (int loopIndex = 0; loopIndex < files.length; loopIndex++) {
            System.out.println(files[loopIndex]);
        }
    }
}
```

Project.java is the only *.java* file in the project, and that's the file the custom project task picks up:

```
C:\ant\ch12\fileset>ant
Buildfile: build.xml

compile:
    [javac] Compiling 1 source file to /home/steven/ant/ch12/fileset/output

jar:
      [jar] Building jar: /home/steven/ant/ch12/fileset/Project.jar

main:
   [project] src/Project.java

BUILD SUCCESSFUL
Total time: 4 seconds
```

Extending MatchingTask to support includes and excludes nested elements, you can make your task support filesets.

Running External Programs

Custom Ant tasks are often wrappers for existing programs. You can launch an external program from the support code for a custom task if you use the org.apache. tools.ant.taskdefs.Execute class. Example 12-13 shows how this works and launches Windows WordPad and opens the project's build file in it.

Example 12-13. Executing external programs (ch12/executetask/src/Project.java)

```
import java.io.IOException;
import org.apache.tools.ant.Task;
import org.apache.tools.ant.taskdefs.Execute;
import org.apache.tools.ant.types.Commandline;

public class Project extends Task
{
    public void execute()
    {
        Commandline commandline = new Commandline();
        commandline.setExecutable("C:\\Program Files\\Windows NT\\Accessories\\wordpad.
                                   exe");
        commandline.createArgument().setValue("C:\\ant\\ch12\\executetask\\build.xml");
```

Example 12-13. Executing external programs (ch12/executetask/src/Project.java) (continued)

```
        Execute runner = new Execute( );
        runner.setCommandline(commandline.getCommandline( ));

        try {
            runner.execute( );
        }
        catch (IOException e) {
            System.out.println(e.getMessage( ));
        }
    }
}
```

In this case, the code creates an org.apache.tools.ant.types.Commandline object holding the path and name of the executable to launch, uses the Commandline object's createArgument( ).setValue method to specify the file to open, and uses the execute( ) method of the org.apache.tools.ant.taskdefs.Execute class to open WordPad.

The build file for this custom task appears in Example 12-14.

Example 12-14. Build file for executing external programs (ch12/executetask/build.xml)

```
<?xml version="1.0"?>
<project basedir="." default="main">

    <property name="src" value="src"/>
    <property name="output" value="output"/>

    <target name="main" depends="jar">
        <taskdef name="project" classname="Project" classpath="Project.jar"/>
        <project/>
    </target>

    <target name="compile">
        <mkdir dir="${output}"/>
        <javac srcdir="${src}" destdir="${output}" />
    </target>

    <target name="jar" depends="compile">
        <jar destfile="Project.jar" basedir="${output}"/>
    </target>

</project>
```

If you run this build file in Windows (after updating the hardcoded paths in the Java code as needed), it'll launch WordPad, opening *build.xml*.

Running Scripts

While discussing how to execute external programs, Ant includes an optional task named script that can run scripts such as those written in JavaScript. You need *bsf.jar*, from *http://jakarta.apache.org/bsf/* (not the IBM version), in the Ant *lib* directory to run this task. You'll need one or more of these *.jar* files, depending on the scripting language you want to use:

jacl.jar and tcljava.jar
> Resources to run TCL scripts. Get them from *http://www.scriptics.com/software/ java/*.

jruby.jar
> Resources to run Ruby scripts. Get this from *http://jruby.sourceforge.net/*.

js.jar
> JAR file for running JavaScript code. Get it from *http://www.mozilla.org/rhino/*.

judo.jar
> Resources to run Judoscript code. Get this from *http://www.judoscript.com/ index.html*.

jython.jar
> JAR file to run Python scripts. Get it from *http://jython.sourceforge.net/*.

netrexx.jar
> Resources to run Rexx scripts. Get this from *http://www2.hursley.ibm.com/ netrexx/*.

The BeanShell JAR files
> You need these to run BeanShell scripts. Get them from *http://www.beanshell.org/*. (Ant 1.6 and later require Beanshell Version 1.3 or later.)

The attributes for the `script` task appear in Table 12-4.

Table 12-4. The script tasks's attributes

Attribute	Description	Required
language	Specifies the script's language. Must be a supported Apache BSF language.	Yes
src	Specifies the location of the script if it's stored in a file (as opposed to being inline).	No

In script, you can access Ant tasks with the *Name*`.createTask` method, where *Name* is the project's name. For instance, Example 12-15 shows how to use the echo task from JavaScript to display numbers using a loop. Ant properties are available to your script's code, as in this case, where the `message` property's value is displayed.

 You have access to a built-in project object in scripts, so, for example, you could find the value of the `message` property as `project. getProperty("message")`.

Example 12-15. Build file for executing JavaScript (ch12/script/build.xml)

```
<project name="js" default="main" basedir=".">

    <property name="message" value="No worries."/>
```

Example 12-15. Build file for executing JavaScript (ch12/script/build.xml) (continued)

```
<target name="main">

    <script language="javascript"> <![CDATA[

        echo = js.createTask("echo");
        main.addTask(echo);

        for (loopIndex = 1; loopIndex <= 10; loopIndex++) {
            echo.setMessage(loopIndex);
            echo.execute( );
        }
        echo.setMessage(message);
    ]]> </script>

</target>
</project>
```

Here's what this build file looks like at work, where JavaScript is executing the Ant echo task. Cool.

```
%ant
Buildfile: build.xml

main:
      [echo] 1
      [echo] 2
      [echo] 3
      [echo] 4
      [echo] 5
      [echo] 6
      [echo] 7
      [echo] 8
      [echo] 9
      [echo] 10
      [echo] No worries.

BUILD SUCCESSFUL
Total time: 1 second
```

Want to work with Ant types like filesets in script? Use the project object's createDataType( ) method. Here's an example that creates Java File objects from a fileset, all in JavaScript:

```
importClass(java.io.File);

fileset = project.createDataType("fileset");
fileset.setDir(new File(dir));
fileset.setIncludes(includes);

directoryscanner = fileset.getDirectoryScanner(project);
files = directoryscanner.getIncludedFiles( );
```

```
for (loopIndex=0; loopIndex < files.length; loopIndex++) {
    var filename = files[loopIndex];
    var file = new File(fileset.getDir(project), filename);
}
```

Creating Custom Listeners

Ant tracks build events, such as when tasks start and finish, and you can catch those events with a *listener*. Listeners implement the `org.apache.tools.antBuildListener` interface and will receive `BuildEvents` for these events:

- Build started
- Build finished
- Target started
- Target finished
- Task started
- Task finished
- Message logged

To add a listener in code, you can create an ant `Project` object and then call its `addBuildListener()` method to add a listener to the project. You can attach a listener to a build from the command line as in this example:

```
ant -listener org.apache.tools.ant.XmlLogger
```

which runs Ant with a listener that generates an XML version of the build progress.

 Listeners and loggers must not access `System.out` and `System.err` because output on these streams is redirected by Ant's core to the build event system. In other words, accessing these streams may cause an infinite loop.

To implement the listener interface, you implement methods such as `buildStarted()`, `buildFinished()`, `targetStarted()`, and so on. In *SoundListener.java*, shown in Example 12-16, the listener code uses the `org.apache.tools.ant.taskdefs.optional.sound.AntSoundPlayer` class to play a sound when the build is finished. The `addBuildSuccessfulSound(java.io.File file, int loops, java.lang.Long duration)` method is used to add a sound to play for build success, and `addBuildFailedSound(java.io.File fileFail, int loopsFail, java.lang.Long duration)` to add a sound indicating build failure. In the listener's `buildFinished()` method, the sound player's `buildFinished()` method is called to play the sound.

If you run this example, substitute your own local filenames for *file1.wav* and *file2.wav* in *SoundListener.java*. The AntSoundPlayer can play sound files in *.wav* and *.aiff* format.

Example 12-16. A new listener (ch12/listener/SoundListener.java)

```java
import java.io.File;
import org.apache.tools.ant.BuildEvent;
import org.apache.tools.ant.BuildListener;
import org.apache.tools.ant.taskdefs.optional.sound.AntSoundPlayer;

public class SoundListener implements BuildListener
{
    AntSoundPlayer soundplayer = new AntSoundPlayer( );

    public SoundListener( )
    {
        soundplayer.addBuildSuccessfulSound(new File("file1.wav"), 1,
            new Long(500));

        soundplayer.addBuildFailedSound(new File("file2.wav"), 1, new Long(500));
    }

    public void buildStarted(BuildEvent event) {}

    public void buildFinished(BuildEvent event)
    {
        soundplayer.buildFinished(event);
    }

    public void targetStarted(BuildEvent event) {}

    public void targetFinished(BuildEvent event) {}

    public void taskStarted(BuildEvent event) {}

    public void taskFinished(BuildEvent event) {}

    public void messageLogged(BuildEvent event) {}
}
```

To build this listener, include *ant-jmf.jar* in the classpath to pick up AntSoundPlayer. Here's the file this example builds, *Project.java*:

```java
public class Project
{
    public void execute( )
    {
        System.out.println("No worries.");
    }
}
```

Here's the build file. Nothing special.

```
<?xml version="1.0"?>
<project basedir="." default="main">

    <property name="src" value="src"/>
    <property name="output" value="output"/>

    <target name="main" depends="jar">
        <taskdef name="project" classname="Project" classpath="Project.jar"/>
        <project/>
    </target>

    <target name="compile">
        <mkdir dir="${output}"/>
        <javac srcdir="${src}" destdir="${output}"/>
    </target>

    <target name="jar" depends="compile">
        <jar destfile="Project.jar" basedir="${output}"/>
    </target>

</project>
```

To attach the listener to the build, run Ant this way:

```
%ant -listener SoundListener
```

If the build finishes successfully, you'll hear the sound you've added for a build; otherwise, you'll hear the sound you've set for failure.

 Want to know what task or target fired a build event? Use the BuildEvent object's getTask( ) or getTarget( ) methods, in which a BuildEvent object is passed to each listener method.

Creating Custom Loggers

You can handle build events with custom loggers as well if you extend the Ant DefaultLogger class. Example 12-17 shows a logger that will log each task as it's executed. Like listeners, loggers must not access System.out and System.err directly, so to display messages to the standard out device, this code uses the Ant log( ) method (which defaults to standard out).

Example 12-17. A new logger (ch12/logger/ProjectLogger.java)

```
import org.apache.tools.ant.BuildEvent;
import org.apache.tools.ant.DefaultLogger;
import org.apache.tools.ant.util.StringUtils;

public class ProjectLogger extends DefaultLogger
{
    public void taskStarted(BuildEvent event)
    {
        String text = "Running task " + event.getTask().getTaskName( )
```

Example 12-17. A new logger (ch12/logger/ProjectLogger.java) (continued)

```
            + StringUtils.LINE_SEP;
        printMessage(text, out, event.getPriority());
        log(text);
    }
}
```

For this example, use a simple custom task:

```
public class Project
{
    public void execute()
    {
        System.out.println("No worries.");
    }
}
```

Here's the build file:

```
<?xml version="1.0"?>
<project basedir="." default="main">

    <property name="src" value="src"/>
    <property name="output" value="output"/>

    <target name="main" depends="jar">
        <taskdef name="project" classname="Project" classpath="Project.jar"/>
        <project/>
    </target>

    <target name="compile">
        <mkdir dir="${output}"/>
        <javac srcdir="${src}" destdir="${output}"/>
    </target>

    <target name="jar" depends="compile">
        <jar destfile="Project.jar" basedir="${output}"/>
    </target>

</project>
```

When you execute this build file with the custom logger, each task will be displayed as it's executed. To attach the logger to the build, use this command line:

```
%ant -logger ProjectLogger
```

When the build runs, you'll see each task logged like this:

```
%ant -logger ProjectLogger
Buildfile: build.xml
Running task property

Running task property

compile:
Running task mkdir
```

```
    [mkdir] Created dir: C:\ant\ch12\logger\output
Running task javac

    [javac] Compiling 1 source file to C:\ant\ch12\logger\output

jar:
Running task jar

      [jar] Building jar: C:\ant\ch12\logger\Project.jar

main:
Running task taskdef

Running task project

  [project] No worries.

BUILD SUCCESSFUL
Total time: 3 seconds
```

Creating Custom Filters

You can implement custom Ant filters. To do that, you can extend Ant classes like
org.apache.tools.ant.filters.BaseParamFilterReader. If you want your filter to be
chainable, implement the org.apache.tools.ant.filters.ChainableReader interface.

Example 12-18 shows how to write a filter. In this example, the code reads each line
of a Java file using the read( ) method and adds a Java single-line comment, //, at the
beginning of each line. When the code reaches the end of the file, it returns a value of
-1 to quit.

Example 12-18. A new filter (ch12/filter/src/ProjectFilter.java)

```java
import java.io.Reader;
import java.io.IOException;
import org.apache.tools.ant.filters.ChainableReader;
import org.apache.tools.ant.filters.BaseParamFilterReader;

public final class ProjectFilter extends BaseParamFilterReader implements ChainableReader
{
    String data = null;

    public ProjectFilter( )
    {
        super( );
    }

    public ProjectFilter(final Reader reader)
    {
        super(reader);
    }
```

Example 12-18. A new filter (ch12/filter/src/ProjectFilter.java) (continued)

```
    public final Reader chain(final Reader reader)
    {
        ProjectFilter filter = new ProjectFilter(reader);
        filter.setInitialized(true);
        return filter;
    }

    public final int read( ) throws IOException
    {
        int leadChar = -1;

        if(data != null) {
            leadChar = data.charAt(0);
            data = data.substring(1);
            if(data.length( ) == 0) {
                data = null;
            }
        }
        else {
            data = readLine( );

            if(data == null) {
                leadChar = -1;
            }
            else {
                data = "// " + data;
                return read( );
            }
        }
        return leadChar;
    }
}
```

You can see how to use this new filter in the build file in Example 12-19. This build file copies all *.java* files in the project, comments out each line, and stores the result in a directory named *commented*.

Example 12-19. Build file for the new filter (ch12/filter/build.xml)

```xml
<?xml version="1.0"?>
<project basedir="." default="main">

    <property name="src" value="src"/>
    <property name="output" value="output"/>
    <property name="commented" value="commented"/>

    <target name="main" depends="jar">
        <copy todir="${commented}">
            <fileset dir="${src}" includes="**/*.java"/>
            <filterchain>
                <filterreader
                  classname="ProjectFilter"
```

```
                        classpath="Project.jar"/>
            </filterchain>
        </copy>
    </target>

    <target name="compile">
        <mkdir dir="${output}"/>
        <mkdir dir="${commented}"/>
        <javac srcdir="${src}" destdir="${output}"/>
    </target>

    <target name="jar" depends="compile">
        <jar destfile="Project.jar" basedir="${output}"/>
    </target>

</project>
```

When you run this build file, every line in the copied *Project.java* file is commented out when filtered and copied:

```
// import java.io.Reader;
// import java.io.IOException;
// import org.apache.tools.ant.filters.ChainableReader;
// import org.apache.tools.ant.filters.BaseParamFilterReader;
//
// public final class ProjectFilter extends BaseParamFilterReader implements
ChainableReader
// {
//     String data = null;
        .
        .
        .
```

Creating Custom Selectors

Writing custom Ant selectors is possible if you extend a class like org.apache.tools. ant.types.selectors.BaseExtendSelector. In code, selectors are passed File objects and return true or false depending on whether or not a file is acceptable. Say, for example, that you want to copy files less than a megabyte in length. Example 12-20 shows a selector that tests file length and returns true if the file is OK, false otherwise.

Example 12-20. A new selector (ch12/selector/src/ProjectSelector.java)

```
import java.io.File;
import org.apache.tools.ant.BuildException;
import org.apache.tools.ant.types.selectors.BaseExtendSelector;

public class ProjectSelector extends BaseExtendSelector
{
```

```
    public boolean isSelected(File basedir, String filename, File file)
    throws BuildException
    {
        if(file.length( ) < 1024 * 1024){
            return true;
        }
        else {
            return false;
        }
    }
}
```

Example 12-21 is a build file that uses this new selector when copying files; in particular, it copies over its own source code to a directory named *sizeOK*.

Example 12-21. Build file for the new selector (ch12/selector/build.xml)

```
<?xml version="1.0" ?>
<project basedir="." default="main">

    <property name="src" value="src"/>
    <property name="output" value="output"/>
    <property name="sizeOK" value="sizeOK"/>

    <target name="main" depends="jar">

        <copy todir="${sizeOK}">
            <fileset dir="${src}">
                <selector>
                    <custom classname="ProjectSelector" classpath="Project.jar"/>
                </selector>
            </fileset>
        </copy>

    </target>

    <target name="compile">
        <mkdir dir="${output}"/>
        <mkdir dir="${sizeOK}"/>
        <javac srcdir="${src}" destdir="${output}"/>
    </target>

    <target name="jar" depends="compile">
        <jar destfile="Project.jar" basedir="${output}"/>
    </target>

</project>
```

Here's what you see when you run this build file:

```
%ant
Buildfile: build.xml
```

```
compile:
    [mkdir] Created dir: /home/steven/ant/ch12/selector/output
    [mkdir] Created dir: /home/steven/ant/ch12/selector/writeable
    [javac] Compiling 1 source file to /home/steven/ant/ch12/selector/output

jar:
    [jar] Building jar: /home/steven/ant/ch12/selector/Project.jar

main:
    [copy] Copying 1 file to /home/steven/ant/ch12/selector/sizeOK

BUILD SUCCESSFUL
Total time: 3 seconds
```

In this case, the code only copies files less than a megabyte in length, but custom seletors like this can select on anything, e.g., file creation date, read/write status, file-name, and so on.

Creating New Types

When creating new tasks, it's sometimes useful to create new data types to be used by those tasks. In this example, I'll create a new data type that extends the Ant FileList type and interfaces easily to attributes in a custom task.

This example centers around a new data type, ProjectType, which extends the Ant FileList class. To use that data type, I'll develop a new custom task, projectTask, that supports nested elements named multiFile, each of which supports an attribute named files. You can set the files attribute to a string containing multiple file-names such as *ed.txt* and *george.txt*, and the code will create an object of a custom data type, ProjectType, to contain that list of files.

Example 12-22 holds the code for the new data type, ProjectType, which extends the org.apache.tools.ant.types.FileList class. In this example, the code simply passes the list of files on back to the FileSet base class, but you can adapt this code to handle the list of files any way you want.

Example 12-22. The new data type (ch12/type/src/ProjectType.java)

```
package data;

import org.apache.tools.ant.types.FileList;

public class ProjectType extends FileList
{
    public void setFiles(String files)
    {
        super.setFiles(files);
    }
}
```

The build file for the custom task appears in Example 12-23; the nested multiFile element's files attribute takes the list of files that will be stored in internal filelist of the object of the custom data type.

Example 12-23. Build file for the data type example (ch12/type/build.xml)

```xml
<?xml version="1.0" ?>
<project basedir="." default="main">

    <property name="src" value="src"/>
    <property name="output" value="output"/>

    <target name="main" depends="jar">

    <taskdef name="projectTask" classname="ProjectTask" classpath="Project.jar" />

        <projectTask>
            <multiFile dir="src" files="ed.txt george.txt"/>
        </projectTask>
    </target>

    <target name="compile">
        <mkdir dir="${output}"/>
        <javac srcdir="${src}" destdir="${output}"/>
    </target>

    <target name="jar" depends="compile">
        <jar destfile="Project.jar" basedir="${output}"/>
    </target>

</project>
```

ProjectTask.java, which implements the projectTask task and uses the new data type, appears in Example 12-24.

Example 12-24. Task that uses the new type (ch12/type/src/ProjectTask.java)

```java
import data.ProjectType;
import org.apache.tools.ant.Task;
import org.apache.tools.ant.BuildException;

public class ProjectTask extends Task
{
    ProjectType multiFile = null;

    public void execute( ) throws BuildException
    {
        String[] files = multiFile.getFiles(getProject( ));

        for(int loopIndex = 0; loopIndex < files.length; loopIndex++)
        {
            System.out.println(files[loopIndex]);
```

```
        }
    }

    public ProjectType createMultiFile()
    {
        multiFile = new ProjectType();
        return multiFile;
    }
}
```

Here's how it works. *ProjectTask.java* handles the nested `multiFile` element with a `createMultiFile()` method, which creates a new object of the `ProjectType` class (our custom data type, based on the `FileList` class):

```
ProjectType multiFile = null;
        .
        .
        .
    public ProjectType createMultiFile()
    {
        multiFile = new ProjectType();
        return multiFile;
    }
```

The `setFiles()` method in the custom data type's support code creates a filelist from the list of files in the `multiFile` element's `files` attribute:

```
public void setFiles(String files)
{
    super.setFiles(files);
}
```

The files are now stored in the new data type object named `multiFile`. When the task executes, it will display their names, using that object:

```
public void execute() throws BuildException
{
    String[] files = multiFile.getFiles(getProject());

    for(int loopIndex = 0; loopIndex < files.length; loopIndex++)
    {
        System.out.println(files[loopIndex]);
    }
}
```

When this build file executes, the custom task creates a new object of the custom data type and displays the files in it:

```
%ant
Buildfile: build.xml

compile:
    [javac] Compiling 3 source files to /home/steven/ant/ch12/type/output
```

```
jar:
      [jar] Building jar: /home/steven/ant/ch12/type/Project.jar

main:
[projectTask] ed.txt
[projectTask] george.txt

BUILD SUCCESSFUL
Total time: 3 seconds
```

Customizing data types for use with custom tasks can be a powerful technique as
you develop and extend Ant to better fulfill your needs.

Index

Symbols

* (asterisk), 38, 48, 58
@ (at sign), 219
\ (backslash), 57
: (colon), 266
$ (dollar sign), 57, 246
! (exclamation point), 194
/ (forward slash), 18, 57, 91, 282
( ) (parentheses), 56
; (semicolon), 266

A

Abbot framework (JUnit extension), 148
absolute paths, 74
AbstractCvsTask class, 260
access attribute (javadoc task), 77
action attribute
    ftp task, 107, 109
    serverdeploy task, 202
actions, conditional, 35
adapter attribute (taskdef task), 258
adaptto attribute (taskdef task), 258
add command (CVS), 152
addBuildFailed-Sound method, 278
addBuildListener method (Project class), 263
addBuildSuccessfulSound method, 278
addedTags attribute
    ejbdoclet task, 223
    webdoclet task, 219
additionalparam attribute (javadoc task), 77
addproperty attribute (input task), 68
address attribute (mail task), 115
addsourcefile attribute (apply task), 179

addTarget method (Project class), 263
addTaskDefinition method (Project class), 263
addText method, 262, 269
admin command (CVS), 152
.aiff format, 278
algorithm attribute (checksum task), 97
all set property, 33
and element (condition task), 34
annotate command (CVS), 152
Ant build files, 67
    absolute path, 74
    Ant view and, 255
    calling tasks in, 68–72
    checksums and, 97
    custom tasks and, 267
    editing, 237
    EJB example, 200
    importing, 72, 74
    projects and, 6
    properties and, 18–23, 42, 211
    reformatting, 247
    running, 144–148
        in Eclipse, 247–253
    scp task example, 190
    servlet example, 221–223
    targets and, 7, 25
    taskdef task example, 259
    tasks and, 8–18
    Tomcat servers and, 188, 194
    .war files and, 184
    writing in Eclipse, 244–247
    XDoclet example, 226–230
    XML declaration and, 6

We'd like to hear your suggestions for improving our indexes. Send email to *index@oreilly.com*.

Ant build process, 4–6
    Anthill and, 119
    controlling, 32
    failure during, 26–28, 268
    scheduling automatic builds, 118–124
    stopping, 36
    testing, 125
Ant build tool
    alternatives to, 1
    debugger support, 28
    editions, 2
    installing, 2
    origins, 2
    process example, 4–6
    running, 23–31
    testing, 4
Ant classpath, 249, 253
Ant editor (Eclipse), 245, 251
Ant Home Entries item (Eclipse), 254
Ant Launcher, 24
ant task, 9, 71
Ant view (Eclipse), 255
ANT_ARGS environment variable, 26
ant.bat file, 26
antcall task, 9, 68–71
antfile attribute (ant task), 71
ant.file property, 22, 74
Anthill build tool, 119–123
ANT_HOME environment variable, 43
    filename length, 3
    installing Ant, 3
    library files and, 31
Antidote IDE, 241
ant.java.version property, 22
antlr task, 11
ANT_OPTS environment variable, 26
ant.project.name property, 22
antrc_post.bat file, 26
AntSoundPlayer class, 278
antstructure task, 9, 206, 213
ant.version property, 23
apachesoap element (ejbdoclet task), 223
append attribute
    apply task, 179
    cvs task, 154
    exec task, 172
    java task, 169
    sshexec task, 113
application attribute (weblogic element), 203
applications
    deploying by copying, 102–106
    moving files, 106

packaging for deployment, 88–99
remote deployment
    using FTP, 107–111
    using SSH, 112
    using Telnet, 111
    via email, 114–116
    setting file protections with chmod, 116, 118
apply task, 9, 56, 179–181
appxml attribute (ear task), 201
arg element
    arguments and, 170, 181
    example, 168
    exec task and, 174
    generic element and, 203
    jonas element and, 205
args attribute
    java task, 169
    weblogic element, 232
argument element, 155
ASCII characters, 12
Assert class (JUnit), 128
assertEquals method (JUnit), 128–130, 132
assertFalse method (JUnit), 128
assertions element, 137, 170
Assertions type, 44
assertNotNull method (JUnit), 128, 132
assertNotSame method (JUnit), 128
assertNull method (JUnit), 128, 130
assertSame method (JUnit), 128, 130
assertTrue method (JUnit), 128, 130, 132
asterisk (*), 38, 48, 58
at command (Windows), 116, 118
at sign (@), 219
attrib task, 11
attribute element
    manifest task, 84
    xmlvalidate element and, 207
    xslt/style task and, 217
attributes
    handling for custom tasks, 266–268
    for project elements, 7
    for property elements, 18–22
    for target elements, 8
author attribute (javadoc task), 77
authserver command (CVS), 152
available element (condition task), 34
available task, 9, 33, 37, 178
axisdeploy element (ejbdoclet task), 223
axisundeploy element (ejbdoclet task), 223

B

backslash (\), 57
backups attribute (patch task), 166
basedir attribute
 cab task, 187
 ear task, 201
 jar task, 82
 project element, 7, 23, 72
 tar task, 89
 war task, 185
 xslt/style task, 216
 zip task, 92
BaseExtendSelector class, 284
basejarname attribute (ejbjar task), 231
basename task, 9, 102
bash shell (Unix), 3, 5
batch execution, 179–181
batch testing, 142, 144
batchtest element, 136
batchtest task, 144
bcc element (mail task), 115
bcclist attribute (mail task), 114
begintoken attribute (FilterSet type), 52
binary attribute (ftp task), 110
binary release (Ant), 2
blgenclient task (EJB), 14, 230
boolean data type, 266
bootclasspath attribute
 javac task, 60, 62
 javadoc task, 77
 path type, 45
bootclasspath element
 java task and, 170
 path type and, 45
bootclasspathref attribute
 javac task, 60
 javadoc task, 77
borland element
 ejbdoclet task, 223
 nesting and, 232
bottom attribute (javadoc task), 77
branching (see forking)
breakiterator attribute (javadoc task), 77
brief formatter, 135, 139
build files (see Ant build files)
build numbers, 84, 119
build process (see Ant build process; Java
 build process)
build property (deploy task), 193
BuildEvent object, 280
BuildException constructor, 269
-buildfile option, 23, 25

buildFinished method, 278
buildnumber task, 9, 84
buildStarted method, 278
build.xml file, 6, 25, 71
bunzip2 task, 9, 92
byline attribute (replaceregexp task), 238
bzip2 task, 9, 91

C

.cab files
 Ant tasks and, 11
 creating, 187
 deploying, 188
cab task, 11, 187
cabarc tool (Microsoft), 187
cabfile attribute (cab task), 187
cache attribute (depend task), 239
carriage returns, fixing, 94–96
casesensitive attribute
 DirSet type, 49
 FileSet type, 47
castormapping element (ejbdoclet task), 223
catalogpath element (xmlcatalog
   element), 207
cc element (mail task), 115
CCCheckin task, 14
CCCheckout task, 14
cclist attribute (mail task), 114
CCLock task, 14
CCMCheckin task, 16
CCMCheckinTask task, 16
CCMCheckout task, 16
CCMCreateTask task, 16
CCMkattr task, 14
CCMkbl task, 14
CCMkdir task, 14
CCMkelem task, 14
CCMklabel task, 14
CCMklbType task, 14
CCMReconfigure task, 16
CCRmtype task, 14
CCUnCheckout task, 14
CCUnluck task, 14
CCUpdate task, 14
<CDATA> section (XML), 74
chacl command (CVS), 152
change logs, 161–164
char data type, 266
charset attribute
 javadoc task, 77
 mail task, 114
 message element, 116

checkout command (CVS), 152
checksum element (condition task), 34
checksum task, 9, 97
chgrp task, 12
chmod attribute (ftp task), 110
chmod task, 9, 103, 116, 118
Choose Location dialog box (Eclipse), 255
chown command (CVS), 152
chown task, 12
classconstants element (FilterChain
    type), 54, 56
classes element (war task), 186
classname attribute
    available task, 37
    formatter task, 135
    generic element, 203
    java task, 169
    jonas element, 205
    mapper element, 57
    taskdef task, 258
    xmlvalidate task, 206
classpath attribute
    available task, 37
    depend task, 239
    ejbjar task, 231
    generic element, 203
    java task, 169
    javac task, 60, 62
    javadoc task, 77
    jonas element, 205
    jspc task, 199
    junit task, 138
    mapper element, 57
    path type, 45
    property element, 18
    taskdef task, 226, 258
    weblogic element, 203, 232
    xslt/style task, 216
classpath element, 168
    depend task and, 239
    ejbjar task, 231
    java task and, 170
    jonas element and, 205
    nesting, 134
    path type and, 45
    serverdeploy task and, 203
    taskdef task and, 259
    weblogic element and, 233
    xmlcatalog element and, 207
    xslt/style task and, 217
classpathref attribute
    available task, 37
    java task, 169

javac task, 60
javadoc task, 77
jspc task, 199
    mapper element, 57
    property element, 18
    xmlvalidate task, 206
    xslt/style task, 216
classpathref element (jspc task), 199
clearcase task, 150
Clearcase version control system, 13, 150
closure attribute (depend task), 239
cmpversion attribute (ejbjar task), 231
code assist (Eclipse), 245
collapseAttributes attribute (xmlproperty
    task), 212
colon (:), 266
command attribute
    cvs task, 154, 158, 160
    exec task, 172
    sshexec task, 113
command line
    environment variables and, 44
    options for, 23, 64
commandline element, 155, 160
Commandline object, 275
commit command (CVS), 152
committers, 2
compilearg element, 64
compiler attribute
    compilearg element, 65
    javac task, 60, 65
    jspc task, 199
    weblogic element, 232
compilerclasspath attribute (jspc task), 199
compiling
    documentation and, 74
    JSPs, 196–199
    source code, 60–63
    source files, 63
component attribute (weblogic
    element), 204
compress attribute
    cab task, 187
    ear task, 201
    jar task, 82
    war task, 185
    zip task, 92
compression attribute
    cvs task, 154
    cvstagdiff task, 164
    tar task, 89, 90
compressionlevel attribute (cvs task), 154
concat task, 9, 53

concatfilter element (FilterChain type), 54
Concurrent Version System (see CVS)
condition task, 9, 33, 111
conditions, 32–36
configParam element
    ejbdoclet task, 223
    webdoclet task, 219
Console view (Eclipse), 247–249
constants, 42, 56
containers, EJB and, 200–205, 223–230
contains element
    condition task, 34
    linecontains filter and, 55
contains selector, 50
containsregexp selector, 50
content assist (Eclipse), 245
Continuous source control servers, 15
Continuus commands, 150
copy task
    deployment and, 102–106
    description, 9
    file filtering, 51
    file sets and, 46
    filterchain element, 53
    mappers and, 56
copydir task, 9
copyfile task, 9
cr attribute (fixcrlf task), 95
createDataType method, 277
createResult method (JUnit), 130
createTask method (Project class), 263, 276
creation date, 98
creation time, 98
crontab utility (Unix), 116, 118
Cruise Control build tool, 123
csc compiler, 187
Csc task, 13
CVS (Concurrent Version System)
    Anthill and, 119
    change logs, 161–164
    changes between versions, 164
    commands, 152
    creating patches, 165
    CVSROOT environment variable
        and, 156
    logging in and, 153
    servers and, 154–160
    source control and, 151–153
    version data and, 161
cvs task
    checking out modules, 155
    CVS commands and, 152

CVS servers and, 154
    description, 9, 150
cvschangelog task, 9, 151, 163
cvsclientproperty attribute (cvsversion
        task), 161
cvspass task, 9, 151
    checking out modules, 155
    logging in with, 153
    updating shared code, 157
cvsroot attribute
    cvs task, 154–156
    cvschangelog task, 163
    cvspass task, 153
    cvstagdiff task, 164
    cvsversion task, 161
CVSROOT environment variable
    CVS servers and, 156
    cvs task and, 154
    cvspass task and, 155
    cvstagdiff task and, 164
    cvsversion task and, 161
    Windows and, 153
cvsrsh attribute
    cvs task, 154
    cvschangelog task, 163
    cvstagdiff task, 164
    cvsversion task, 161
CVS_RSH environment variable, 154, 161,
        164
cvsserverproperty attribute (cvsversion
        task), 161
cvsServerVersion property (cvsversion
        element), 161
cvstagdiff task, 9, 151, 164
cvsversion task, 9, 161
Cygwin environment, 174

D

-D option, 23, 42
-d option, 23
daemons element (parallel task), 182
dao element (ejbdoclet task), 223
data (see types)
dataobject element (ejbdoclet task), 223
date attribute (cvs task), 154
date selector, 50, 51
datetime attribute (touch task), 99
davidhost attribute (jonas element), 204
davidport attribute (jonas element), 204
Davidson, James Duncan, 2
daysinpast attribute (cvschangelog task), 163
dbUnit framework (JUnit extension), 148

ddcreator task (EJB), 14, 230
debug attribute
    javac task, 61
    weblogic element, 204
-debug option, 23, 28
debuglevel attribute (javac task), 61
default attribute (project element), 7
defaultexcludes attribute
    cab task, 187
    chmod task, 117
    delete task, 100
    ear task, 201
    FileSet type, 47
    fixcrlf task, 95
    jar task, 82
    javadoc task, 77
    tar task, 90
    war task, 186
    xslt/style task, 216
    zip task, 92
defaultexcludes task, 9, 48
defaultInput method (Project class), 263
DefaultLogger class, 280
defaultvalue attribute (input task), 68
delete action (weblogic tool), 203
delete task, 9, 66, 99–101
deletecharacters element (FilterChain
            type), 54
delimOutput attribute (FilterChain type), 54
deltree task, 9
depend attribute (javac task), 61
depend selector, 50
depend task, 12, 63, 238–240
dependencies
    antcall task and, 68
    depend task, 63
    handling, 238–240
    parallel task and, 182
    recommendations, 71
    tasks and, 16–18
dependency attribute (ejbjar task), 231
depends attribute
    build example, 17
    ftp task, 110
    target element, 8
dependset task, 9
deploy action
    JOnAS servers, 204
    weblogic tool, 203
deploy task, 192
deployment
    by copying, 102–106
    to EJB containers, 200–205

hot, 202–205
    by moving files, 106
    packaging applications for, 88–99
    preparing for, 99–102
    scheduling automatic builds, 118–124
    scp task, 189–192
    setting file protections, 116, 118
    Tomcat web servers and, 192–196
    using
        email, 114–116
        FTP, 107–111
        SSH, 112
        Telnet, 111
    .war files, 185
    web, 188
deploymentdescriptor element
    ejbdoclet task, 224, 226
    webdoclet task, 219
deprecation attribute (javac task), 61
depth selector, 50
description attribute (target element), 8, 30
Description type, 44
descriptordir attribute (ejbjar task), 231
dest attribute
    apply task, 179, 181
    cvs task, 154
    cvsversion task, 161
    get task, 195
    unjar task, 84
destdir attribute
    depend task, 239
    ejbdoclet task, 223
    ejbjar task, 231
    fixcrlf task, 95
    javac task, 61
    javadoc task, 77
    jspc task, 199
    webdoclet task, 219
    weblogic element, 232
    xslt/style task, 216
destfile attribute
    cvschangelog task, 163
    cvstagdiff task, 164
    ear task, 201
    gzip/bzip2 tasks, 92
    jar task, 82
    patch task, 166
    tar task, 90
    war task, 186
    zip task, 93
-diagnostics option, 23
diff command (CVS), 152, 155, 159
different selector, 50

dir attribute
  ant task, 71
  apply task, 179
  build.xml file and, 71
  chmod task, 117
  custom tasks and, 273
  cvschangelog task, 163
  delete task, 101
  DirSet type, 49
  exec task, 173
  FileList type, 49
  FileSet type, 47
  ftp task, 109
  java task, 169
  junit task, 133
  mkdir task, 102
  patch task, 166
dir command (Windows), 176
directories
  copying to new locations, 102
  creating, 101
  default excludes, 48
  deleting, 99
  dependencies and, 239
  ejbjar task and, 231
  ftp task and, 107
  jspc task and, 199
  manipulating remotely, 99
  modules and, 151
  moving, 106
  scanning, 273
  working with groups of, 48
DirectoryScanner class, 273
dirmode attribute
  tarfileset element, 91
  zipfileset element, 93
dirname task, 9, 102
dirset element
  apply task, 181
  chmod task, 118
DirSet type, 44, 48, 102
displayname attribute (user element), 164
docencoding attribute (javadoc task), 77
doclet attribute (javadoc task), 77
doclet task (XDoclet), 218
docletpath attribute (javadoc task), 77
docletpathref attribute (javadoc task), 77
doctitle attribute (javadoc task), 78
document element, 6
documentation
  of code, 74–80
  fixing carriage returns in, 94–96

JUnit, 127
  (see also reports)
dollar sign ($), 57, 246
DSTAMP property (tstamp task), 85
dtd element
  ejbjar task, 231
  xmlcatalog element and, 207
  xmlvalidate task and, 207
DTDs
  antstructure task and, 206
  creating for Ant tasks, 213
  validating with, 209–211
  XMLCatalog and, 207
dump attribute (depend task), 239
duplicate attribute
  ear task, 201
  jar task, 82
  war task, 186
  zip task, 93
duration attribute (success/fail
        elements), 235

E

-e option, 23
ear task, 9, 201
easerver element (ejbdoclet task), 224
echo task, 9, 277
  creating text files, 98
  JavaScript and, 276
  output and, 28, 56
echoproperties task, 12
Eclipse IDE, 241–244
  Ant versions and, 253, 255
  Ant view and, 255
  running Ant build files, 247–253
  writing Ant build files, 244–247
eclipse.org consortium, 241
edit command (CVS), 152
editors command (CVS), 152
EJB (Enterprise JavaBeans)
  Ant tasks for, 14
  deploying to containers, 200–205
  developing, 230–233
  working with containers, 223–230
ejbc task (EJB), 14, 230
ejbcclass attribute (weblogic element), 232
ejbClassNameSuffix attribute (ejbdoclet
        task), 223
ejbdoclet task (XDoclet), 218, 223–230
ejbjar task (EJB), 14, 230–233
ejbSpec attribute (ejbdoclet task), 223

elements, nesting, 45, 270–272

-emacs option, 23

email, remote deployment, 114–116

enablemultiplemappings attribute (copy task), 104

encoding attribute
    copy task, 104
    ear task, 201
    fixcrlf task, 95
    jar task, 82
    javac task, 61
    javadoc task, 78
    loadfile task, 41
    mail task, 114
    manifest task, 84
    replaceregexp task, 238
    war task, 186
    zip task, 93

end attribute (cvschangelog task), 163

enddate attribute (cvstagdiff task), 164

end-of-line (EOL) characters, 95

endtag attribute (cvstagdiff task), 165

endtoken attribute (FilterSet type), 52

Enterprise JavaBeans (see EJB)

entitybmp element (ejbdoclet task), 224

entitycmp element (ejbdoclet task), 224

entityfacade element (ejbdoclet task), 224

entitypk element (ejbdoclet task), 224

env element, 134, 170, 174, 181

environment attribute (property element), 18, 43

environment variables
    customizing, 26
    env element and, 170, 174
    forked JVM and, 134
    JDK and, 3
    setting, 251
    setting properties using, 18, 43

eof attribute (fixcrlf task), 95

eol attribute (fixcrlf task), 96

EOL (end-of-line) characters, 95

equals element (condition task), 34

error attribute
    apply task, 179
    cvs task, 154
    exec task, 173
    java task, 169

errorproperty attribute
    apply task, 180
    batchtest element, 136
    exec task, 173

java task, 169

junit task, 133, 138

test task, 136

errors
    brief formatter and, 139
    build process and, 27
    Eclipse and, 246
    external programs and, 175
    Java code and, 170–172
    Java development and, 241
    responding to, 32
    validating XML documents, 209

escapeunicode element (FilterChain type), 54

events
    custom listeners, 278–280
    custom loggers, 280

exclamation point (!), 194

exclude attribute (delete task), 100

exclude element
    cab task and, 188
    depend task and, 239
    DirSet type and, 48
    fileset element and, 47
    FileSet type, 46
    jar task and, 83
    javac task, 62
    PatternSet type and, 50
    support element and, 231
    xslt/style task and, 217
    zip task and, 94

excludedTags attribute
    ejbdoclet task, 223
    webdoclet task, 219

excludepackagenames attribute (javadoc task), 78

excludes attribute
    cab task, 187
    chmod task, 117
    delete task, 101
    DirSet type, 49
    ear task, 201
    FileSet type, 47
    fixcrlf task, 96
    jar task, 82
    javac task, 61
    PatternSet type, 50
    tar task, 90
    war task, 186
    xslt/style task, 216
    zip task, 93

---

excludes element
    jspc task and, 199
    MatchingTask class, 274
excludesfile attribute
    cab task, 187
    delete task, 100
    DirSet type, 49
    ear task, 201
    FileSet type, 47
    fixcrlf task, 96
    jar task, 82
    javac task, 61
    PatternSet type, 50
    tar task, 90
    war task, 186
    xslt/style task, 216
    zip task, 93
excludesfile element
    DirSet type and, 48
    fileset element and, 47
    FileSet type, 46
    PatternSet type and, 50
exdirs element, 45
exec task, 9, 172–178
    arguments and, 181
    file permissions and, 103
execon task, 9
executable attribute
    apply task, 180
    exec task, 173, 177
    javac task, 61
Execute class, 274
execute method
    Ant tasks and, 257, 260, 262
    Execute class, 275
    nested elements and, 271
    Task class, 261
executeTarget method (Project class), 263
executeTargets method (Project class), 263
executing
    Ant, 24
    batch programs, 179–181
    external programs, 172–178
    Java code, 167–172
    setting order and, 182
exit method (System), 77
expandproperties element (FilterChain
        type), 54
export command (CVS), 152
expression attribute
    containsregexp selector, 51
    param element, 217

extdirs attribute
    javac task, 61
    javadoc task, 78
    path type, 45
extension attribute
    formatter task, 135
    xslt/style task, 216
external programs
    executing, 172–178
    running, 274
External Tools dialog box (Eclipse), 255

F

-f option, 23, 25
factory element (TraX), 218
fail element (sound task), 234
fail method (JUnit), 130
fail task, 9, 36, 171
failifexecutionfails attribute
    apply task, 180
    exec task, 173, 175
failonany attribute (parallel task), 182
failonerror attribute
    apply task, 180
    copy task, 104
    custom tasks and, 268
    cvs task, 154
    cvschangelog task, 163
    cvstagdiff task, 165
    cvsversion task, 161
    delete task, 101
    exec task, 173, 175
    java task, 169, 171
    javac task, 61
    javadoc task, 78
    jspc task, 199
    loadfile task, 41
    mail task, 114
    scp task, 191
    sshexec task, 113
    tasks and, 27
    xmlvalidate task, 207
failureproperty attribute
    batchtest element, 136
    junit task, 133
    test task, 136
file attribute
    available task, 37
    buildnumber task, 85
    checksum task, 97
    chmod task, 117
    compilearg element, 65

copy task, 104
delete task, 101
echo task, 98
env element, 174
FileSet type, 47
import task, 73
manifest task, 84
property element, 18
property task, 39
replaceregexp task, 238
scp task, 191
taskdef task, 258
touch task, 99
xmlproperty task, 212
xmlvalidate task, 207
file mappers, 44, 56–59
-file option, 23, 25
fileext attribute (checksum task), 97
filelist element (apply task), 181
FileList type, 44, 49, 102, 286
filemode attribute (zipfileset element), 93
filename selector, 46, 50
filepath attribute (available task), 37
files
    checking contents of, 97
    checking modification dates, 38
    comparing, 159, 165
    compressing, 91
    copying
        to local machines, 189
        to new locations, 102
        using filesets, 189
    creating empty, 98
    default excludes, 48
    deleting, 99–101
    filters and, 51, 53
    lists of, 49
    mappers and, 44, 56–59
    moving, 106, 107
    property, 39–43
    retrieving using ftp task, 109
    selecting to compile, 63
    setting creation time/date, 98
    setting protections with chmod, 116, 118
    working with groups of, 46–48
    XML, 211
files attribute
    FileList type, 49
    mail task, 114
fileset element, 46–48
    cab task and, 188
    catalogpath element and, 207

delete task and, 100
depend task and, 239
ejbdoclet task, 224
junitreport task and, 141
nesting, 93, 101, 106, 111, 118
replaceregexp task and, 238
scp task and, 192
war task and, 186
webdoclet task, 219
xslt/style task and, 217
FileSet type, 44, 46
    attributes, 47
    batch testing and, 144
    cab task and, 188
    chmod task and, 118
    defaultexcludes, 48
    delete task and, 99
    depend task and, 239
    fixcrlf task and, 94
    jar task and, 83
    javac task and, 62
    pathconvert task and, 102
    PatternSet type and, 49
    tar task and, 89
    tarfileset elements and, 90
    zip task and, 94
filesetmanifest attribute (jar task), 82
filesets, 189, 272–274
filesmatch element (condition task), 34
filesonly attribute
    ear task, 201
    jar task, 82
    war task, 186
    zip task, 93
filter task, 9, 52
FilterChain type, 44, 53–56, 106
filtering attribute (copy task), 104
filterreader element (FilterChain type), 54
FilterReaders, 53–56
filters
    copy task and, 106
    custom, 282–284
    files and, 51, 53
    FileSets as, 49
    text and, 53–56
FilterSet type, 44, 51–53
filtersfile attribute (filter task), 53
filtertrace attribute
    batchtest element, 136
    junit task, 133
    test task, 136
-find option, 23, 25

firewalls, 236
fixcrlf task, 10, 94–96
fixlast attribute (fixcrlf task), 96
flags attribute (replaceregexp task), 238
flatdestdir attribute (ejbjar task), 231
flatten attribute (copy task), 105
flatten mapper, 57
followsymlinks attribute
    DirSet type, 49
    FileSet type, 47
footer attribute (javadoc task), 78
force attribute
    ejbdoclet task, 223
    webdoclet task, 219
    xslt/style task, 216
forceoverwrite attribute (checksum task), 97
fork attribute
    batchtest element, 136
    java task, 169
    javac task, 61
    junit task, 133
    test task, 136
forking
    based on true/false properties, 68
    compiler, 64
    java task and, 167
    JVM, 167, 169
    jvmarg elements and, 134
format attribute
    report task, 141
    taskdef task, 258
Format command (Eclipse), 247, 251
format element (tstamp task), 86
formatter element (junit task), 135, 138
formatter task, 135
formatting
    Ant build files, 247
    test results, 135
forward slash (/), 18, 57, 91, 282
forwardslash attribute (apply task), 180
from attribute
    glob mapper and, 58
    mail task, 115
    mapper element, 57
    regular expressions and, 56, 58
    slashes and, 57
from element (mail task), 115
FTP, remote deployment, 107–111
ftp: schema, 193
ftp task, 12, 102, 107–111, 188
fullpath attribute
    tarfileset element, 91
    zipfileset element, 93, 201

G

generic element (serverdeploy task), 203
genericjarsuffix attribute
    ejbjar task, 231
    weblogic element, 232
genkey task, 10
get task, 10, 102, 193–196
getBaseDir method (Project class), 263
getBuildListeners method (Project class), 263
getDefaultInputStream method (Project
        class), 263
getDefaultTarget method (Project class), 263
getDescription method
    Project class, 263
    Task class, 261
getElementName method (Project class), 263
getIncludedFiles method (DirectoryScanner
        class), 273
getLocation method (Task class), 261, 265
getName method
    JUnit framework, 130
    Project class, 263
getOwningTarget method (Task class), 261
getProject method (Task class), 262
getProperties method
    Project class, 263
    System class, 22
getProperty method (Project class), 262, 276
getReference method (Project class), 263
getReferences method (Project class), 263
getRuntimeConfigurableWrapper method
        (Task class), 261
getTarget method (BuildEvent), 280
getTargets method (Project class), 263
getTask method (BuildEvent), 280
getTaskDefinitions method (Project
        class), 264
getTaskName method (Task class), 261
getTaskType method (Task class), 261
getUserProperties method (Project
        class), 264
getUserProperty method (Project class), 264
getWrapper method (Task class), 261
glob mapper, 12, 57
group attribute
    javadoc task, 78
    tarfileset element, 91
Gump build tool, 123
gunzip task, 10, 92
gzip task, 10, 90–92

H

-h option, 23
haltonerror attribute
    batchtest element, 136
    junit task, 134
    test task, 136
haltonfailure attribute
    batchtest element, 136
    junit task, 134, 138
    test task, 136
handleErrorFlush method (Task class), 261
handleErrorOutput method (Task class), 261
handleFlush method (Task class), 261
handleInput method (Task class), 261
handleOutput method (Task class), 261
header attribute (javadoc task), 78
headfilter element (FilterChain type), 54
-help option, 23
helpfile attribute (javadoc task), 78
hibernatedoclet task (XDoclet), 218
history command (CVS), 152
homeinterface element (ejbdoclet task), 224
host attribute (sshexec task), 113
hot deployment, 202–205
hpas element (ejbdoclet task), 224
HTML reports, 165
HtmlUnit framework (JUnit extension), 148
http element (condition task), 34, 111
http: schema, 193
https: schema, 193
HttpUnit framework (JUnit extension), 148
hyphen (-), 25

I

IBM, Eclipse and, 241
icontract task, 12
id attribute
    FilterSet type, 52
    patterns and, 49
    xmlcatalog element, 207
identity mapper, 57
ieplugin attribute (jspc task), 199
if attribute
    batchtest element, 136
    elements and, 47
    elements supporting, 35
    fail task and, 36
    formatter task, 135
    param element, 217

target element, 8
test task, 136
if statement (see conditions)
ignoreerrors attribute (get task), 195
ignoreNoncriticalErrors attribute (ftp
        task), 110
ignoresystemclasses attribute (available
        task), 37
ignorewhitespace attribute (patch task), 166
ilasm task, 13
ildasm task, 13
image task, 12
imageurl attribute (splash task), 236
import command (CVS), 152
import task, 10, 72, 74
ImportTypelib task, 13
in attribute (xslt/style task), 216
include element
    cab task and, 188
    depend task and, 239
    DirSet type and, 48
    fileset element and, 47
    FileSet type, 46
    filesets and, 272
    jar task and, 83
    javac task, 62
    PatternSet type and, 50
    support element and, 231
    xslt/style task and, 217
    zip task and, 94
includeantruntime attribute
    javac task, 61
    junit task, 134
includeEmptyDirs attribute
    copy task, 105
    delete task, 101
includefilenames attribute (mail task), 115
includeJavaRuntime attribute (javac task), 61
includes attribute
    cab task, 187
    chmod task, 117
    delete task, 100
    DirSet type, 49
    ear task, 201
    FileSet type, 47
    fixcrlf task, 96
    jar task, 83
    javac task, 61
    PatternSet type, 50
    tar task, 90
    war task, 186

---

xslt/style task, 216
zip task, 93
includes element
  jspc task and, 199
  MatchingTask class, 274
includeSemanticAttribute attribute
      (xmlproperty task), 212
includesfile attribute
  cab task, 187
  delete task, 100
  DirSet type, 49
  ear task, 201
  FileSet type, 47
  fixcrlf task, 96
  jar task, 83
  javac task, 62
  PatternSet type, 50
  tar task, 90
  war task, 186
  xslt/style task, 216
  zip task, 93
includesfile element
  DirSet type and, 48
  fileset element and, 47
  FileSet type, 46
  PatternSet type and, 50
index attribute (jar task), 83
info command (CVS), 152
inheritAll attribute
  ant task, 71
  antcall task, 69
inheritRefs attribute
  ant task, 71
  antcall task, 69
init command (CVS), 152
init method
  Ant tasks and, 262
  Project class, 264
  Task class, 261
initialCR attribute (telnet task), 112
input attribute
  apply task, 180
  exec task, 173
  java task, 169
input task, 10, 66–68, 107
-inputhandler option, 23
inputstring attribute
  apply task, 180
  exec task, 173
  java task, 169
installing
  Ant, 2
  Anthill, 119

int data type, 266
Internet Service Providers (ISPs), 31
IP addresses, 107, 189
iPlanet element, 232
iplanet-ejbc task (EJB), 14, 230
isfalse element (condition task), 34
isInvalid method (Task class), 261
ISPs (Internet Service Providers), 31
isreference element (condition task), 34
isset element (condition task), 34
istrue element (condition task), 34

J

jar attribute (java task), 169
.jar files
  adding, 249
  creating, 81–84
  ejbjar task and, 231–233
  optional tasks and, 11
  running scripts and, 275
  unpacking, 11
jar: schema, 193
jar task, 10
  creating .jar files, 81–83
  ear task and, 201
  jlink task and, 12
  nesting and, 83
  war task and, 184
  zipfileset element and, 201
jarlib-available task, 12
jarlib-manifest task, 12
jarlib-resolve task, 12
jarsign task, 82
Jasper JSP compiler, 196
Java build process
  calling other tasks, 68–72
  compiling code, 60–66
  creating .jar files, 81–84
  documenting code, 74–80
  importing build files, 72, 74
  setting build numbers, 84
  setting timestamps, 85–87
  user input and, 66–68
Java classes
  data types and, 267
  dependencies and, 238, 240
  filters and, 54
  generic element and, 203
  java task and, 167
  recognizing updated, 193
  test element and, 135
Java Development Kit (see JDK)

Java Media Framework, 234
Java Native Interface (JNI), 12
java task, 10, 167–172
    running test cases, 137
    timeouts and, 177
JavaBean Tester tool, 148
javac task, 10
    alternatives, 65
    compiling
        code, 60–63
        JSPs, 196, 198
        source files, 63
    depend task and, 238
    file sets and, 47
    forking compiler, 64
    java task and, 170
    setting command-line options, 64
    src element and, 45
    srcdir attribute, 48
JavaCC compiler, 12
javacc task, 12
JAVACMD environment variable, 26
javadoc task, 10, 74–80
Javadoc wizard (Eclipse), 247
javadoc2 task, 10
javafiles attribute (fixcrlf task), 96
javah task, 12
JAVA_HOME environment variable, 3
java.io.File data type, 266
JavaServer Pages (see JSPs)
JAXP (Sun), 206
jboss element (ejbdoclet task), 224, 232
jbosswebxml element (webdoclet task), 219
JcovMerge task, 12
JcovReport task, 12
JDBCTask class, 260
jdepend task, 12
JDK (Java Development Kit), 3, 215
jdodoclet task (XDoclet), 218
Jemmy (Java library), 148
Jenerator, 148
JFCUnit, 148
JJDoc documentation generator, 12
jjdoc task, 12
JJTree preprocessor, 12
jjtree task, 12
jlink task, 12
jmxdoclet task (XDoclet), 218
JNDI DataSource helper package, 149
JNI (Java Native Interface), 12

JOnAS
    deployment tool, 204
    servers
        ejbdoclet task and, 224
        EJBs and, 230
        hot deployment and, 202
        jonas element and, 204
jonas element
    ejbdoclet task, 224
    nesting, 232
    serverdeploy task, 203, 204–205
JOnAS servers
jonasroot attribute (jonas element), 204
jonaswebxml element (webdoclet task), 219
JPCoverage task, 12
jprobe task, 12
jrun element (ejbdoclet task), 224
jrunwebxml element (webdoclet task), 219
jsharpc task, 13
jspc task, 12, 196–199
JSPs (JavaServer Pages), 192, 196–199
jsptaglib element (webdoclet task), 219
JUnit framework, 127–130
    Ant tasks and, 12
    batch testing, 142, 144
    extending, 148–149
    performing tests, 133–137
    running build file, 144–148
    running test cases, 137–142
    writing tests, 130–133
junit task, 12, 125, 138, 142
    packager mapper and, 58
    performing tests with, 133–137
    testing with, 126
JUnitDoclet, 149
JUnitPerf, 149
junitreport task, 12, 141
JUnitX, 149
JVM
    accessing system properties, 135
    Eclipse and, 247
    forking, 167, 169
    mixed environments and, 174
    passing environment variables to, 134
jvm attribute
    java task, 169
    junit task, 134
jvmarg element
    arguments and, 170
    generic element and, 203

jonas element and, 205
  nesting and, 134
jvmargs attribute
  java task, 169
  weblogic element, 233
jvmdebuglevel attribute (weblogic
      element), 233
jWebUnit, 149

K

-k option, 23
keepcompression attribute
  ear task, 202
  jar task, 83
  war task, 186
  zip task, 93
keepgenerated attribute (weblogic
      element), 233
keepgeneric attribute (weblogic
      element), 233
-keep-going option, 23
keepRoot attribute (xmlproperty task), 212
key attribute
  env element, 174
  system properties and, 135
keyfile attribute
  scp task, 191
  sshexec task, 113
knownhosts attribute
  scp task, 191
  sshexec task, 113
knownhosts file, 189

L

-l option, 23
language attribute (script task), 276
lenient attribute (xmlvalidate task), 207
lib directory (Ant), 11, 31
lib element (war task), 186
-lib option, 23, 31
libcabinet tool, 187
line attribute
  argument element, 155
  compilearg element, 65
line feed (carriage return), 94–96
linecontains element (FilterChain type), 54
linecontainsregexp element (FilterChain
      type), 54
link attribute (javadoc task), 78
linkoffline attribute (javadoc task), 78
linksource attribute (javadoc task), 78

Linux environment, 176
list action
  JOnAS servers, 204
  weblogic tool, 203
-listener option, 23
listeners, custom, 278–280
listfiles attribute (javac task), 62
listing attribute (ftp task), 110
loaderRef attribute (taskdef task), 258
loadfile task, 10, 41, 53
loadproperties task, 10, 53, 56
locale attribute
  format task, 87
  javadoc task, 78
Locale class (Java), 87
localhomeinterface element (ejbdoclet
      task), 224
localinterface element (ejbdoclet task), 224
location attribute
  dtd element, 207
  pathelement element, 45
  property element, 19
log command (CVS), 152
log method
  loggers and, 280
  Project class, 264
  Task class, 261
Log4Unit, 149
logError attribute
  apply task, 180
  exec task, 173
  java task, 169
-logfile option, 30
-logger option, 23
loggers/logging
  custom, 280
  output, 30, 278
logging in, source control and, 153
login command (CVS), 152
logout command (CVS), 152
longfile attribute (tar task), 90
loops attribute (success/fail elements), 235
ls command (CVS), 152, 176
lsacl command (CVS), 152

M

Mac OS environment, 33
macrodef task, 10
mail task, 10, 12, 114–116
mailhost attribute (mail task), 114
MailLogger.failure.notify property, 116
MailLogger.failure.subject property, 116

MailLogger.failure.to property, 116
MailLogger.from property, 116
MailLogger.mailhost property, 116
MailLogger.port property, 116
MailLogger.success.notify property, 116
MailLogger.success.subject property, 116
MailLogger.success.toSpecifies property, 116
mailport attribute (mail task), 115
manifest attribute
    ear task, 202
    jar task, 83
    war task, 186
manifest element (jar task), 83
manifest files, 86
    creating, 81, 84
    default, 185
    jar task and, 83
    plug-in, 247
manifest task, 10, 84
manifestencoding attribute (jar task), 83
mapped attribute (jspc task), 199
mapper element
    attributes, 57
    batch execution and, 181
    copying files and, 103
    nesting, 57, 69, 106
mappers, 44, 56–59
master targets, 16
match attribute (replaceregexp task), 238
MatchingTask class, 260, 273
maudit task, 12
maxmemory attribute
    java task, 169
    javadoc task, 78
    junit task, 134
maxparallel attribute
    apply task, 180
    chmod task, 117
maybeConfigure method (Task class), 261
MD5 checksum, 97
memoryInitialSize attribute (javac task), 62
memoryMaximumSize attribute (javac
    task), 62
merge mapper, 57
mergeDir attribute
    ejbdoclet task, 223
    webdoclet task, 219
message attribute
    fail task, 36
    input task, 68
    mail task, 115
message element (mail task), 116

messagefile attribute (mail task), 115
messagemimetype attribute (mail task), 115
metainf element
    jar task and, 83
    war task and, 186
Metamata Metrics/WebGain Quality
    Analyzer, 12
methods
    attributes in custom tasks, 266–268
    Project class and, 262
    Property class, 263–265
    Task class, 261
Microsoft, 3, 15, 151, 187
millis attribute (touch task), 99
mimemail task, 12
mimetype attribute (message element), 116
mkdir task, 10, 20, 99, 101
mmetrics task, 12
mockdoclet task (XDoclet), 218
mode attribute
    manifest task, 84
    tarfileset element, 91
modification dates, files, 38, 39
modification sets, 124
modificationset task, 124
modified selector, 50
modules, 151
    checking out, 155
    updating shared code, 157
move task, 10
    deployment and, 102, 106
    filterchain element, 53
    mappers and, 56
    renamextension task and, 12
MParse compiler (Metamata), 12
mparse task, 12
multithreading tasks, 181
mvcsoft element (ejbdoclet task), 224

N

name attribute
    attribute element, 84, 207
    elements supporting, 47, 115
    factory element, 218
    outproperty element, 218
    param element, 217
    project element, 7, 22
    property element, 19
    section element, 84
    target element, 8
    taskdef task, 258
    test task, 136

name property (input task), 107
name=value format, 40
naming attribute (ejbjar task), 231
native2ascii task, 12
nesting
    arg elements, 174
    batchtest element, 136
    catalogpath element and, 207
    checksum task and, 98
    chmod task and, 118
    classpath element, 134
    dependencies and, 17
    DirSet type and, 48
    ejbdoclet task and, 223
    ejbjar task and, 231
    elements, 34, 45, 270–272
    fileset elements, 93, 101, 106, 111, 181
    FilterChain type, 53
    generic element and, 203
    jar task and, 83
    javac task and, 62
    jonas element and, 205
    jspc task and, 199
    mail task and, 115
    mapper element and, 57, 69, 106
    message elements, 116
    param elements, 69
    PatternSet type, 49
    property elements, 72
    propertyset elements, 69, 72
    read elements, 112
    reference elements, 69, 72
    replaceregexp task and, 238
    selectors, 51
    tarfileset elements, 90
    taskdef task and, 259
    text data, 269
    user element, 164
    webdoclet task and, 219
    weblogic element and, 233
    write elements, 112
    xmlcatalog elements and, 207
    xmlvalidate task and, 207
    xslt/style task and, 217
    zipgroupfileset elements, 94
.NET, 13, 187
netrexxc task, 12
New Java Class dialog box (Eclipse), 243
New Project dialog box (Eclipse), 243
newCMP attribute (weblogic element), 233

newenvironment attribute
    apply task, 180
    exec task, 173
    java task, 169
    junit task, 134
newer attribute (ftp task), 110
newline (/n), 94
nodeprecated attribute (javadoc task), 78
nodeprecatedlist attribute (javadoc task), 78
noEJBC attribute (weblogic element), 233
noexec attribute (cvs task), 154
nohelp attribute (javadoc task), 79
noindex attribute (javadoc task), 79
-noinput option, 24
nonavbar attribute (javadoc task), 79
NonStop Kernel (Tandem), 117
noqualifier attribute (javadoc task), 79
not element (condition task), 34
notree attribute (javadoc task), 79
nowarn attribute (javac task), 62

O

oc4j element (ejbdoclet task), 224
offset attribute (format task), 87
old attribute (javadoc task), 79
onerror attribute (taskdef task), 259
open source
    Ant and, 2
    CVS and, 151
    Eclipse and, 241
    JUnit and, 127
    XDoclet and, 206
openejb element (ejbdoclet task), 224
operating systems
    Ant support, 5
    build process and, 6
    determining name, 22
    exec task and, 176
optimize attribute (javac task), 62
optional attribute (import task), 73
options attribute (cab task), 188
or element (condition task), 34
orb attribute (jonas element), 204
originalfile attribute (patch task), 166
orion element (ejbdoclet task), 224
os attribute
    apply task, 180
    exec task, 173, 176
os element (condition task), 34
out attribute (xslt/style task), 216

outfile attribute (test task), 136
Outline view (Eclipse), 245
outproperty element, 218
output
  build process and, 27
  controlling, 28–30
  logging, 30
output attribute
  ant task, 71
  antstructure task, 213
  apply task, 180
  cvs task, 155
  exec task, 173
  java task, 170
  sshexec task, 113
outputdir attribute (weblogic element), 233
outputencoding attribute (copy task), 105
outputproperty attribute
  apply task, 180
  exec task, 173
  java task, 170
  sshexec task, 113
overview attribute (javadoc task), 79
overwrite attribute
  copy task, 105
  move task, 106

P

-p option, 24
P4Add task, 15
P4Change task, 14
P4Counter task, 15
P4Delete task, 15
P4Edit task, 14
P4Fstat task, 15
P4Have task, 14
P4Integrate task, 15
P4Label task, 14
P4Labelsync task, 14
P4Reopen task, 15
P4resolve task, 15
P4Revert task, 15
P4Submit task, 14
P4Sync task, 14
Pack class, 260
package attribute
  cvs task, 155
  cvschangelog task, 163
  cvstagdiff task, 165
  cvsversion task, 161
  javadoc task, 79
  jspc task, 199

Package Explorer (Eclipse)
  build.xml file and, 245, 247
  creating
    build files, 244
    projects, 243
package mapper, 57
packagelist attribute (javadoc task), 79
packagenames attribute (javadoc task), 79
packageSubstitution element
  ejbdoclet task, 224
  webdoclet task, 219
packaging applications/deployment, 88–99
parallel attribute
  apply task, 180
  chmod task, 117
parallel task, 10, 181
param element
  nesting, 69
  xslt/style task and, 217
parentheses [()], 56
parser attribute (xmlvalidate task), 208
passfile attribute
  cvs task, 155
  cvschangelog task, 163
  cvspass task, 154
  cvstagdiff task, 165
  cvsversion task, 161
passive attribute (ftp task), 110
passphrase attribute
  scp task, 191
  sshexec task, 113
passwd command (CVS), 152
password attribute
  cvspass task, 154
  ftp task, 110
  generic element, 203
  get task, 195
  mail task, 115
  scp task, 189, 191
  sshexec task, 113
  telnet task, 112
  weblogic element, 204
password property (input task), 107
passwords, 153, 191
patch task, 10, 160, 165
patchfile attribute (patch task), 166
path attribute
  compilearg element, 65
  env element, 174
PATH environment variable, 3
path type, 44, 102
pathconvert task, 10, 102

pathelement element
    catalogpath element and, 207
    location attribute, 45
    nesting and, 45
path-like structures, 45
    core Ant types, 44
    javac task and, 62
    junit task and, 134
paths
    absolute, 74
    converting references to, 102
    exec task and, 174
    nested elements and, 45
pattern attribute (format task), 87
patterns, 49
    DirSet type attributes and, 49
    fixcrlf task and, 96
    glob mapper and, 58
    replaceregexp task and, 236–238
    selectors and, 50
patternset element
    cab task and, 188
    conditional actions, 35
    depend task and, 239
    DirSet type and, 48
    fileset element and, 47
    jar task and, 83
    javac task, 62
    xslt/style task and, 217
    zip task and, 94
PatternSet type, 44, 49
Perforce, Ant tasks for, 14
perforce task, 151
perform method (Task class), 261
perm attribute (chmod task), 117
permissions
    setting with chmod, 116
    tarfileset type and, 90
    Unix and, 103, 191
permissions element, 137, 170
Permissions type, 44
plain formatter, 135, 138
plug-in manifest files, 247
pollInterval attribute (parallel task), 182
port attribute
    cvs task, 155
    cvschangelog task, 163
    cvstagdiff task, 165
    cvsversion task, 161
    ftp task, 110
    scp task, 191
    sshexec task, 113
    telnet task, 112

portletdoclet task (XDoclet), 218
pramati element (ejbdoclet task), 224
prefix attribute
    property element, 19
    tarfileset element, 91
    tstamp task, 86
    xmlproperty task, 212
    zipfileset element, 94, 201
prefixlines element (FilterChain type), 54, 56
present selector, 51
preservelastmodified attribute
    copy task, 105
    ftp task, 111
preserveLeadingSlashes attribute (tarfileset
    element), 91
presetdef task, 10
printsummary attribute (junit task), 134
private attribute (javadoc task), 79
Problems view (Eclipse), 248
processor attribute (xslt/style task), 217
Project class, 263, 276
project element, 7, 72
<project> tags, 73
-projecthelp option, 24, 30
projects, 6
    accessing in code, 262–266
    creating, 243
    modules and, 151
    setting classpath, 249
properties, 18
    accessing in code, 262–266
    built-in, 22
    conditional actions, 35–36
    declaring outside targets, 19
    loading from XML files, 211–212
    loading text files, 41
    name=value format, 40
    overriding, 41–43
    passing with ant task, 72
    setting
        conditions, 32–35
        values, 250
        with environment variables, 43
        with tasks, 37
    stopping builds, 36
    text strings and, 40
    values as tooltips, 247
    (see also types)
property attribute
    available task, 37
    checksum task, 97
    condition task, 33
    format task, 87

property attribute *(continued)*
    loadfile task, 41
    update task, 39
Property class, 263–265
property element
    attributes, 18–22
    environment variables, 18, 43
    nesting, 72
property files, 39–43
property task, 10, 39
    declaring properties, 19
    param elements and, 69
-propertyfile option, 24, 39
propertyfile task, 12, 40
propertyref element, 69
propertyset element, 69, 72
PropertySet type, 44
protected attribute (javadoc task), 79
provider attribute (checksum task), 97
public attribute (javadoc task), 79
publicId attribute (dtd element), 207
pvcs task, 12, 151

Q

-q option, 24
quiet attribute
    cvs task, 155
    cvstagdiff task, 165
    delete task, 101
    patch task, 166
-quiet option, 24, 28

R

rannotate command (CVS), 152
rdiff command (CVS), 152, 160, 165
read element (telnet task), 112
readbuffersize attribute (checksum task), 97
reallyquiet attribute (cvs task), 155
rebuild attribute (weblogic element), 233
reconfigure method (Task class), 262
record task, 10
reference element, 69, 72
refid attribute
    FilterSet type, 52
    path element, 45
    property element, 19
    reference element, 69
    xmlcatalog element, 207
regexp element, 238
regexp mapper, 56–58

regular expressions
    from attribute and, 56
    mappers and, 57
    substituting text, 236–238
relative attribute (apply task), 180
release command (CVS), 152
reload task, 192
reloading attribute (junit task), 134
reloadstylesheet attribute (xslt/style task), 217
remotedir attribute (ftp task), 109, 111
remotefacade element (ejbdoclet task), 224
remoteinterface element (ejbdoclet task), 224
remove command (CVS), 152
rename task, 10
renameextensions task, 12
replace attribute (replaceregexp task), 238
replace task, 10, 53
replaceProperties method (Project class), 264, 270
replaceregexp task, 13, 236–238
replacetokens element (FilterChain type), 54
replyto attribute (mail task), 115
replyto element (mail task), 115
report element, 141
reports
    brief formatter, 139
    change logs, 161–164
    cvstagdiff task and, 164
    junitreport task and, 141
    plain formatter, 138
    XML formatter, 140
repositories, 151
resin-ejb-xml element (ejbdoclet task), 224
resin-web-xml element (webdoclet task), 219
resolveExecutable attribute
    apply task, 180
    exec task, 173
resolveFile method (Project class), 264
resource attribute
    available task, 38
    property element, 19
    taskdef task, 259
resultproperty attribute
    apply task, 180
    exec task, 173, 175
    java task, 170
return codes, 170–172, 175
reverse attribute (patch task), 166
rexec task, 13
rlog command (CVS), 152

rmic task, 10
rootDirectory attribute (xmlproperty task), 212
rpm task, 13
rtag command (CVS), 153
run method (JUnit), 130
runBare method (JUnit), 130

S

-s option, 23
SAX Parser, 207
SAX2 parser, 206
scanincludeddirectories attribute (xslt/style task), 217
Schema Unit Test (SUT), 149
schema, validating with, 208
scp command (Unix), 191
scp task, 13, 112, 189–192
Scripdef task, 13
script task, 13, 275–278
section element (manifest task), 84
selector element (fileset element), 47
selectors, 50, 51, 284
Selectors type, 44
semanticAttributes attribute (xmlproperty task), 212
semicolon (;), 266
separator attribute (ftp task), 111
sequential task, 10, 182
serialwarn attribute (javadoc task), 79
server attribute
    ftp task, 107, 111
    generic element, 203
    jonas element, 205
    telnet task, 112
    weblogic element, 204
server command (CVS), 153
serverdeploy task, 13, 202–205
servlets, 188, 192–195, 221–223
session element (ejbdoclet task), 224
setBaseDir method (Project class), 264
setDefault method (Project class), 264
setDefaultInputStream method (Project class), 264
setDescription method
    Project class, 264
    Task class, 262
setInheritedProperty method (Project class), 264
setKeepGoingMode method (Project class), 264

setLocation method (Task class), 262
setName method
    JUnit framework, 130
    Project class, 264
setNewProperty method (Project class), 264
setOwningTarget method (Task class), 262
setProjectReference method (Project class), 264
setProperty method (Project class), 264
setproxy task, 13, 236
setRuntimeConfigurableWrapper method (Task class), 262
setTaskName method (Task class), 262
setTaskType method (Task class), 262
setUp method (JUnit), 130, 133
setUserProperty method (Project class), 265
setValue method
    Commandline object, 275
    EnumeratedAttribute class, 267
shell commands, 177, 178
short data type, 266
showduration attribute (splash task), 236
showoutput attribute (junit task), 134
signjar task, 10
SimpleDateFormat class (Java), 86, 87
size selector, 51
skipemptyfilesets attribute (apply task), 181
skipFailedTransfers attribute (ftp task), 111
sleep task, 10, 109, 205
SMTP servers, 114, 115
socket element (condition task), 34, 111
Soscheckin task, 16
Soscheckout task, 16
Sosget task, 16
Soslabel task, 16
sound task, 13, 234, 235
source attribute
    javac task, 62
    javadoc task, 79
    serverdeploy task, 202
    success/fail elements, 235
source code
    accessing projects/properties in, 262–266
    checking out, 119
    compiling, 60–63
    patches to, 165
source control (see CVS)
source release (Ant), 2
sourcefiles attribute (javadoc task), 80
SourceOffsite (SourceGear), 16
sourceoffsite task, 151

sourcepath attribute
    javac task, 62
    javadoc task, 80
    path type, 45
sourcepath element, 45
sourcepathref attribute
    javac task, 62
    javadoc task, 80
spaces, 95, 153, 237
spawn attribute
    apply task, 181
    exec task, 173
    java task, 170
splash screens, 13, 235
splash task, 13, 235
splitindex attribute (javadoc task), 80
sql task, 10
SQLUnit, 149
src attribute
    get task, 195
    gzip/bzip2 tasks, 92
    message element, 116
    script task, 276
    unjar task, 84
    zipfileset element, 94, 202
src element, 45
srcdir attribute
    depend task, 239
    ejbjar task, 231
    fixcrlf task, 96
    javac task, 48, 62
    jspc task, 199
    path type, 45
srcfile attribute
    example, 38
    loadfile task, 41
    purpose, 38
    update task, 39
srcfile element, 181
SSH protocol, 112, 189
sshexec task, 13, 112
ssl attribute (mail task), 115
start attribute (cvschangelog task), 163
startdate attribute (cvstagdiff task), 165
StarTeam, 15, 151
starteam task, 151
starttag attribute (cvstagdiff task), 165
status command (CVS), 153
STCheckin task, 15
STCheckout task, 15
STLabel task, 15
STList task, 15

stripjavacomments element (FilterChain
        type), 54
striplinebreaks element (FilterChain
        type), 54
striplinecomments element (FilterChain
        type), 54
strutsconfigxml element (webdoclet
        task), 219
strutsform element (ejbdoclet task), 224
strutsvalidationxml element (webdoclet
        task), 219
style attribute (xslt/style task), 217
style task, 11, 206, 214–218
stylebook task, 13
styledir attribute (report task), 141
stylesheetfile attribute (javadoc task), 80
subant task, 10
subject attribute (mail task), 115
subroutine calls, 71
substitution element (replaceregexp
        task), 238
subTask element
    ejbdoclet task, 224
    webdoclet task, 219
success element (sound task), 234
suffix attribute (weblogic element), 233
sunone element (ejbdoclet task), 224
support element (ejbjar task), 231
SUT (Schema Unit Test), 149
symlink task, 13
sync task, 10
syntax checking, 246
sysproperty element
    junit task, 135
    purpose, 170
    weblogic element and, 233
syspropertyset element, 137, 170
System.err, 278, 280
System.out, 278, 280

T

tab attribute (fixcrlf task), 96
tablength attribute (fixcrlf task), 96
tabs, manipulating, 95
tabstospaces element (FilterChain type), 54
tag attribute
    cvs task, 155
    cvschangelog task, 164
tag command (CVS), 153
tailfilter element (FilterChain type), 54
tar task, 10, 89–91
tarfileset element (tar task), 90

target attribute
  ant task, 71
  antcall task, 69
  javac task, 62
target element, 8, 30, 35
targetfile attribute
  update task, 39
  uptodate task, 38
targetfile element, 181
targets, 7
  Ant view and, 255
  antcall task and, 68
  build example, 16–18
  build files and, 25, 71
  declaring properties and, 19
  DirSet type and, 48
  FileSet type and, 46
  hyphens and, 25
  master, 16
  running
    multiple, 25
    test cases, 137
targetStarted method, 278
Task class, 260–262
taskdef element, 192
taskdef task, 10
  attributes, 258
  creating tasks, 257
  ejbdoclet task and, 226
  target element and, 19
  webdoclet task and, 220
tasks, 8
  adding, 252
  built-in, 8–11
  calling other, 68–72
  creating custom, 257–260
  creating DTDs for, 213
  declaring outside targets, 19
  dependent, 16–18
  DirSet type and, 48
  failonerror attribute, 27
  FileSet type and, 46
  grouping, 7
  handling attributes, 266–268
  implicit file sets, 47
  life cycle of, 262
  multithreading, 181
  optional, 11–16
  property-setting, 32–38
  setting execution order, 182
  third-party, 16
  as wrappers, 274
  (see also types)

tearDown method (JUnit), 130, 133
telnet task, 13, 111
tempdir attribute
  javac task, 62
  junit task, 134
tempfile task, 10, 98
test cases, 130, 133, 137–142
test element, 135
test suites, 142
test task, 13, 136
TestCase class (JUnit), 128, 130
TestCases method (JUnit), 130
testEquals method (JUnit), 130
testNotNull method (JUnit), 130
TestRunner class (JUnit), 137
tests/testing
  Ant, 4
  build process, 125
  criteria, 33
  formatting results, 135
  in batches, 136, 137, 142, 144
  junit task and, 126
  performing, 133–137
  running test cases, 137–142
  writing, 130–133
TestSuite class (JUnit), 142
testTrue method (JUnit), 130
text data
  as attribute values, 266
  filtering, 53–56, 106
  loading, 41
  nesting, 269–270
  os attribute and, 174
  properties, 40
  replaceregexp task and, 236–238
threadCount attribute (parallel task), 182
threadsPerProcessor attribute (parallel task), 182
timediffauto attribute (ftp task), 111
timediffmillis attribute (ftp task), 111
timeout attribute
  apply task, 181
  exec task, 174, 177
  java task, 170
  junit task, 134
  parallel task, 182
  sshexec task, 113
  telnet task, 112
timeouts, handling, 177
timestamp property (format element), 86
timestamps, 84–87
timezone attribute (format task), 87
TimeZone class (Java), 87

to attribute
    glob mapper and, 58
    mapper element, 57
    regular expressions and, 58
    slashes and, 57
to element (mail task), 115
TODAY property (tstamp task), 85
todir attribute
    batchtest element, 136
    checksum task, 98
    copy task, 105
    junitreport task, 141
    report task, 141
    scp task, 192
    test task, 136
tofile attribute
    copy task, 105
    junitreport task, 141
token attribute (filter task), 53
tokenfilter element (FilterChain type), 54
tokens, 51
tolist attribute (mail task), 115
Tomcat web servers
    Anthill and, 119
    deploying to, 192–196
    Jasper JSP compiler, 196
    .war files and, 188
tooltips, 247
torefid attribute (reference element), 69
toString method (JUnit), 130
totalproperty attribute (checksum task), 98
touch task, 98
translate task, 13
translatePath method (Project class), 265
TraX processor, 218
true/false tests, 33, 68
trust attribute
    scp task, 189, 192
    sshexec task, 113
TSTAMP property (tstamp task), 85
tstamp task, 11, 85–87
type attribute
    apply task, 181
    available task, 38
    chmod task, 117
    formatter task, 135
    mapper element, 57
type selector, 51
typedef task, 11, 19
types
    adding, 252
    core, 44
    creating, 286–289
    file filters, 51, 53
    filtering/modifying text, 53–56
    lists of files, 49
    mappers as, 56–59
    path-like structures, 45
    selectors as, 50
    with groups of directories, 48
    with groups of files, 46–48
    with patterns, 49
    (see also properties)

U

umask attribute (ftp task), 111
UMASK permissions (Unix), 103, 191
undeploy action
    JOnAS servers, 204
    weblogic tool, 203
undeploy task, 192
unedit command (CVS), 153
Unicode characters, 6, 54
unit attribute (format task), 87
Unix environment
    build process, 5, 21
    chmod task and, 117
    crontab utility, 116, 118
    end-of-line characters, 94
    exec task and, 174
    executing shell commands, 177
    file permissions and, 103
    installing Ant, 3
    MAC OS and, 33
    permissions and, 191
    scheduling automatic builds, 118
    verbose build, 28
unjar task, 11, 84
unless attribute
    batchtest element, 136
    elements supporting, 35, 47
    fail task and, 36
    formatter task, 135
    param element, 217
    target element, 8
    test task, 136
Unpack class, 260
unpackage mapper, 57, 59
untar task, 11, 91
unwar task, 11
unzip task, 11, 94
update action
    JOnAS servers, 204
    weblogic tool, 203

update attribute
  ear task, 202
  jar task, 83
  war task, 186
  zip task, 93
update command (CVS), 153, 157
uptodate element (condition task), 34
uptodate task, 11
  attributes for, 39
  file modification dates and, 38
  mappers and, 56
  package mapper and, 58
uri attribute (taskdef task), 259
uribase attribute (jspc task), 199
uriroot attribute (jspc task), 199
url attribute
  property element, 19
  property task, 39
URL schemas, 193
use attribute (javadoc task), 80
useexternalfile attribute (javadoc task), 80
usefile attribute
  formatter element, 135
  formatter task, 135
user attribute (mail task), 115
user element, 164
userid attribute
  ftp task, 111
  telnet task, 112
  user element, 164
username attribute
  generic element, 203
  get task, 195
  sshexec task, 113
  tarfileset element, 91
  weblogic element, 204
usernames, 191
usersfile attribute (cvschangelog task), 164
usetimestamp attribute (get task), 196
utilobject element (ejbdoclet task), 224

V

-v option, 24
vajexport task, 13
vajimport task, 13
vajload task, 13
validargs attribute (input task), 68
validate attribute (xmlproperty task), 212
value attribute
  argument element, 155
  attribute element, 84, 207

available task, 38
compilearg element, 65
condition task, 33
env element, 174
filter task, 53
outproperty element, 218
property element, 19
property task, 40
setting property values, 37
system properties and, 135
update task, 39
valueobject element (ejbdoclet task), 224
vbc task, 13
verbose attribute
  apply task, 181
  cab task, 188
  chmod task, 117
  copy task, 105
  delete task, 101
  ejbdoclet task, 223
  ftp task, 111
  get task, 196
  javac task, 62
  javadoc task, 80
  jspc task, 199
  webdoclet task, 219
-verbose option, 24, 28–30
verifyproperty attribute (checksum task), 98
version attribute (javadoc task), 80
version command (CVS), 153
-version option, 24
Visual Source Safe (Microsoft), 15, 151
vmlauncher attribute
  apply task, 181
  exec task, 174
Vssadd task, 15
Vsscheckin task, 15
Vsscheckout task, 15
Vsscp task, 15
Vsscreate task, 15
vssget task, 15
Vsshistory task, 15
Vsslabel task, 15

W

waitfor task, 11, 109, 205
war task, 11, 184–186
warfile attribute (war task), 186
warn attribute (xmlvalidate task), 207
watch command (CVS), 153
watchers command (CVS), 153

.wav format, 278
web applications
    compiling JSPs, 196–199
    creating CAB files, 187
    creating WAR archives, 184–186
    EJB containers and, 200–205
    scp task and, 189–192
    simple web deployment, 188
    Tomcat servers and, 192–196
    XDoclet and, 218–223
webdoclet task (XDoclet), 218–223
webinc attribute (jspc task), 199
webinf element (war task), 186
weblogic element, 203, 224, 232
WebLogic servers, 14, 202, 204, 230, 233
weblogic.deploy deployment tool, 203
weblogicwebxml element (webdoclet
    task), 219
websphere element, 224, 232
webspherewebxml element (webdoclet
    task), 219
webworkactiondocs element (webdoclet
    task), 219
webworkactionsxml element (webdoclet
    task), 219
webworkconfigproperties element (webdoclet
    task), 219
webxml attribute
    jspc task, 199
    war task, 186
whenempty attribute
    jar task, 83
    zip task, 93
whichresource task, 11
wildcards, 38, 57
Windows environment
    at command, 116, 118
    build process, 5, 22
    CVS servers, 151
    EOL characters and, 95
    exec task and, 174, 176, 177
    executing shell commands, 177
    filename lengths, 3
    installing Ant, 3
    scheduling automatic builds, 118

    spaces in username, 153
    verbose build, 29
windowtitle attribute (javadoc task), 80
wlclasspath attribute (weblogic
    element), 233
wlclasspath element (weblogic element), 233
wljspc task, 13
wlrun task (EJB), 14, 182, 230
wlstop task (EJB), 14, 230
write element, 112
WsdlToDotNet task, 13

X

Xalan processor, 215, 217
XDoclet, 206
XML
    documents, 6, 141, 206–211
    files, 211
    formatter, 135, 140
    transforming, 214–218
xmlcatalog element, 207, 217
XMLCatalog type, 44
xmlproperty task, 11, 206, 211
xmlvalidate task, 13, 206–211
XSLT, 165, 214–218
xslt task, 11, 206, 214–218

Z

zip task, 92–94
    description, 11
    jlink task and, 12
    .war files and, 185
    zipfileset element and, 201
zipfile attribute
    gzip/bzip2 tasks, 92
    zip task, 93
zipfileset element
    attributes, 93
    ear task and, 202
    war task and, 186
    zip task and, 93
ZipFileSet type, 44
zipgroupfileset element, 94

About the Author

Steve Holzner is an award-winning author who has been writing about Java topics since Java first appeared. He's a former *PC Magazine* contributing editor whose many books have been translated into 18 languages around the world. His books have sold more than 1.5 million copies, and many of his bestsellers have been about Java. Steve has also written *Eclipse* for O'Reilly.

Steve graduated from MIT and got his Ph.D. from Cornell; he's been a very popular member of the faculty at both MIT and Cornell, teaching thousands of students over the years and earning an average student evaluation of over 4.9 out of 5.0. Steve and his team of over 50 instructors teach classes onsite to corporate programmers through his company at *http://www.onsiteglobal.com*.

Colophon

Our look is the result of reader comments, our own experimentation, and feedback from distribution channels. Distinctive covers complement our distinctive approach to technical topics, breathing personality and life into potentially dry subjects.

The animal on the cover of *Ant: The Definitive Guide*, Second Edition, is a horned lizard. There are 13 species of the horned lizard in North America. Horned lizards prefer a dry, warm climate, such as the desert or a dry woodland, and they can be found in Texas, Oklahoma, Kansas, and New Mexico. Adults grow to 3–5 inches. They depend on their environment to control their body temperature, and use burrows and shade to prevent overheating. The horned lizard has a wide, flat body ideal for desert camouflage, and a short neck and short legs. It has spines on its body and prominent horns on its head. It is also known as the horny "toad."

Despite the horned lizards' fierce appearance, they are not aggressive. Their primary diet consists of ants, although they sometimes eat beetles, grasshoppers, and other insects, which they catch with their long tongues. The horned lizards' first line of defense from predators is their camouflage, but they are also known to hiss and inflate their bodies to appear more intimidating. As a last resort, they have the ability to squirt blood from the corners of their eyes in an attempt to confuse attackers. In Texas and Oklahoma, horned lizards are considered a threatened species. It is illegal to possess a horned lizard without a scientific permit.

Matt Hutchinson was the production editor for *Ant: The Definitive Guide*, Second Edition. GEX, Inc. provided production services. Mary Brady, Sanders Kleinfeld, and Darren Kelly provided quality control.

Hanna Dyer designed the cover of this book, based on a series design by Edie Freedman. The cover image is a 19th-century engraving from the Dover Pictorial Archive. Karen Montgomery produced the cover layout with Adobe InDesign CS using Adobe's ITC Garamond font.

David Futato designed the interior layout. This book was converted by Keith Fahlgren to FrameMaker 5.5.6 with a format conversion tool created by Erik Ray, Jason McIntosh, Neil Walls, and Mike Sierra that uses Perl and XML technologies. The text font is Linotype Birka; the heading font is Adobe Myriad Condensed; and the code font is LucasFont's TheSans Mono Condensed. The illustrations that appear in the book were produced by Robert Romano, Jessamyn Read, and Lesley Borash using Macromedia FreeHand MX and Adobe Photoshop CS. The tip and warning icons were drawn by Christopher Bing. This colophon was written by Colleen Gorman.

Buy *Ant: The Definitive Guide* and access the digital edition

FREE on Safari for 45 days.

Go to **www.oreilly.com/go/safarienabled**
and type in coupon code **X8H7-LETH-HR96-1FHW-4J9Z**

Better than e-books

Search
over 2000 top
tech books

Download
whole chapters

Cut and Paste
code examples

Find
answers fast

Read books from cover
to cover. Or, simply click
to the page you need.

**Search Safari! The premier electronic reference
library for programmers and IT professionals**

Part# 40421

Keep in touch with O'Reilly

1. Download examples from our books

To find example files for a book, go to:

www.oreilly.com/catalog

select the book, and follow the "Examples" link.

2. Register your O'Reilly books

Register your book at *register.oreilly.com*

Why register your books?
Once you've registered your O'Reilly books you can:

- Win O'Reilly books, T-shirts or discount coupons in our monthly drawing.
- Get special offers available only to registered O'Reilly customers.
- Get catalogs announcing new books (US and UK only).
- Get email notification of new editions of the O'Reilly books you own.

3. Join our email lists

Sign up to get topic-specific email announcements of new books and conferences, special offers, and O'Reilly Network technology newsletters at:

elists.oreilly.com

It's easy to customize your free elists subscription so you'll get exactly the O'Reilly news you want.

4. Get the latest news, tips, and tools

www.oreilly.com

- "Top 100 Sites on the Web"—PC Magazine
- CIO Magazine's Web Business 50 Awards

Our web site contains a library of comprehensive product information (including book excerpts and tables of contents), downloadable software, background articles, interviews with technology leaders, links to relevant sites, book cover art, and more.

5. Work for O'Reilly

Check out our web site for current employment opportunities:

jobs.oreilly.com

6. Contact us

O'Reilly Media
1005 Gravenstein Hwy North
Sebastopol, CA 95472 USA

TEL: 707-827-7000 or 800-998-9938
(6am to 5pm PST)

FAX: 707-829-0104

order@oreilly.com
For answers to problems regarding your order or our products. To place a book order online, visit:

www.oreilly.com/order_new

catalog@oreilly.com
To request a copy of our latest catalog.

booktech@oreilly.com
For book content technical questions or corrections.

corporate@oreilly.com
For educational, library, government, and corporate sales.

proposals@oreilly.com
To submit new book proposals to our editors and product managers.

international@oreilly.com
For information about our international distributors or translation queries. For a list of our distributors outside of North America check out:

international.oreilly.com/distributors.html

adoption@oreilly.com
For information about academic use of O'Reilly books, visit:

academic.oreilly.com

O'REILLY®

Our books are available at most retail and online bookstores.
To order direct: 1-800-998-9938 • *order@oreilly.com* • *www.oreilly.com*
Online editions of most O'Reilly titles are available by subscription at *safari.oreilly.com*